REVOLUTIONARY WAR RECORDS
MECKLENBURG COUNTY
VIRGINIA

Compiled by:
Katherine B. Elliott

Southern Historical Press, Inc.
Greenville, South Carolina

Please direct all correspondence and orders to:

www.southernhistoricalpress.com
or
SOUTHERN HISTORICAL PRESS, Inc.
PO BOX 1267
Greenville, SC   29601
southernhistoricalpress@gmail.com

ISBN #0-89308-381-X

Printed in the United States of America

FOREWORD

This is not a definitive history of Mecklenburg County during the Revolutionary War, but a collection of records of the county for that period.

It has been the purpose of the compilers to present in this volume the records of military and patriotic services recorded in the order books, and from other sources pertaining to the county which could be documented.

While the order books contain, apparently, all of the names of the militia officers recommended and commissioned, it is regretted that so few names of privates and the non-commissioned officers have been found. With the exception of one militia company muster roll for 1779, no militia records have been found or are known to exist.

Mecklenburg County had eighteen companies of militia in two battalions throughout the war, but only a part of these were ordered out or were in service at any one time. That nearly all saw some service or action is without doubt true. That all were completely armed is unlikely. In 1781, when Lord Cornwallis was marching towards Virginia, Col. Lewis Burwell wrote Governor Jefferson that the militia would fight, but that there was a shortage of guns and ammunition in the county.

Several companies of Mecklenburg militia were ordered to Georgia under the command of Col. David Mason in 1779. Again in 1780, the Mecklenburg militia was ordered out and marched to South Carolina under the command of Col. Lewis Burwell. The number of companies ordered out, however, is not known.

Governor Jefferson appointed Col. Lewis Burwell as County Lieutenant for Mecklenburg County in February 1781, and shortly thereafter, the militia was ordered out again to march to Guilford Court House, N. C. The number of companies ordered out is not known. They were commanded by Col. Robert Munford.

The militia was again ordered out in August 1781, and marched to the Siege of Yorktown. Col. Lewis Burwell, although serving as County Lieutenant, personally took command of the militia. The number of companies called out is not definitely known, but a part, if not all, of both battalions of militia were ordered out then. An examination of pension applications indicates that Major Henry Walker and Major Samuel Dedman were in command of militia at Yorktown. Probably ten or more of the companies were called out at this time.

In addition to those serving in the militia, many from Mecklenburg County served in the state and continental lines. The early companies commanded by Captain Robert Ballard, Captain Henry Delony, Jr. and Captain Samuel Hopkins appear to have been incorporated into the state line. The Minutemen Company commanded by Captain James Anderson was discharged at Portsmouth after service at Hampton.

Since the militia records have not been preserved, most of the information now available is found in the applications of those who applied for pensions. It was not possible for the compilers to examine all of pension applications known to have been made by soldiers who served from Mecklenburg County. A selected alphabetical list was compiled as being representative, and these applications were examined. The pension records examined reveal much information not to be found now in any other source. Many names in the following pages were taken from these applications. It is to be regretted that hundreds of those serving from Mecklenburg County cannot now be documented.

The public claims listed in this volume do not cover all such claims of record in the order books. One or more claims are listed for each name found in the order books. The claims listed were selected to show the diversity of the services performed. It was not deemed advisable to list every claim.

The number of claims for beef furnished the army may puzzle the reader. Under an Act of the General Assembly of October 1780 for clothing and provisioning the army, every freeholder was assessed, or taxed, 300 hundred pounds of beef. This did not mean slaughtered beef, but beef on the hoof. The collectors of cattle, under the Act, were required to judge the weight of each animal impressed, and, as an example, if the beef was judged to weigh 650 pounds, a certificate for the 350 pounds was given which became a public claim against the government. The 300 pounds was assessed as his contribution under the Act.

Included in this volume are excerpts from the Acts of the General Assembly, and from the Pension Act of 1832 and the Regulations issued thereunder, which are deemed of interest and pertinent to the records compiled. The full Acts of the General Assembly are found in Henings Statutes. Included, also, are Bible records copied from the pension applications examined.

The few records now extant do not show the importance of Taylor's Ferry, Mecklenburg County, in the Revolutionary War. The order books have few entries in regard to this ferry.

The road from Petersburg, Va., to Hillsborough, N. C. crossed the Roanoke River at Taylor's Ferry in Mecklenburg County; and was the principal road used for military travel north and south. The Store House at Petersburg and the Magazine at Taylor's Ferry were important points for military supplies. Detachments of militia were stationed at Taylor's Ferry to guard the ferry, the magazine and the supplies kept there. The location of this ferry and the magazine today are under the waters of Buggs Island Lake. A pension application states that the magazine was located at Banks Old Store one-half mile from the ferry.

I am indebted to the University of North Carlina Library for their courteous permission to include the muster roll of Captain Reuben Vaughan in this volume. This roll is in the Hubard Papers in the Southern Historical collection of papers in the library. I am indebted, also, to the staff and personnel of the Virginia State Library for their patience and courtesy while searching records in the library.

I must also express my indebtedness to Mr. N. G. Hutcheson, Clerk of Mecklenburg County, and his staff for the assistance and courtesy extended in making available the order books and other records of the county for search in collecting material for this volume.

Words cannot express my appreciation for the assistance given by Mrs. Olive Yancey Vassar, South Hill, Va., and Mrs. Verna Bracey, Bracey, Va., in searching records for names of Mecklenburg County soldiers; and the aid given me by Miss Anne Waller Reddy, Richmond, Va., whose knowledge of sources of search and the records in the Virginia State Library were invaluable.

The Prestwould Chapter, DAR, South Hill, Va., presented to Mr. N. G. Hutcheson, Clerk of Mecklenburg County, at an open meeting held in the Courthouse on February 20, 1960, a framed roster containing the names of 768 soldiers and citizens of Mecklenburg County who aided the cause of the American Revolution.

This volume is a continuation of this original project; and has been compiled with the collaboration of my husband, Herbert A. Elliott, who assisted in compiling, indexing and preparing the manuscript for printing.

                                    Katherine Blackwell Elliott
                            Historian, Prestwould Chapter, DAR

CONTENTS

Title   1

Foreword   3

Abbreviations - Sources   9

Mecklenburg County Soldiers and Patriots   11

Committee of Safety   157

Gentleman Justices - 1775-1783   158

Notes on Pension Applications   160

Muster Roll of Captain Reuben Vaughan   162

Commission of Captain Reuben Vaughan   164

Rev. War Officers in Meck. County Records   165

Brief List - Pay for Militia Service   168

Notes on Military Regulations   170

Militia Officers - Mecklenburg County   173

Sundry Notes from Order Books   181

Notes on Pension Regulations   183

Mecklenburg County Records   188

Notes on Pension Certificates   191

Bible Records from Pension Applications   192

Notes on Acts of the General Assembly   198

Mecklenburg County Legislative Petition   203

Index   207

ABBREVIATIONS - SOURCES

PC   - Public Claims Recorded in Mecklenburg County
          Order Books
O.B. - Mecklenburg County Order Books
W.B. - Mecklenburg County Will Books
D.B. - Mecklenburg County Deed Books
M.R. 1765-1810 - Mecklenburg County Marriage
          Records 1765-1810 - Published 1963
M.R. 1811-1863 - Mecklenburg County Marriage
          Records 1811-1853 - Published 1962
Early Wills - Early Wills, 1765-1799, Mecklenburg
                County - Published 1963
Census 1782 - Mecklenburg County Census Year 1782
Min. Book - Mecklenburg County Minute Books
Meck. Co. Pet.) Legislative Petitions from Mecklen-
Leg. Pet.   ) burg County in Archives,
Pet.   ) Virginia State Library
Aud. Acct Book - Auditor's Account Book *
Comm. Book - Commissioner's Book *
Meck. Book Lists - Mecklenburg County Lists *
Meck. Cert. - Mecklenburg Certificates *
Exec. Comm. - Executive Communications *
EP - Executive Papers *
* Records in Archives, Virginia State Library
CJV - Council Journals of Virginia
JHD - Journals of the House of Delegates
JCS - Journals of Council of State of Virginia
(G) - Gwathmey: Virginians in the Revolution
(E) - Eckenrode: List of Revolutionary Soldiers of
                Virginia - 1910-1911, 1912-1913
CS(E) - Eckenrode: Chesterfield Supplement
Pen. S- Pension Application of Soldier **
Pen. W- Pension Application of Wife **
Pen. R- Pension Application Rejected **
** National Archives, Washington, D. C.
BLWt. - Bounty Land Warrants
VMH - Virginia Magazine of History and Biography
Va. Gazette - Newspaper Published at Williamsburg,
                Virginia
Hubard Papers - Papers in Southern Historical Coll-
ections, University of North Carolina Library,
Chapel Hill, N. C.
Burgess: Virginia Soldiers of 1776
McAllister: Virginia Militia in Revolutionary War
DAR - Georgia DAR Roster
        Tennessee DAR Roster
        DAR Lineage Books
        Va. DAR Register

ABERCROMBY, Robert   **Patriot**

    For Continental Use   PC April 10, 1782
    1. Service of a wagon, team and driver, one day, with
       provisions being found by the public   O.B. 5, p 135

ADAMS, David   **Patriot**

    For Continental Use   PC April 9, 1782
    1. 2 bu. Corn - 375 cwt Beef
    2. 100 bundles Fodder
    3. 1 Gun taken into the service and not returned -
       Value 4 pounds   O.B. 5, pp 128-130
    4. Served as Grand Juror - Nov. 9, 1778

                                          O.B. 4, p 444

ADAMS, John   Private Militia

    Meck. Mil. (E)(G) 3   Pen. W-881
    b. 13 Feb. 1758 - d. 30 April 1835
    Muster Roll, Captain Reuben Vaughan's Company, 1779 -
    Hubard Papers
    Capt. Reuben Vaughan, Lt. John Holmes - Served 9 months
    Drafted 1777 - At battle of Stono
    Entered service 1778 under Capt. Asa Oliver, Col. Binns
    Jones - Served 5 months.
    Entered service 1779 under Capt. Richard Witton - serv-
    ed 3 months. 1781 went to Little York (Yorktown) und-
    er Capt. William Roffe - Served 3 months.
    Wife Calarine - Moved to Montgomery County, Tenn.

ADAMS, Thomas   Private Militia

    Mec. Mil. (E)(G) 3
    Muster Roll, Captain Reuben Vaughan's Company, 1779 -
    Hubard Papers - Wife Lucy - Will - W.B. 4, p 360

ADKINS, Thomas Durham   **Patriot**

    For Continental Use   PC April 9, 1782
    1. 275 cwt Beef   O.B. 5, p 125

ADKINS, William   Private Militia

    Muster Roll, Captains Reuben Vaughan's Company - 1779
    Hubard Papers - Substituted for Richard Lewis

AKIN, Thomas   **Patriot**

    For Continental Use   PC April 9, 1782
    1. 225 cwt Beef   O.B. 5, p 125

ALEXANDER, Col. Robert   Patriot

    For Continental Use   PC April 9, 1782
    1. 1125 cwt Beef   O.B. 5, p 124
    Early Wills, pp 136-140-146

ALLEN, Darling   Soldier Militia

    Received pay as soldier in militia - Auditors' Acct Bk
    No. 22 p 20
    M.R. 1765-1810 p 8 - Early Wills, p 9

ALLEN, David   Soldier Militia
                                                       22
    Received pay as soldier in militia - Aud. Acct Bk p 317
    See pension Francis Farrar

ALLEN, Robert   Patriot

    For Continental Use   PC April 9, 1782
    1. 350 cwt Beef   O.B. 5, p 124
    Census 1782

ALLEN, Robert   Soldier Militia

    Received pay as soldier in militia - Aud. Acct Bk No.
    15, p 533

ALLEN, Thomas   Soldier Militia

    Received pay as soldier in militia - Aud. Acct Bk No.
    15, p 34

ALLEN, Thomas   Patriot

    For Continental Use   PC April 9, 1782
    1. 375 cwt Beef   O.B. 5, p 124
    Census 1782

ALLEN, William   Patriot

    For Continental Use   PC April 9, 1782
    1. 600 cwt Beef   O.B. 5, p 124
    2. 1 smooth gun - Value 40 s   PC May 14, 1782
    Early Wills, p 8   O.B. 5, p 147

ALLIN, Philip (Allen)   Soldier

    b. 1760 - King and Queen County   Pen. S-31514
    Entered service 1776 Meck. Co. Mil. under Capt. William
    Lucas. Served 1777 in Va. Line under Capt. James Ander-
    son and Col. Lewis Burwell. Moved to Clarke County, Ga.

ALLGOOD, John   Soldier Militia

    b. Meck. Co.   Pen. S-15357
Served three tours of duty in Meck. Co. Mil. under
Captains Asa Oliver and Richard Swepson, Major Binns
Jones and Col. Lewis Burwell
Moved to Washington Co., Tenn. and then to Breckinridge
Co., Kentucky.

ALLGOOD, John, Senr.   Soldier Militia

    b. 12 May 1751 in Richmond County   Pen. R-153
Entered service in Meck. Co. in Militia - Served under
Capt. William Lucas, Captain Asa Oliver, Captain Achil-
les Jeffries and Col. Lewis Burwell
Moved to Elbert Co., Ga. in 1788 and then to Walton Co.
Ga. in 1826.

ALLGOOD, John   Soldier

    b. 1760 in Meck. Co.   Pen. W-1350
BLWt36518-160-55
Entered service in 1778 under Capt. (John) Overton and
Col. (James) Fleming, marched from Meck. Co. to New
York. Entered service as a substitute for his father,
Ishmael Allgood. Wounded at Monmouth - served 18 months
Drafted in Meck. Co. in fall 1779 - Served under Capt.
Asa Oliver, Lt. Edward Goode and Ensign John Bevill -
served 6 months. Moved to Elbert Co., Ga. in 1786 and
to Monroe Co., Tenn. in 1826. d. Monroe Co., Tenn. on
17 Nov. 1854. Married Seleta Lankford 12 March 1835 in
Monroe Co., Tenn.

ALLGOOD, Moses   Patriot

    For Continental Use   PC Aug. 12, 1782
1. 1 smooth gun taken into service and not returned -
    Value 6 pounds   O.B. 5, p 182
Early Wills, p 174

ALLGOOD, Spencer   Soldier

    b. Amelia Co. 1759 - Resident of Meck. Co.
Enlisted 27 Aug. 1780 - Served 8 months in militia
Roll Call of troops at Chesterfield Courthouse, 1780,
CS(E) p 1 - Planter, Ht. 5 ft 9 in, Hair fair, Eyes
blue, Complexion fair.

ALLGOOD, William   Soldier

    b. Amelia Co. 1761 - Resident of Meck. Co.
Roll Call of troops C. Ch. 1780 - CS(E) p 70 - Planter,
Moved to Surry Co., N.C. after Revolutionary War.

ANDERSON, Major James   Militia Officer

    Meck. Mil. (E)(G) p 15
    Recommended as Major in first Battalion 13 Oct. 1777
    Took oath as militia officer 8 Dec. 1777
                                 O.B. 4, pp 374-382
    Gent. Justice, Member Committee of Safety, Vestryman
    St. James Parish, furnished supplies, served in many
    public capacities.
    Captain in command of Minutemen Company called out in
    1776.
    Moved to North Carolina after Revolutionary War and
    then to Bedford County, Tenn.   Early Wills, p 9.

ANDERSON, Thomas, Senr.   Patriot

    Public Service - Furnished supplies
    1. Appointed overseer of road from Taylor's Ferry to
       Daniel Hutt's in room of William Daniel, deceased.
    Early Wills, p 9.   See below.

ANDERSON, Sarah   Patriot

    (Widow of Thomas Anderson, above)
    For Continental Use   PC May 14, 1782
    Pasturage 14 days for 17 horses - pasturage 10 days
    for 18 horses - Continental Army   O.B. 5, p 148
    Early Wills, p 9.

ANDERSON, Thomas, Junr.   Patriot

    For Continental Use   PC May 12, 1782
    1. 100 days pasturage for livestock for army
                             O.B. 5, p 148
    2. 150 bundles Fodder, 19 bu. Corn, 90 bundles Fodder,
       80 bu. Oats, 100 bundles Fodder, 80 bu. Oats, 70
       diets, 12½ bu. corn, 30 bu. corn, Pasturage: 22
       horses 10 days, 16 horses 20 days, 18 horses 10
       days, 2 horses 37 days.   O.B. 5, p 149
    Early Wills, p 9.

ANDREWS, Ephraim Senr.   Patriot

    For Continental Use   PC May 14, 1782
    1. 300 cwt Beef   O.B. 5, p 148
    2. Served as Juror 10 Nov. 1777 O.B. 4, p 379, Juror
       11 Nov. 1782 O.B. 5, p 336, Juror 12 May 1783 O.B.
       5, p 294.   M.R. 1765-1810, p 22.

ANDREWS, Ephraim, Junr.   Private Militia

    Muster Roll, Captain Reuben Vaughan's Company - 1779
    Hubard Papers.

ANDREWS, Ephraim   <u>Soldier</u>

    b. Meck. Co.   BLW 5468-100
    Enlisted in Halifax County 24 April 1781 in Lee's
    Legion - Discharged 15 Nov. 1783.
    Served in Troop commanded by Capt. James Armstrong.
    Son of William Andrews of Meck. Co., and brother of
    Varney Andrews. See below.   <u>Burgess,Vol. I, p 67</u>
    Moved to Hawkins County, Tenn.

ANDREWS, George   <u>Patriot</u>

    For Continental Use   PC April 9, 1782
    1. 8 bu. Wheat, 10 bu. Oats   <u>O.B. 5, p 129</u>
    2. 2 empty hogsheads - Value 6 shillings each
       300 bundles Fodder   <u>O.B. 5, p 136</u>

ANDREWS, Knacy H.   <u>Militia Officer</u>

    Recommended as an Ensign in the Militia March 8, 1779.
                                     <u>O.B. 4, p 457</u>

ANDREWS, Rowland   <u>Patriot</u>

    For Continental Use   PC April 9, 1782
    1. 305 cwt Beef   <u>O.B. 5, p 124</u>

ANDREWS, Varney   <u>Soldier</u>

    b. Meck. Co. 1754   d. Meck. Co. 1847
    Mpl. (G) p 17 - Pension Roll - Sec. of War Vol. 2
    Enlisted in Halifax Minutemen in 1776 - Moved to Lunen-
    burg County where he served on tour of duty, then ret'd
    to Meck. Co. where he was drafted in 1781.
    Militia pensioner - McAlister, p 234

ANDREWS, William   <u>Soldier</u>

    b. Meck. Co. d. in service in winter of 1779.
    Enlisted in Meck. Co. under Capt. Robert Ballard as a
    soldier in 1st Va. Regiment in Continental service.
    Cert. of Capt. Ballard that William Andrews enlisted
    for three years and served in his company until his
    death. Meck. Co. Pet. 5 Dec. 1785 Va. State Library

ARCHER, William   <u>Private Militia</u>

    Muster Roll, Captain Reuben Vaughan's Company - 1779
    Hubard Papers.

ARMISTEAD, John   <u>Patriot</u>

```
        For Continental Use                    PC April 9, 1782
        1. 325 cwt Beef                        O.B. 5, p 125
        2. Overseer of road  - 8 June 1778     O.B. 4, p 414
        M.R. 1765-1810, p 10
```

ARNOLD, Elisha   Soldier

```
        b. Meck. Co. 1758                          Pen. S-6523
        Enlisted in 1776 for 2 years under Capt. James Johnson
        In battle at Germantown - Discharged at Valley Forge
        23 March 1778.
        Moved to Franklin Co. 1797, and to Henry Co. Va. 1802
        Early Wills, p 10
```

ARNOLD, Elisha *   Patriot

```
        For Continental Use                    PC April 9, 1782
        1. 225 cwt Beef                        O.B. 5, p 126
        2. 1 smooth gun - Value 50 shillings   O.B. 5, p 147
        * May be same as above
```

ARNOLD, James   Patriot

```
        For Continental Use                    PC April 9, 1782
        1 275 cwt Beef                         O.B. 5, p 126
        Wife Mary Arnold  - Early Wills, p 10
```

ARNOLD, James (Jr.)   Private Militia

```
        Muster Roll, Captain Reuben Vaughan's Company - 1779
        Hubard Papers
        See Will of John Arnold - Early Wills, p 10
```

ARNOLD, John   Patriot

```
        For Continental Use                    PC April 9, 1782
        1. 275 cwt Beef                        O.B. 5, p 126
        Early Wills, p 10
```

ARRINGTON, John   Soldier

```
        b. 1757 Lunenburg Co.  d. 26 Nov. 1837 Meck. Co.
        m. Granville Co. N. C. 30 April 1790 Susanna Vaughan,
        dau. of William Vaughan.
        BLWt 28552-160-55                          Pen. W-5653
        Entered service in Halifax Co. under Capt. John Faulk-
        ner.  Elijah Griffin made affidavit that John Arring-
        ton was at Yorktown when Cornwallis surrendered.
        Susanna Arrington, age 90, gave Power of Attorney on
        9 Aug. 1867.
        M.R. 1811-1853, p 199
```

AVERY, Henry   Patriot

    For Continental Use   PC May 14, 1782
    1. 175 cwt Beef   O.B. 5, p 146
    Census 1782

AVERY, John   Patriot

    For Continental Use   PC April 9, 1782
    1. 325 cwt Beef   O.B. 5, p 127
    2. Overseer of road in room of William Hudson
    3. Served as Juror - 9 Nov. 1778   O.B. 4, p 444

BABER, William   Private Militia

    Pensioned 1 Jan. 1786 under Act of   Pen. S-10333
    7 June 1785 for disability
    Served in Rev. War from Meck. Co. under Capt. Elijah
    Graves and Col. Lewis Burwell

BAGLEY, William   Patriot

    For Continental Use   PC Oct. 10, 1783
    1. 350 cwt Beef   Comm. Book IV, p 40
    Meck. Cert. No. 411

BAGWELL, Lunsford   Patriot

    For Continental Use   PC April 9, 1782
    1. For Philip Mealer - Service of a wagon and team for
       82 days, provision and a driver being found by the
       public.   O.B. 5, p 132

BAILEY, George   Patriot

    Civil Service
    1. Served as Juror   O.B. 4, pp 536-537-538
    2. Served on Grand Jury 8 May 1780   O.B. 5, p 34
    Census 1782

BAILEY, Howard   Patriot

    Civil Service   1782-83
    1. Served as Juror   O.B. 5, 193-259-347-419

BAILEY, Peter   Soldier

    b. 9 Oct. 1762 Henrico Co.   Pen. S-21618
    Entered service in Granville Co., N. C. Served under
    Capt. William Gill (Jr.) and Col. Thornton Yancey
    Moved from Meck. Co. to Montgomery Co. Tenn. 1831

BAILEY, William   Patriot

    For Continental Use   PC April 9, 1782
    1. 350 cwt Beef   O.B. 5, p 126
    2. 4 diets - 1/2 bu Corn   PC May 14, 1782
                                                   O.B. 5, p 150

BAILEY, William (Jr.)   Private Militia

    Pay for riding express for Militia marching to South
    Carolina.   Aud. Acct Bk 79, p 39
    EP 10 June 1783

BAILS, David   Patriot

    For Continental Use   PC Aug. 11, 1783
    1. Allowed 23 pounds 15 shillings for horse taken for
        use of militia - Ordered charged to Continental.
                                                   O.B. 5, p 401

BAKER, Jane   Patriot

    For Continental Use   PC April 9, 1782
    1. 575 cwt Beef   O.B. 5, p 127
    Early Wills, p 11

BALLAD, Dudley   Soldier

    "Late of Capt. Ballard's Company of Minutemen from
    Mecklenburg ... ordered to wait on the commanding off-
    icer at Williamsburg immediately, of failure .... will
    be treated as a deserter".
                                       Virginia Gazette, Feb. 21, 1777

BALLARD, John (Senr.)   Patriot

    For Continental Use   PC April 9, 1782
    1. 600 cwt Beef, 7 cwt Bacon, 6 bu. Wheat, 2 bu. Corn,
        100 bundles Fodder - Supper for 9 men.
    Early Wills, p 12   O.B. 5, p 130

BALLARD, John (Jr.)   Captain Militia

    Captain Meck. Militia (E). Minute Men of '76; Mecklen-
    burg Co. Mss Orderly Book W.D. (G)
    Received pay for service in militia, Aud. Acct Bk 22, p
    20.
    Ord. that a warrant issue to Capt. John Ballard of
    Mecklenburg for 50 pounds 6 shillings 4 pence for prov-
    issions, etc., for his Minute Company.
                                       18 June 1776 - CJV, Vol. 1, p 27

BALLARD, Robert   Officer

    Captain 1 CL Oct. 7, 1775; Major 1777; Lieut. Col. 4th
Oct. 1777; trans, 4 CL; resigned July 4, 1779. "Comp-
any enlisted in Mecklenburg District 1775". Mss. War
Dept. Awarded 6,000 acres. (G) p 36.
Two companies of regulars are just arrived, viz: Capt.
John Fleming's from Henrico and Capt. Robert Ballard's
from Mecklenburg.   Virginia Gazette, Oct. 21, 1775
                                      Williamsburg
Lt. Col. Ballard will superintend the recruiting busi-
ness of my Brigade and receive his orders from his Ex.
(Officer). General Washington   VMH. Vol. 17, p 417

BALLARD, William   Patriot

    For Continental Use   PC April 9, 1782
1. 171 cwt Beef   O.B. 5, p 124
                                        PC May 14, 1782
2. 45 cwt Bacon   O.B. 5, p 151
Court 13 March 1786
3. For 73 days collecting public cattle for which he
    received 150 pounds in Oct. 1781   O.B. 6, p 482

BALLARD, William (Jr.)   Private Militia

    Received pay for militia service. Aud. Acct Bk 22 p 18

BAPTIST, William Glanvil   Patriot

    Civil Service
1. Served as Juror   10 May 1779   O.B. 4, p 466
2. Served as Grand Juror 13 May 1782   O.B. 5, p 142
3. Served as Grand Juror 11 Nov. 1782   O.B. 5, p 236

BARBEE, William   Soldier

    Private in Continental Line - Enlisted at age 17 in
Regiment of Col. Lewis Burwell - Married Mary Smith of
Mecklenburg County.   Burgess, Vol. II, p 554

BARNS, James (Barnes)   Private Militia

    b. 14 Dec. 1748 Cumberland Co., Va.   Pen. S-1894
Entered service in Meck. Co. under Capt. John Burton.
Served under Capt. Elijah Graves and Lt. James Brown.
Served under Capt. Achilles Jeffries, in detail guard-
ing prisoners taken from Yorktown to Winchester.
Moved after war (1) to Burke Co., N.C., (2) to Blunt
Co., Tenn. and to Vigo County, Indiana.

BASKERVILL, George   Patriot

Member of Mecklenburg County Committee of Safety. Appointed 8 May 1775. Died in 1777.
Early Wills, p 12

BASKERVILL, John   Militia Officer

Recommended as second lieutenant in second battalion
of Mecklenburg County Militia under Benjamin Ferrell,
8th captain, 13 Oct. 1777.   O.B. 4, p 374
For Continental Use   PC April 10, 1782
1. 900 cwt Beef   O.B. 5, p 135
                                              PC March 10, 1783
2. 2 empty hogsheads at 7sh. 6 pence each
Census 1782 - Early Wills, p 12   O.B. 5, p 278
Early Wills, p 185 - M.R. 1765-180 p 14

BASKERVILL, William   Officer

Appointe^d a lieutenant in the Continental service 20th
Nov. 1776.   JHD, March 12, 1778
Lt. in 15th Va. Regiment Nov. 21, 1777
                          Virginia Gazette, Nov. 28, 1777
Appointed as Deputy Clerk under John Brown, Clerk of
Meck. Co., 9 July 1781   O.B. 5, p 99
Took oath as captain in Meck. Co. militia 8 July, 1782
M.R. 1765-1810 p 166 - Early Wills p 12   O.B. 5, p 159

BAUGH, Daniel   Patriot

For Continental Use   PC May 14, 1782
1. 350 cwt Beef   O.B. 5, p 152
Census 1782 - M.R. 1765-1810 p 14

BAUGH, James   Patriot

For Continental Use   PC April 9, 1782
1. 1 bu. Corn
2. 600 cwt Beef   PC May 14, 1782
3. 1 smooth gun taken into service and   Sept. 9, 1782
   not returned - 4p 7s 6 p   O.B. 5, 126-152-216
Early Wills, p 13

BAXTER, Peter   Patriot

For Continental Use   PC April 9, 1782
1. 250 cwt Beef   O.B. 5, p 129

BEAVERS, John   Soldier

Resident of Meck. Co.   Pen. S-30853
Entered service at Chesterfield Courthouse in 1780
Served under Capt. Barbee in 2nd Va. Reg. State Line
Served 18 months. In battles 96 S.C., Camden, Eutaw
Springs, Gulford Courthouse. Moved to Barron Co., Ky.

BENNETT, Anthony   Private Militia

    b. Meck. Co. - Soldier in militia - 1782
    EP 10 June 1783 - Moved to Kentucky - Early Wills, p 71
    M.R. 1765-1810 p 71 - Census 1782

BENNETT, Jordan   Private Militia

    BLWt. 31446-160-55   Pen. W-2713
    b. Meck. Co. - d. Meck. Co. 4 Oct. 1822
    In service under Capt. William Lucas and Capt. Richard
    Witton. Discharged after surrender at Yorktown.
    Williamson Rainey, Bartlett Cox and William Coleman
    testified that they served with Jordan Bennett.
    M.R. 1765-1810 p 15.

BENNETT, Joseph, Senr.   Patriot

    For Continental Use   PC May 14, 1782
    1. 675 cwt Beef   O.B. 5, p 147
                                                March 10, 1783
    2. 4 60 gal. Casks at 5 shillings   O.B. 5, p 278
    Census 1782

BENNETT, Joseph   Private Militia

    b. 1757 Meck. Co.   Pen. S-1495
    Vol. in 1776 under Capt. John Ballard, Lt. Malone and
    Ensign Davis in Minutemen Co. of Capt. Ballard, served
    nine months. Entered service in 1781 as a substitute
    for John Bugg under Capt. Asa Oliver, but was trans. to
    Company of Capt. Jesse Saunders as a Drum Major.
    Drafted in late summer 1781 under Capt. Stephen Mahry,
    Lt. Taylor and Ensign Fox in Regt. of Col. Lewis Bur-
    well. Marched to Gloucestor where they remained until
    after the surrender of Cornwallis.
    Moved (1) to Rutherford County, Tenn. and then to
    Davidson County, Tenn.

BENTLEY, Samuel   Patriot

    Public Service
    1. Served as Juror - 12 Oct. 1779   O.B. 4, p 536

BERRY, Andrew   Patriot

    For Continental Use   PC April 10, 1782
    1. 3 bu. Corn   O.B. 5, p 136
    Census 1782

BERRY, Hugh   Patriot

    For Continental Use   PC May 14, 1782

21

1. For putting on 25 pr. horseshoes, mending wagon
   tongue, pasturage 1 day for 21 horses, pasturage
   for 56 horses, putting on 11 pr horse shoes.
2. 30 cwt Lamb   O.B. 5, p 150
Early Wills, pp 127/147

BERRY, John   Private Militia

Soldier in first Battalion of Meck. Co. Militia - 1782
EP - 10 June 1783

BERRY, Thomas   Patriot

For Continental Use   PC April 9, 1782
1. 300 cwt Beef   O.B. 5, p 131
                                         PC Apr.10, 1782
2. 15 diets, 2 days pasturage for 50 head cattle, 10
   diets, 4 bu. Oats.   O.B. 5, p 133
3. 1 horse, price 120 pounds, 12½ bu. corn, 8 diets
Census 1782   O.B. 5, p 137

BERRY, Thomas   Private Militia

b. 8 June 1757 in King and Queen County   Pen. S-14941
Moved to Meck. Co. where he entered service in 1776 in
Minutemen Company commanded by Capt. James Anderson.
Drafted in 1779 under Capt. Charles Clay and Col. Lewis
Burwell. Served in 1781 under Capt. Robert Smith and
Col. Robert Munford. Moved in 1784 to North Carolina
and in 1788 to Mercer County, Kentucky, and later to
Clarke County, Kentucky. Mentions sisters Elizabeth
Brasfield and Sarah Harris in pension application.

BEVILL, Edward   Patriot

For Continental Use   PC April 9, 1782
1. 350 cwt Beef   O.B. 5, p 128
2. Service of wagon, team and driver 35 days,
   provision being found by the public.
3. 1 smooth gun taken into service and not returned.-
Early Wills, p 13   O.B. 5, p 132

BEVILL, Edward   Private Militia

b. 16 Sept. 1762 in Meck. Co.   Pen. S-16648
Entered service in Meck. Co. militia in 1778 under
Capt. Charles Clay. Served in 1780 under Capt. Richard
Witton. Entered service in 1781 under Capt. Asa Oliver
as a substitute for John Easter, a Methodist Minister,
who had been drafted. Moved to Guilford County, N. C.
and then in 1825 to Madison County, Alabama.

BEVILL, John   Patriot

    For Continental Use   PC June 10, 1782
    1. Service of wagon, team and driver for 7½ days, prov-
       ision found by the public.
    2. 225 cwt Beef   O.B. 5, p 154
    Census 1782

BILBO, James (Sr.)   Patriot

    For Continental Use   PC April 9, 1782
    1. 12 cwt Beef, 12 cwt Flour, 5 bu. Corn O.B. 5, p 126
    2. 750 cwt Beef, 1 1/2 BB Corn   O.B. 5, p 129
                                   PC May 14, 1782
    3. 6 bu. Oats, 20 diets   O.B. 5, p 148
    4. 14 bu. Salt - March 10, 1783   O.B. 5, p 278
    Early Wills, p 14 - Census 1782

BILBO, James (Jr.)   Officer Militia

    Took oath as officer in militia 11 May 1778
    M.R. 1765-1810 p 166   O.B. 4, p 403

BILBO, John   Patriot

    For Continental Use   PC April 9, 1782
    1. 350 cwt Beef   O.B. 5, p 129
    2. 1 smooth gun taken into service and not returned
    PC 9 Sept. 1782   O.B. 5, p 216
                     Census 1782

BILBO, Joseph   Patriot
    For Continental Use
    1. 1 gun taken into service and not   PC April 10, 1782
       returned.   O.B. 5, p 133
    M.R. 1765-1810 p 15 - Census 1782

BILBO, Nathan   Private Militia

    Received pay for service in militia. Aud. Acct. Bk 22
    page 19.

BILBO, William (Sr.)   Patriot

    For Continental Use   PC April 10, 1782
    1. 3 bu. Meal   O.B. 5, p 133
              Census 1782

BILBO, William   Private Militia

    Received pay for service in militia - Aud. Acct Bk 22,
    page 20.   Early Wills p 14

BLACKBOURN, Clement   Private Militia

    b. City of Lisbon 11 Feb. 1760   Pen. S-10388
Entered service in Meck. Co. in 1776 under Capt. James
Anderson as a substitue for William Toone.
Drafted in Feb. 1779 under Capt. Charles Clay. Served
in 1780 and 1781 - two months each time - under Capt.
James Hester and Col. Lewis Burwell. Moved to Madison
County, Alabama in 1816. Died in Limestone Co. Ala. on
7 Feb. 1843. His wife died in June 1842.
Early Wills, p 15 - M.R. 1765-1810 p 16

BLACKBOURN, Thomas   Patriot

    For Continental Use   PC April 9, 1782
1. 475 cwt Beef   O.B. 5, p 128
2. 1 pole axe   O.B. 5, p 135
Early Wills, p 15

BLAKE, Robert   Private Militia

    Serving in militia in South Carolina and Georgia - 1779
                                            O.B. 4, p 474

BLANTON, James   Patriot

    For Continental Use   PC May 10, 1782
1. 675 cwt Beef   O.B. 5, p 146
2. 1 smooth gun taken into service and not returned.
3. 1 flat boat destroyed by Major Hogg's orders - value
    10 pounds. 9 cwt Bacon. 16 pr horseshoes put on.
4. Ferriage of 116 men, 3 wagons and teams and 6 horses
    over Roanoke River.   O.B. 5, p 151
                    Census 1782

BLANTON, John   Patriot

    Bacon furnished for Continental use - Comm. Bk 4, p 36

BOOKER, Richard   Soldier

    Soldier in 3rd. Va. Regiment on Continental establish-
ment.   O.B. 5, p 86

BOOTH, Thomas (Sr.)   Patriot

    For Continental Use   PC April 9, 1782
1. 975 cwt Beef   O.B. 5, p 130
                    Census 1782

BOOTH, Thomas   Officer Militia

Took oath as (second) lieutenant in militia 13 Sept.
1779.   O.B. 4, p 517
Recommended as first lieutenant in militia 11 August
1780.   O.B. 5, p 72

BOSWELL, David (Bazwell)   Private Militia

    b. Meck. Co. 1759   Pen. R-645
    Entered service in Meck. Co. (1) as a substitute for
    William Minor, and (2) for George Stanback. Moved with
    father to Person County, N. C., and served in North
    Carolina militia. Stated brother Robert Boswell kill-
    ed at Eutaw Springs, and that brother John Boswell was
    too young to serve. Married Susan Price 29 June 1793
    in Caswell Co. N. C. Moved to Williamson Co. Tenn. in
    1822.

BOSWELL, Joseph   Patriot

    For Continental Use   PC April 9, 1782
    1. 350 cwt Beef   O.B. 5, p 129
    2. 1 gun taken into service and not returned
    3. 300 bu. Oats   O.B. 5, p 132
    Early Wills, p 16

BOSWELL, Robert
                                            Private Militia
    Named in pension application of David Boswell
    Killed at battle of Eutaw Springs.

BOTTOM, James   Patriot

    For Continental Use   PC April 10, 1782
    1. 1 smooth gun taken into service and not returned
                                             O.B. 5, p 136

BOTTOM, John   Patriot

    For Continental Use   PC April 10, 1782
    1. 1 smooth gun taken into service and not returned
                                             O.B. 5, p 136

BOTTOM, William   Patriot

    For Continental Use   PC April 10, 1782
    1. 1 gun taken into service and not returned
                                             O.B. 5, p 136

BOWEN, Alexander   Private Militia

    Muster Roll, Captain Reuben Vaughan's Company - 1779
    Hubard Papers - Substituted for Hicks Bowen

25

BOWEN, Bracey   Private Militia

    Muster Roll, Captain Reuben Vaughan's Company - 1779
    Hubard Papers - Substituted for Jesse Bowen
    Moved to Rutherford County, N. C. 1822   Pen. S-6693
    b. Meck. Co. 1762.

BOWEN, Charles   Patriot

    For Continental Use   PC April 9, 1782
    1. 200 cwt Beef   O.B. 5, p 126

BOWEN, David   Private Militia

    Muster Roll, Captain Reuben Vaughan's Company - 1779
    Hubard Papers - Substituted for James Bowen
    Early Wills, p 17

BOWEN, Hicks   Private Militia

    Muster Roll, Captain Reuben Vaughan's Company - 1779
    Hubard Papers - Early Wills, p 17

BOWEN, Isham   Private Militia

    Received pay for militia service - Aud. Acct. Bk 22, p
    18.

BOWEN, James   Private Militia

    Muster Roll, Captain Reuben Vaughan's Company - 1779
    Hubard Papers. Received pay for militia service. Aud.
    Acct. Bk 22, page 18.

BOWEN, Jesse   Private Militia

    Muster Roll, Captain Reuben Vaughan's Company - 1779
    Hubard Papers. Census 1782 - Early Wills, p 17

BOWEN, John   Private Militia

    Received pay for militia service.   Pen. S-32124
    Aud. Acct. Bk 22, page 18, b. Meck. Co. 1763.
    Entered service (1) under Capt. Binns Jones in June
    1780. Drafted 15 Feb. 1781 under Capt. Benjamin Ferrel
    for 3 months. Entered service again in Aug. 1781 under
    Capt. Samuel Marshall and Col. Lewis Burwell and was at
    Yorktown until after surrender and then discharged.
    Died in Gwinnett County, Ga. 24 Jan. 1850.

BOWEN, Sterling   Private Militia

    Received pay for militia service - Aud. Acct. Bk 22,
    page 20.   Census 1782

BOWEN, William   Patriot

    For Continental Use   PC May 14, 1782
    1. 275 cwt Beef   O.B. 5, p 151

BOYD, Alexander   Patriot

    For Continental Use   PC April 9, 1782
    1. 400 cwt Beef   O.B. 5, p 124
                    Census 1782

BRAGG, John   Patriot

    For Continental Use
    1. Musquet furnished April 1782   Comm. Bk 4, p 349

BRAGG, Newman   Patriot

    Public Service
    1. Served as Juror - 12 Oct. 1779   O.B. 4, p 536
    2. Served as Grand Juror - May, July and Sept. 1782
    Census 1782   O.B. 5, pp 142-172-219

BRAME, James   Patriot

    Public Service
    1. Served on Grand Jury - 12 May 1777   O.B. 4, p 356

BRAME, John   Patriot

    For Continental Use   PC April 10, 1782
    1. 13 cwt Bacon   O.B. 5, p 138
    Public Service
    2. Served as Grand Juror - May-Oct 1779 - Nov. 1781 -
       May-Nov. 1782   O.B. 4, pp 464-527O.B. 5, 109-142-236
    Early Wills, p 18

BRAME, Richins (Sr.)   Patriot

    For Continental Use   PC April 9, 1782
    1. 100 cwt Bacon   O.B. 5, p 123
    2. 1400 cwt Beef   O.B. 5, p 146
    3. 10 diets - 3/4 bu. Corn   O.B. 5, p 150
    Early Wills, p 18

BRAME, Samuel   Patriot

    For Continental Use   PC April 9, 1782
    1. 325 cwt Beef   O.B. 5, p 132

BRANDON, Thomas   Private Militia

    b. 1746 in Hanover Co. d. Meck. Co. 17 Dec. 1834

Moved to Meck. Co. before Revolutionary War. Drafted
in Meck. Co. June 1780 under Capt. Richard Swepson, Lt.
John Clay and Ensign Laughlin Fanning. Drafted in Aug.
1781. Marched to Yorktown and was at surrender of Lord
Cornwallis. Served in Meck. Co. Militia under Capt.
Elijah Graves, Capt. Achilles Jeffries, Capt. Thompson
Fowlkes, Col. Lewis Burwell and Col. Samuel Dedman.

BRANDON, William   Private Militia

Muster Roll, Captain Reuben Vaughan's Company - 1779
Hubard Papers.

BRIDGEWATER, William   Patriot

For Continental Use   PC April 10, 1782
1. 1 horse valued at 110 pounds   O.B. 5, p 135

BRODIE, John   Patriot

For Continental Use   PC Sept. 9, 1782
1. Medicines, etc. for sick soldiers at Taylor's Ferry
    as per account of 11 pounds 2 shillings.
                                           O.B. 5, p 216

BROOKS, David   Patriot

For Continental Use   PC March 10, 1783
1. 275 cwt Beef   O.B. 5, p 278

BROOKS, Robert   Patriot

For Continental Use   PC May 14, 1782
1. 675 cwt Beef, 56 diets, 34 diets   O.B. 5, p 152

BROOKS, Robert   Private Militia

Entered service in Meck. Co. 10 Jan. 1781 under Capt.
Asa Oliver, Major Binns Jones and Col. James Fleming.
Discharged 10 April 1781. Enlisted July 1781 in Meck.
Co. under Capt. Stephen Mabry and Col. Lewis Burwell.
At Yorktown when Cornwallis surrendered. Discharged at
Richmond in November 1781.   Pen. S-10422
Moved to Edgefield Dist. S. C. in Jan. 1800, then to
Washington Co., Ga. in 1818 and finally to Pike Co.
Alabama.

BROUGH, Robert   Soldier

Adjutant of Militia. Served as Adjutant to the Meck.
Co. Militia. (E)(G) - Va. Mag. Hist. Vol. 6, p 403

BROWN, Aris   Soldier

  Corporal in Continental Forces   Pen. W-8386
  Enlisted for three years in 1776 in Meck. Co. Dischar-
  ged after term of enlistment and returned to Meck. Co.
  Entered service in Aug. 1781 as a substitute for John
  Simmons, was at Yorktown, discharged after three months
  Married Joanna Crocksin in Meck. Co. in 1779. Moved to
  Spartanburg Dist., S. C. after the war.
  Early Wills, p 19

BROWN, Henry   Patriot

  For Continental Use   PC May 13, 1782
  1. Gun taken into service and not returned
  Early Wills p 19   O.B. 5, p 143

BROWN, James   Officer Militia

  Recommended as ensign in militia 12 Dec. 1780
  Lieut. in militia June 1781.   O.B. 5, p 90

BROWN, John   Patriot

  Public Service
  Took oath of office as Clerk of the Court 12 Aug. 1776
                                          O.B. 4, p.338

BROWN, John   Patriot

  For Continental Use   PC April 9, 1782
  1. 325 cwt Beef   O.B. 5, p 125

BROWN, John   Officer Militia

  Recommended as a captain in the second Battalion of the
  Meck. Co. militia 13 Oct. 1777.   O.B. 4, p 344
  Took oath required of militia officer on 8 Dec. 1777.
                                            O.B. 4, p 382

BROWN, Mordecai   Officer Militia

  Recommended as an ensign in the Meck. Co. militia 10th
  Dec. 1781.   O.B. 5, p 113
  Took oath as an ensign in the militia 11 Nov. 1782.
  Early Wills, p 19   O.B. 5, p 237

BROWN, Thomas   Patriot

  For Continental Use   PC April 9, 1782
  1. 400 cwt Beef   O.B. 5, p 128

BROWN, Thomas   Private Militia

    Received pay for militia service - Aud. Acct. Book 22,
    page 19.

BRUCE, John   Patriot

    For Continental Use   PC April 9, 1782
    1. 275 cwt Beef   O.B.5, p 125

BUCHANAN, William Willis   Soldier

    b. Meck. Co. 1754   Pen. R-1401
    Entered service in 1776 under Capt. James Johnson in
    Lunenburg County. Served in State Line. At battles of
    Trenton, White Plains and Stony Point. Moved to Clark
    Co. Ga. after war, and then to Fayette Co., Alabama.
    Living in Baltimore County, Md. in 1844 - age 90.

BUGG, Jacob   Patriot

    For Continental Use   PC April 9, 1782
    1. 1375 cwt Beef   O.B. 5, p 124
    2. 208 bu. Wheat   O.B. 5, p 128
    3. 1 Mutton, 66 cwt Beef, 15 bu. Corn, 300 bundles of
        Fodder, 398 cwt Beef   O.B. 5, p 130

BUGG, Jacob   Officer Militia

    Recommended as an ensign in second Battalion of Militia
    under Capt. Benjamin Ferrell   O.B. 4, p 374

BUGG, Jesse   Patriot

    For Continental Use   PC April 9, 1782
    1. 275 cwt Beef   O.B. 5, p 130
    2. 1 Rifled gun taken into service and not returned
    3. 100 bundles Fodder   O.B. 5, p 148

BUGG, Jesse   Private Militia

    Muster Roll, Captain Reuben Vaughan's Company - 1779
    Hubard Papers.

BUGG, John   Patriot

    For Continental Use   PC April 9, 1782
    1. 575 cwt Beef   O.B. 5, p 124
    2. 20 diets, 4 bu Corn
    3. 1 smooth gun taken into service and not returned
                                              O.B. 5, p 136

BUGG, John   Soldier

    b. Meck. Co. 1745 - d. Georgia 1825   DAR Lineage Book 1
    See Joseph Bennett - Pen. S-1495

BUGG, Samuel,Gent.   Patriot

    Public Service
    Gentleman Justice - 1775-1777
    Appointed to take list of tithables 8 April 1776
                              O.B. 4, p 334
    Estate of Samuel Bugg   PC April 2, 1782
    1. 725 cwt Beef   O.B. 5, p 129
    Early Wills, p 20

BUGG, Samuel   Patriot

    For Continental Use
    725 cwt Beef   Comm. Book 4, page 37

BUGG, William   Soldier

    b. Meck. Co. 1757 - d. 29 Jan. 1804 in Georgia
    Georgia Land Grant - Ga. Rev. Soldiers, Vol. 1, p 586 -
    1769-1782

BULLINGTON, William   Patriot

    For Continental Use   PC April 10, 1782
    1. 1 Saddle and bridle - value 5 pounds   O.B. 5, p 135

BURNETT, Barnett   Private Militia

    Muster Roll, Captain Reuben Vaughan's Company - 1779
    Hubard Papers

BURNETT, Benjamin   Private Militia

    Muster Roll, Captain Reuben Vaughan's Company - 1779
    Hubard Papers

BURNETT, John   Private Militia

    Muster Roll, Captain Reuben Vaughan's Company - 1779
    Hubard Papers

BURNETT, Nathan   Private Militia

    Received pay for service in militia - Aud. Acct. Book
    22, page 19

BURNETT, William   Private Militia

Received pay for service in militia - Aud. Acct. Book
22, page 20.

BURRUS, Wm. Jennings   Patriot

    Public Service
    1. Served as Juror - 12 Oct. 1779   O.B. 4, p 536
    2. 2 bu. Corn   O.B. 5, p 126

BURT, Matthew   Patriot

    Public Service
    1. Served as Grand Juror 12 May 1777   O.B. 4, p 356
    2.   do   11 May 1778   O.B. 4, p 402
    Early Wills, p 117

BURT, William   Private Militia

    b. Meck. Co. 1754 - d. Warren Co., N. C. 8 July 1823
    Private in militia   Va. DAR Register, p 446

BURTE, Moody   Private Militia

    b. York Co. Va. - Res. Meck. Co. 1779 - Enlisted on 17
    March 1779 for eighteen months. Carpenter - 5ft 9in
    brown hair, gray eyes, dark complexion.
    Moved to Georgia.   CS(E), page 25

BURTON, Abraham   Patriot

    For Continental Use   PC April 10, 1782
    1. 300 cwt Beef
    2. 1 Gun taken into service and not returned
    Early Wills, p 22   O.B. 5, p 136

BURTON, Benjamin   Patriot

    For Continental Use   PC April 10, 1782
    1. 2 smooth guns taken into service and not returned
                                               O.B. 5, p 134

BURTON, Charles   Patriot

    For Continental Use   PC April 9, 1782
    1. 350 cwt Beef   O.B. 5, p 126

BURTON, Hutchins   Officer

    First Lieutenant 6th Va. Regiment - Killed at Battle
    of Princeton 17 Jan. 1777.   O.B. 5, p 285
    Early Wills, p 21

BURTON, Hutchins   Private Militia

    Drafted in 1780 in Meck. Co. militia under Col. William
    Lucas, Captain Richard Swepson, Lieut. John Clay and
    Ensign Laughlin Fannin for southern campaign - Served 4
    months.   Joseph Butler - Pen. W-3384

BURTON, Hutchins   Patriot

    For Continental Use   PC April 9, 1782
    1. 275 cwt Beef   O.B. 5, p 128
    2. 1 Wagon and gear taken into service and not returned
    3. 1 Horse taken into service - valued at 30 pounds
                                               O.B. 5, p 132

BURTON, John   Officer Militia

    Recommended as Major in militia 13 Oct. 1777
    Took oath as a militia officer 8 Dec. 1777
                                         O.B. 4, pp 374-382
    Lieut. Colonel 12 July 1779   O.B. 4, p 478
    Recommended as Colonel 12 Dec. 1780   O.B. 5, p 90
    Early Wills, p 21 - Gent. Justice 11 Dec. 1780

BURTON, John   Patriot

    1. Ferriage of 33 men, wagon and team over Roanoke
       River   PC May 14, 1782   O.B. 5, p 152
    2. Ferriage of 10 wagons, 41 horses over Roanoke River
                    PC March 10, 1783   O.B. 5, p 278

BURTON, John   Patriot

    For Continental Use   PC April 9, 1782
    1. 300 cwt Beef, 113 cwt Bacon, 375 cwt Beef
                                               O.B. 5, p 129
    2. 1 Bay horse - value 50 pounds, saddle and bridle,
       1 smooth gun taken into service and not returned,
    Note: The three above may have been same O.B. 5, p 135

BURTON, Peter   Patriot

    For Continental Use   PC April 10, 1782
    1. 250 cwt Beef
    2. Musquet taken into service and not returned
                                               O.B. 5, p 136

BURTON, Peter   Officer Militia

    Took oath as militia officer 14 Sept. 1778
                                               O.B. 4, p 427

33

BURTON, Noel Hunt   Officer

    Lieutenant in Continental Line. He became ill while in
service and returned home where he died. Rejected claim
of Horace A. Burton for additional bounty land for the
service of Hutchins Burton, who was killed at battle at
Princeton.   14 Jan. 1839.

BURTON, Robert   Patriot

    For Continental Use   PC May 14, 1782
1. Rifled gun taken into service and not returned.
                                          O.B. 5, p 150

BURTON, Col. Robert   Officer

    Member of Committee of Safety 8 May 1775
b. in Meck. Co. 20 Oct. 1747 - d. 31 May 1825 in
Granville County, N. C. Moved from Meck. Co. to North
Carolina where he served as a Colonel in Revolutionary
War.

BURTON, Thomas   Patriot

    For Continental Use   PC April 10, 1782
1. Musquet and bayonet taken into service and not returned.   O.B. 5, p 136

BURWELL, Lewis   Officer Militia

    Recommended as a Colonel in Meck. Co. militia in first
Battalion 13 Oct. 1777.   O.B. 4, p 374
Took oath as militia officer 8 Dec. 1777 O.B. 4, p 382
Recommended as County Lieutenant 12 Feb. 1781
                                          EP. (G) p 115
Served as Gentleman Justice, and in many capacities in
Revolutionary War.

BURWELL, Lewis   Patriot

    For Continental Use   PC April 9, 1782
1. 2550 cwt Beef   O.B. 5, p 131
2. 15 cwt Bacon   O.B. 5, p 135
3. One gray horse - value 80 pounds   O.B. 5, p 138

BURWELL, Mary   Patriot

    For Continental Use   PC April 10, 1782
1. Sorrel horse - value 60 pounds   O.B. 5, p 136

BURWELL, Thacker   Officer Militia

Recommended as Lieut. Colonel in Meck. Co. militia in
first Battalion 13 Oct. 1777.   O.B. 4, p 374
Took oath as militia officer 8 Dec. 1777 O.B. 4, p 382
Served as a Gentleman Justice.

BURWELL, Thacker   Patriot

    For Continental Use   PC April 9, 1782
    1. 400 cwt Beef   O.B. 5, p 125
    Estate of Thacker Burwell
    2. 2900 cwt Beef   O.B. 5, p 131
    Early Wills, p 23

BUTLER, James   Private Militia

    b. Hanover Co. 5 June 1758, Res. Meck. Co. CS(E), p 2
    Entered service in Meck. Co. 1778 under Capt. James
    Anderson, Col. John Burton. Drafted 1780 for 18
    months under Capt. Richard Swepson. Moved to Wilkes
    (now Elbert) County, Ga. after Rev. War. Moved to
    Shelby Co. Alabama, in 1837.

BUTLER, John   Patriot

    For Continental Use   PC May 14, 1782
    1. 250 cwt Beef   O.B. 5, p 145

BUTLER, Joseph   Private Militia

    b. 1758 - d. 3 Aug. 1843   Pen. W-3384
    Entered service in Meck. Co. June 1780 under Colonel
    William Lucas, Capt. Richard Swepson, Lt. John Clay
    and Ensign Laughlin Fannin - served 4 months.
    Drafted Aug. 1781 under Col. Lewis Burwell, Captain
    Thompson Fowlkes - at Yorktown at surrender of Lord
    Cornwallis.   M.R. 1765-1810 p 25

BUTLER, Patrick   Private Militia

    b. Hanover Co. 1 March 1760   Pen. S-31587
    Entered service in Meck. Co. where he then resided as
    a substitute for William Allgood. Served 3 months under
    Capt. James Anderson, Lt. John Clay. Entered service
    again in July 1780 in Meck. Co. militia. Served under
    Capt. Richard Swepson and Capt. John Brown. Served 19
    months in all. Moved to Wilkes (now Elbert) Co. Ga.

BUTLER, Zachariah   Private Militia

    b. Hanover Co. - Res. Meck. Co.   CS(E), p 2
    Enlisted 2 Sept. 1780. Age 44 - black hair - blue eyes
    - fair complexion.

CALL, William   Patriot

   For Continental Use   PC Sept. 9, 1782
   1. One horse - value 30 pounds   O.B. 5, p 216
   Census 1782

CAMP, John   Patriot

   Public Service
   Member of Committee of Safety - Gentleman Justice
   Appointed to take annual list of tithables in the Upper
   District 12 May 1777   O.B. 4, p 356
   For Continental Use   PC May 14, 1782
   1. 975 cwt Beef   O.B. 5, p 146
   2. 100 cwt Bacon, wagon, gear and horse, 4 bu. Corn,
      ferriage of 23 dragoons, wagon and team, 2 carts and,
      7 men, 12 horses and 3 men, wagon and 120 men over
      Roanoke River.   O.B. 5, p 149
   3. 2 horses furnished Continental, use of flat and two
      ferrymen for 4 days, ferriage of 8 wagons and team
      over Roanoke River.   O.B. 5, p 150

CARDIN, John   Patriot

   For Continental Use   PC July 8, 1782
   1. Pasturage 10 days for 2 horses and delivery of the
      horses to the Magazine.   O.B. 5, p 160

CARLETON, Gabriel   Patriot

   Public Service - Appointed under (deputy) sheriff, by
   John Murray, Sheriff, Sept. 1781.   O.B. 5, p 103

CARLETON, Henry   Patriot

   For Continental Use   PC April 9, 1782
   1. Sorrel horse - value 100 pounds   O.B. 5, p 131
   2. Service of wagon, team and driver for 90 days, pro-
      vision found by public.   O.B. 5, p 133

CARLETON, Thomas   Officer Militia

   Recommended as second Lieutenant in first Battalion,
   under Capt. John Murray, 13 Oct. 1777.   O.B. 4, p 374

CARLETON, Thomas Junr.   Officer Militia

   Recommended as second Lieutenant in first Battalion,
   under Capt. Asa Oliver, 13 Oct. 1777.   O.B. 4, p 374
   Took oath of a militia officer 8 Dec. 1777
                                                O.B. 4, p 382

CARTER, Alexander   Patriot

    For Continental Use   PC May 14, 1782
    1. 250 cwt Beef   O.B. 5, p 146
    Census 1782

CARTER, James   Private Militia

    b. 13 Nov. 1763 in Meck. Co.   Pen. S-8145
    Enlisted in Meck. Co. 1 Feb. 1781 under Capt. John
    Brown - At battle at Guilford Court House. Moved to
    Chatham County, N. C. after Rev. War.

CARTER, John   Soldier

    b. Meck. Co. - d. Oglethorpe Co. Ga. in 1838
    Served in Rev. War as a soldier in the N. C. Line.
    After War, moved from Meck. Co. to Granville Co., N. C.
-   and then to Oglethorpe County, Ga.
                     Ga. DAR Roster, p 255

CARTER, Matthew   Patriot

    For Continental Use   PC April 10, 1782
    1. 300 cwt Beef   O.B 5, p 136

CARTER, Thomas   Patriot

    For Continental Use   PC May 14, 1782
    1. 300 cwt Beef   O.B. 5, p 151
    2. Gun taken into service and not returned

                             O.B. 5, p 278

CAVANISS, Henry   Patriot

    For Continental Use   PC May 14, 1782
    1. 250 cwt Beef   O.B. 5, p 146
    Census 1782

CHAMBERLAIN, Thomas   Patriot

    For Continental Use   PC May 14, 1782
    1. 365 cwt Beef   O.B. 5, p 147

CHANDLER, Joel   Private Militia

    Soldier in first Battalion of militia 1782
                     EP, 10 June 1783

CHANDLER, Joel   Patriot

    For Continental Use   PC May 14, 1782
    1. 325 cwt Beef   O.B. 5, p 145

CHANDLER, John   Patriot

    For Continental Use   PC April 9, 1782
    1. 275 cwt Beef   O.B. 5, p 128
    Census 1782

CHAVERS, Anthony (Chavous)   Soldier

    Soldier in infantry from Mecklenburg Co. B.W. (G) p 145
                                 Leg. Pet. Jan. 9, 1836

CHAVIS, John   (Chavous)   Soldier

    Private in Continental Line   BLWt. 6300-200
    3 & 7 CL, 5 CL, 5 & 11 CL. (E)(G) p 145
                         Burgess, Vol. 3, p 1450

CHAVIS, John   (Chavous)   Soldier

    b. Brunswick Co. Res. Meck. Co.
    Soldier in Meck. Co. militia - 1780. Planter, age 26,
    5ft 9½in, black hair, black eyes, swarthy complexion.
                                 CS(E), p 26

CHEATHAM, Elizabeth   Patriot

    For Continental Use   PC May 14, 1782
    1. 225 cwt Beef   O.B. 5, p 146
    Early Wills, p 25

CHEATHAM Daniel   Patriot

    For Continental Use   PC April 9, 1782
    1. 325 cwt Beef   O.B. 5, p 125

CHEATHAM, James   Patriot

    For Continental Use   PC April 9, 1782
    1. 225 cwt Beef
    2. Musquet taken into service and not returned
    Census 1782   O.B. 5, p 127

CHEATHAM, Leonard   Patriot

    For Continental Use   PC May 14, 1782
    1. 325 cwt Beef   O.B. 5, p 146
    2. 51 bu. Wheat, 25 bu. Oats, 7 bu. Wheat, 36 bundles
       fodder   O.B. 5, p 150
    Early Wills, p 25

CHRISTOPHER, David   Patriot

    Public Service - Gentleman Justice 11 March 1776 - Ap-
    pointed to take annual list of tithables in the Upper
    District 9 June 1777   O.B. 4, p 358

CHRISTOPHER, David   Patriot

    For Continental Use   PC April 9, 1782
    1. 325 cwt Beef   O.B. 5, p 125
    2. 1 Empty hogshead, 15½ bu. Oats   O.B. 5, p 138
    Early Wills, p 25

CHRISTOPHER, Robert   Patriot

    For Continental Use   PC April 9, 1782
    1. 350 cwt Beef   O.B. 5, p 127
    Census 1782

CHRISTOPHER, William   Patriot

    For Continental Use   PC July 8, 1782
    1. 250 cwt Beef   Meck. Book Lists, p 12
    2. 350 cwt Beef   O.B. 5, p 530

CLARK, Alexander   Soldier

    b. Dinwiddie Co. - Res. Meck. Co.
    Enlisted 1 Sept. 1780. Age 26, Planter - 6ft, brown hair
    grey eyes, dark complexion.   CS(E), p 3

CLARK, Archibald   Patriot

    For Continental Use   PC May 14, 1782
    1. 350 cwt Beef   O.B. 5, p 146
    Census 1782

CLARK, Bolling   Patriot

    Public Service
    Served as Juror - 12 Aug 1783   O.B. 5, p 417

CLARK, Carter   Officer Militia

    Recommended as an Ensign in Meck. Co. militia 10 July
    1780.   O.B. 5, p 60
    M.R. 1765-1810 p 29 - Early Wills, p 26
    Will of Thomas Clark 12/1/1750-2/13/1752 Southampton Co.

CLARK, Edward   Soldier

    b. Dinwiddie Co. - Res. Meck. Co.   CS(E), p 41
    Enlisted 2 June 1780 - Age 26 - Planter 6ft - dark
    brown hair, hazel eyes, fair complexion.

CLARK, James   Patriot

    For Continental Use   PC April 15, 1783
    1. 2 Guns taken into service   O.B. 5, p 289

CLARK, James   Private Militia

    b. Meck. Co. 18 Nov. 1759   Pen. S-30941
    Entered service in Meck. Co., as substitute for Harold
    Jones, under Capt. Tignal Jones (Jr.). At Guilford
    Court House. Detached to guard wagon train, and later
    transferred to Taylor's Ferry, Meck. Co., as guard at
    the Magazine there. Moved to Mercer County, Kentucky,
    in 1782.

CLARK, John   Patriot

    For Continental Use   PC May 14, 1782
    1. 30 cwt Bacon
    2. 2 Guns taken into service, not returned O.B 5, p 147
    Moved to Granville County, N. C. and then to Edgefield
    County, S. C.

CLAUSEL, Clausel   Officer Militia

    Recommended as second Lieutenant in Meck. Co. militia
    under Capt. James Hester 13 Oct. 1777   O.B. 5, p 374
    Recommended as first Lieutenant in militia 12 Aug. 1782
                                               O.B. 5, p 181
    Appointed as Escheator for county 12 Aug. 1782
                                               O.B. 5, p 178
    Gentleman Justice 29 April 1783

CLAUSEL, Clausel   Patriot

    For Continental Use   PC April 10, 1782
    1. 300 cwt Beef   O.B. 5, p 134
    2. 1 smooth gun taken into service   O.B. 5, p 149

CLAUSEL, Richard   Patriot

    Public Service
    1. Served as Grand Juror 13 May 1782   O.B. 5, p 142
    2. Served   do   12 May 1783   O.B. 5, p 294

CLAY, Charles   Officer Militia

    Recommended as a Captain in Meck. Co. militia in first
    Battalion 13 Oct. 1777   O.B. 4, p 374
    Took oath as militia officer 8 Dec. 1777   O.B. 4, p 382
    Recommended as Major in militia 12 Dec. 1780
                                               O.B. 5, p 90

CLAY, Charles   Patriot

    For Continental Use   PC April 9, 1782
    1. 800 cwt Beef   O.B. 5, p 125

CLAY, John   Patriot

    For Continental Use   PC April 10, 1782
    1. 325 cwt Beef   O.B. 5, p 134

CLAY, John, Junr.   Officer Militia

    Recommended as second Lieutanant in first Battalion,
    under Capt. Charles Clay, 13 Oct. 1777   O.B. 4, p 374
    Took oath as a militia officer 9 March 1778
                               O.B. 4, p 394

CLAY, Samuel   Private Militia

    Soldier in first Battalion of militia - 1782
                                EP, 10 June 1783

CLEMONS, Edmund (Clements)   Patriot

    For Continental Use   PC May 14, 1782
    1. 350 cwt Beef   O.B. 5, p 147
    Early Wills, p 27 - Census 1782

CLEATON, John   Patriot

    For Continental Use   PC April 9, 1782
    1. 475 cwt Beef   O.B. 5, p 129
    Census 1782

CLEATON, John   Private Militia

    Received pay for militia service - Aud. Acct. Book 22,
    page 18.   (E)(G) p 157

CLEATON, Poythress   Patriot

    For Continental Use   PC Sept. 8, 1783
    1. Gun taken into service and not returned
                                O.B. 5, p 431

CLEATON, Thomas   Patriot

    For Continental Use   PC May 14, 1782
    1. Saddle and bridle taken for service and not return-
       ed.   O.B. 5, p 152

CLEATON, William   Patriot

    For Continental Use   PC April 9, 1782
    1. 325 cwt Beef   O.B. 5, p 129

CLEMONDS, William   (Clements)   Patriot

    For Continental Use   PC April 9, 1782
    1. 450 cwt Beef   O.B. 5, p 129

CLIBOURN, William   Private Militia

    b. Chesterfield Co. 21 Sept. 1766   Pen. W-10620
    Mecklenburg Mpl. (G) p 158   BLWt. 77535-160-55
    Served 12 months in Virginia Line.

COCKERHAM, Benjamin   Patriot

    For Continental Use   PC May 14, 1782
    1. 235 cwt Beef   O.B. 5, p 145
    2. Rifle taken into service and not returned.
                                              O.B. 5, p 147

COLEMAN, Cluverius   Patriot

    Member Committee of Safety - Gentleman Justice 11.
    Aug. 1776. Appointed to take the annual list of tith-
    ables in Middle District 11 May 1778   O.B. 4, p 400
    For Continental Use   PC April 9, 1782
    1. 1575 cwt Beef   O.B. 5, p 129
    2. Dark Bay horse taken in service
    3. Service of wagon, team and driver for 35 days, pro-
       vision found by the public.   O.B. 5, p 132
    4. 110 barrels Flour   O.B. 5, p 155

COLEMAN, James   Patriot

    Public Service
    Served as a Juror 12 Aug. 1783   O.B. 5, p 415

COLEMAN, Obadiah   Patriot

    Public Service
    Appointed surveyor of road from the Castle to the old
    Courthouse.   O.B. 5, p 262

COLEMAN, Richard   Patriot

    For Continental Use   PC May 14, 1782
    1. Bay mare taken for army   O.B. 5, p 148

COLEMAN, William   Private Militia

    b. 1760 Meck. Co.   Pen. S-39337
    Enlisted in Meck. Co. 12 Oct. 1776. Served in 3rd Reg.
    in Georgia.

COLEY, Isham   Private Militia

    b. 1764 in Meck. Co.   Pen. R-2167
    Entered service in 1780 under Capt. William Green and
    served three months. Entered service in 1781 under
    Capt. Robert Smith in Meck. Co. militia and served 3
    months.

COLLEY, Daniel   Private Militia

    Soldier in Meck. County Militia, 1781
                                        Exec. Commun., 1781

COLLEY, Edward   Patriot

    For Continental Use   PC April 9, 1782
    1. 275 cwt Beef   O.B. 5, p 129
    2. Smooth gun taken into service and not returned.
                                            O.B. 5, p 134
    3. Service of wagon, team and driver for 28 days, pro-
       vision found by the public.   O.B. 5, p 154
    Early Wills, p 28

COLLIER, Frederick   Private Militia

    Soldier in Meck. County militia, 1782
                                            EP, 10 June 1783
    For Continental Use   PC May 14, 1782
    1. 300 cwt Beef   O.B. 5, p 147

COLLIER, Howell   Patriot

    For Continental Use   PC April 9, 1782
    1. 575 cwt Beef, 5½ bbl. Corn, 3 empty casks
                                            O.B. 5, p 124
    2. 400 bundles fodder   O.B. 5, p 134
    3. 90 cwt fresh pork, 9 bu. Corn, 550 bundles fodder,
       7 bu. Oats   O.B. 5, p 152
    4. 5 flour barrels, 2 60 gal. casks   O.B. 5, p 155
    Early Wills, p 28

COLLIER, William   Private Militia

    b. 1753   Pen. S-39334
    Enlisted in Meck. Co. for 2 years under Capt. Samuel
    Hopkins. Re-enlisted for three years in Company of
    Horse under Col. Thomas Bland.

CONERY, John   Private Militia

    Soldier in Meck. Co. Militia. (E)(G) p 172
    (Meck.) Rev. Army V, 1, Reg. 67 (E)

43

CONNEL, Avery (Connell)   Private Militia

    Soldier in Mecklenburg Militia (E) (G) page 172
    Early Wills, p 29

CONNEL, James (Connell)   Private Militia

    Soldier in Mecklenburg Militia (E) (G) page 172
    Early Wills, p 29

CONNEL, William (Connell)   Private Militia
    Muster Roll, Captain Reuben Vaughan's Company - 1779
    Hubard Papers.

CONNELL, Morris   Patriot

    For Continantal Use   PC Sept. 9, 1782
    1. Gray horse, saddle and bridle   O.B. 5, p 215

COOK, John   Patriot

    For Continental Use   PC April 9, 1782
    1. 325 cwt Beef   O.B. 5, p 128

COOK, Nathaniel   Patriot

    For Continental Use   PC April 9, 1782
    1. 325 cwt Beef   O.B. 5, p 125

COOK, William   PC May 14, 1782
    1. Service of one horse   O.B. 5, p 148
    Census 1782

COPELAND, John   Patriot

    For Continental Use   PC April 10, 1782
    1. Service of a wagon, team and driver for 36 days,
       provision found by the public.   O.B. 5, p 135

COPPAGE, Charles   Patriot

    For Continental Use   PC May 14, 1782
    1. 275 cwt Beef   O.B. 5, p 151

COX, Bartlett   Patriot

    For Continental Use   PC April 9, 1782
    1. 500 cwt Beef   O.B. 5, p 127
    2. Service of wagon, team and driver for 53 days, pro-
       vision found by the public.   O.B. 5, p 134
    3. 15 diets, 6½ bu. Corn, 1 Bell, 1 Saddle, wagon and
       team 8 days   O.B. 5, p 150

COX, Bartlett   Private Militia

    b. 1762 Meck. Co. - d. 12-25-1845   Pen. S-24296
    Enlisted in 1779 - Served in 10th Va. Regiment.
    Served under Capt. William Lucas and Col. Robert Mun-
    ford at Guilford Court House, lost a leg in battle.

COX, James   Private Militia

    Received pay for service in militia - Aud. Acct. Book
    22, page 20.

COX, John - Gent.   Patriot

    Gentleman Justice June 19, 1775. Appointed to take the
    annual list of tithables in the Middle District 12 May
    1777.   O.B. 4, p 356
    Wife Francinia - Early Wills, p 30

COX, John   (Finneywood)   Patriot

    For Continantal Use   PC April 10, 1782
    1. 325 cwt Beef, Service of wagon, team and driver 43
       days, provision found by the public   O.B. 5, p 134

COX, John, Senr.   Patriot

    For Continental Use   PC April 10, 1782
    1. 3½ cwt Flour, 3½ cwt Beef, 17½ bu. Corn, 205 bundles
       fodder.   O.B. 5, p 138
    Wife Lucretia - Early Wills, p 30

COX, John   Officer Militia

    Recommended as an Ensign in Meck. Co. militia 12 Dec.
    1780.   O.B. 5, p 81

COX, John   (Rattler)   Patriot

    For Continental Use   PC April 10, 1782
    1. 320 cwt Beef   O.B. 5, p 134

COX, John   (Stirrup)   Patriot

    For Continental Use   PC May 14, 1782
    1. 375 cwt Beef   O.B. 5, p 146

COX, John, Junr. (Bluestone)   Patriot

    For Continental Use   PC April 9, 1782
    1. 350 cwt Beef   O.B. 5, p 128

COX, Samuel   Officer Militia

Recommended as an Ensign in Meck. Co. militia 10 July
1780.   O.B. 5, p 60

COX, Thomas   Patriot

Public Service - Served as a Juror 8 July 1782
                                                 O.B. 5, p 172

CRADDOCK, Edmund   Patriot

Public Service - Served as a Juror 12 Oct. 1779
                                                 O.B. 4, p 536
Served as a Juror 13 May 1783 - 14 July 1783
                                                 O.B. 5, pp 348-390

CRAGE, Thomas (Craig)   Private Militia

Muster Roll, Captain Reuben Vaughan's Company - 1779
Hubard Papers.

CRAWFORD, Peter   Private Militia

b. 1764 Meck. Co. - d. 19 Feb. 1842   Pen. W-2765
Enlisted early in 1781 under Capt. Richard Swepson,
marched to South Carolina, served 5 months. Drafted in
Aug. 1781 under Capt. Thompson Fowlkes, marched to
Little York. With Meck. Militia in Gloucestor when Lord
Cornwallis surrendered. Moved to Rockingham County, N.
C. where he married Hannah Christy 27 Dec. 1797.

CRAWLEY, Robert   Patriot

For Continental Use   PC May 14, 1782
1. 700 cwt Beef   O.B. 5, p 146
2. 100 bundles fodder, 5 bu. corn, 12½ bu oats, pasturage 8 horses.   m   O.B. 5, p 149
3. Attending and accomodating a sick soldier at his
   house for 35 days.   O.B. 5, p 149

CREDLE, Joseph   (Creedle)   Private Militia

Muster Roll, Captain Reuben Vaughan's Company - 1779
Hubard Papers.

CREDLE, William   (Creedle)   Private Militia

Muster Roll, Captain Reuben Vaughan's Company - 1179
Hubard Papers.

CROOK, James   Patriot

        For Continental Use   PC June 10, 1782
        1. Services for 72 days collecting beef for army.
           Received 150 pounds in paper money in part for the
           same Oct. 1781   O.B. 5, p 155

CROOK, William   Patriot

        For Continental Use   PC June 10, 1782
        1. Smooth gun taken into service and not returned.
                                                 O.B. 5, p 154

CROWDER, Abraham   Patriot

        For Continental Use   PC April 9, 1782
        1. 300 cwt Beef   O.B. 5, p 126

CROWDER, Bartholomew   Patriot

        For Continental Use   PC April 9, 1782
        1. 275 cwt Beef   O.B. 5, p 125
        2. Smooth gun taken into service and not returned
                                                 O.B. 5, p 147

CROWDER, Bartholomew, Junr.   Patriot

        For Continental Use   PC April 9, 1782
        1. 70 bu Oats   O.B. 5, p 125
        2. 1400 bundles fodder, 25 bbl. corn   O.B. 5, p 127

CROWDER, Batt   Patriot
        For Continental Use   PC April 9, 1782
        1. 235 cwt Beef   O.B. 5, p 126

CROWDER, Dorcas   Patriot

        For Continental Use   PC April 9, 1782
        1. 350 cwt Beef   O.B. 5, p 126
        Early Wills, p 135

CROWDER, George   Patriot

        For Continental Use   PC April 9, 1782
        1. 285 cwt Beef   O.B 5, p 126
        2. 21 cwt Bacon   O.B 5, p 151

CROWDER, Godfrey   Patriot

        For Continental Use   PC April 9, 1782
        1. 650 cwt Beef   O.B. 5, p 124

CROWDER, Hezekiah   Private Militia

    Muster Roll, Captain Reuben Vaughan's Company - 1779
    Hubard Papers.
    Received pay for service in militia - Aud. Acct. Book
    22, page 20.

CROWDER, Jeremiah   Patriot

    For Continental Use   PC March 13, 1786
    1. Services for 67 days collecting cattle for which he
       received 150 pounds in Oct. 1781   O.B. 6, p 482

CROWDER, John   Patriot

    For Continental Use   PC April 9, 1782
    1. 300 cwt Beef   O.B. 5, p 126
    2. Smooth gun taken into service and not returned
                          O.B. 5, p 148

CROWDER, Richard   Patriot

    For Continental Use   PC April 9, 1782
    1. 285 cwt Beef   O.B. 5, p 127

CROWDER, Robert   Private Militia

    Muster Roll, Captain Reuben Vaughan's Company - 1779
    Hubard Papers.

CROWDER, William   Patriot

    For Continental Use   PC April 9, 1782
    1. 275 cwt Beef   O.B. 5, p 127

CROWDER, William   Private Militia

    Soldier in militia   Pen. R-2540

CULBREATH, Thomas   Patriot

    For Continental Use   PC April 9, 1782
    1. 20 cwt Bacon   O.B. 5, p 131

CULBREATH, William   Patriot

    For Continental Use   PC April 9, 1782
    1. 1050 cwt Beef   O.B. 5, p 127
    2. 59 cwt Bacon   O.B. 5, p 135

CULBREATH, William, Junr.   Patriot

William Culbreath, administrator of estate of William
Culbreath, Junr., deceased, came into Court and made
oath that a gun was impressed from decedant in his
lifetime. He believed that no certificate was given
and no settlement made. Same is ordered to be certified. 12 May 1783.   O.B. 5, p 294

CUNNINGHAM, Ansel   Private Militia

    Muster Roll, Captain Reuben Vaughan's Company - 1779
    Hubard Papers.
    b. in Meck. Co. 27 July 1763   McAllister, p 142
                                              Pen. S-31636

CUNNINGHAM, James   Private Militia

    Muster Roll, Captain Reuben Vaughan's Company - 1779
    Hubard Papers.

CUNNINGHAM, Josiah   Private Militia

    Muster Roll, Captain Reuben Vaughan's Company - 1779
    Hubard Papers.

CUNNINGHAM, William   Private Militia

    Muster Roll, Captain Reuben Vaughan's Company - 1779
    Hubard Papers.

DAILEY, Josiah   (Daley)   Officer Militia

    Recommended as a first Lieutenant in the second Batta-
    lion of Meck. Co. militia under Capt. Reuben Vaughan
    13 Oct. 1777.   O.B. 4, p 374
    Took oath of a militia officer 9 Feb. 1778
                                           O.B. 4, p 391
    Took oath as a Captain in militia 11 Nov. 1782
                                           O.B. 5, p 237

DAILEY, Josiah   (Senr. ?)   Patriot

    For Continental Use   PC April 9, 1782
    1. 375 cwt Beef   O.B. 5, p 129
    2. Gun taken into service and not returned
                                           O.B. 5, p 136

DAILEY, John   (Daley)   Patriot

    For Continental Use   PC April 9, 1782
    1. 334 cwt Beef, 10 bu. Wheat   O.B. 5, p 127

DAILEY, John   Patriot

    Claim for service performed for Continental
    1. Seventy (70) days collecting public cattle for which
       he received 1920 pounds in Oct. 1781 O.B. 6, p 482
    Court 13 March 1786

DANIEL, William   (Senr.)   Patriot

    Public Service - Appointed overseer of road 15 Sept.
    1778.   O.B. 4, p 439
    Served as Juror 10 Aug. and 12 Oct. 1779 O.B. 4, p 509
    Early Wills, p 32

DANIEL, William (Junr.)   Patriot
                                 PC April 10, 1782
    For Continental Use
    1. 2 wagon loads of corn tops, 10 bu. corn, 17 cwt
       Bacon   O.B. 5, p 136

DANIEL, William Powell   Private Militia

    b. Meck. Co. d. Coffee Co. Tenn. 1841   Pen. R-2655
    Enlisted in Meck. Co. 1777 under Col. (Bennett) Goode.

DARDEN, David   Patriot

    For Continental Use   PC April 9, 1782
    1. 300 cwt Beef   O.B. 5, p 128
    2. Chestnut sorrel stud horse - value 300 pounds -
       Horse impressed by Capt. James Gunn of Col. Washing-
       ton's Corp of Dragoons.   O.B. 5, p 241

DARDEN, David   (Junr.)   Soldier

    Soldier in militia, 1782   EP, 10 June 1783

DAVIS, Baxter   Patriot

    For Continental Use   PC April 9, 1782
    1. 1075 cwt Beef   O.B. 5, p 128
    2. 54 cwt Bacon, Saddle and bridle   O.B. 5, p 130

DAVIS, Baxter (Junr)   Officer Militia

    Recommended as second Lieutenant in Meck. Co. militia,
    under Capt. George Tarry, 13 Oct. 1777 O.B. 4, p 374
    Took oath of militia officer 12 Jan. 1778 O.B. 4, p 388

DAVIS, Charles   Patriot

    For Continental Use   PC April 9, 1782
    1. 665 cwt Beef   O.B. 5, p 129
    2. Bay horse - value 80 pounds   O.B. 5, p 135

DAVIS, Charles   Officer Militia

    Recommended as a Captain in Meck. Co. militia 10 Dec.
1781.   O.B. 5, p 113
Took oath as Captain in militia 9 Sept. 1782
                                                  O.B. 5, p 214

DAVIS, Edward   Patriot

    For Continental Use   PC April 9, 1782
1. 1000 cwt Beef   O.B. 5, p 124

DAVIS, Hardaway   Patriot

    For Continental Use   PC April 9, 1782
1. 1780 cwt Beef   O.B. 5, p 124

DAVIS, Hardaway   Officer Militia

    Recommended as second Lieutenant in second Battalion of
Meck. Co. militia, under Capt. James Lewis, 13 Oct.
1777.   O.B. 4, p 374

DAVIS, James   Patriot

    Public service - Served as Juror 9 Nov. 1778
                                                  O.B. 4, p 444

DAVIS, John   Patriot

    For Continental Use   PC April 9, 1782
1. 1000 cwt Beef   O.B. 5, p 124
2. 619 cwt Beef, pasturage of 57 head of cattle
3. Bay horse - value 90 pounds   O.B. 5, p 135

DAVIS, John   Soldier

    Received pay for service in militia - Aud. Acct. Book
22, page 20.

DAVIS, Joshua   Patriot

    For Continental Use   PC April 9, 1782
1. 400 cwt Beef   O.B. 5, p 124

DAVIS, Joshua   Officer Militia

    Took oath as militia officer 11 May 1778 O.B. 4, p 403

DAVIS, Randolph   Patriot

    For Continental Use   PC April 10, 1782

             1. Rifle taken into service and not returned
                                                    O.B. 5, p 135
             2. 124 cwt Bacon, 525 cwt Beef   O.B. 5, p 151

DAVIS, William   (Cooper)   Patriot
     Forage furnished for Continental use, May 1781
                                          Comm. Book 4, p 47

DAVIS, William Gent.   Patriot

     Public Service - Gentleman Justice 10 July 1775
     Member of Committe of Safety
     Appointed to take the annual list of tithables on south
     side of Roanoke River 8 April 1776   O.B. 4, p 334
     Took oath of office as Sheriff 9 Nov. 1778
                                          O.B. 4, p 449
     Appointed to take the list of tithables, slaves and
     other taxable property 14 March 1782   O.B. 5, p 121

DAVIS, William   Patriot

     For Continental Use   PC April 9, 1782
     1. 475 cwt Beef, 25½ bu. wheat   O.B. 5, p 129
     2. 114 bundles fodder, 2 gal. Tar   O.B. 5, p 131
     3. Gun taken into service and not returned
                                          O.B. 5, p 138

DAVIS, William, Junr.   Patriot

     Appointed to take a list of the number of people, both
     white and black, in Precinct 2, on south side of the
     Roanoke River, and return the list to Court with the
     white and black listed separately. (Meck. Co. Census of
     1782)   Court 9 Sept. 1782   O.B. 5, p 209

DAWS, John   Patriot

     For Continental Use   PC April 9, 1782
     1. 200 cwt Beef   O.B. 5, p 129

DAY, James   Soldier

     Pet. H. D. 1780, p 36   Pen. R-2784
     Hurt in service, and petitions for aid.

DECKER, Fanny   Patriot

     For Continental Use   PC May 14, 1782
     1. 1 bu. corn   O.B. 5, p 150

DECKER, John   Private Militia

     Muster Roll, Captain Reuben Vaughan's Company - 1779
     Hubard Papers.

                            52

DECKER, William   Private Militia

    Received pay for service in militia - Aud. Acct Book 22
    page 20.

DEDMAN, Samuel   Officer Militia

    Recommended as Major in Meck. Co. militia 10 Dec. 1781
                                                 O.B. 5, p 113
    Took oath as Major in militia 8 July 1782 O.B. 5, p 159
    Member of Committee of Safety
    Gentleman Justice 11 Oct. 1779   Early Wills, p 32

DELAFIELD, William   Private Militia

    Muster Roll, Captain Reuben Vaughan's Company - 1779
    Hubard Papers. Received bounty land in Georgia.

DELONY, Henry   Patriot
                         Public Service
    Member of Committee of Safety
    Gentleman Justice 10 July 1775
    Appointed to take annual list of tithables in Lower
    District 8 April 1776   O.B. 4, p 334

DELONY, Henry   Patriot

    For Continental Use   PC April 9, 1782
    1. 100 cwt Beef, 32 bu Corn, 200 bundles of fodder, 33
       gal. Vinegar, 100 bu. Wheat, 8 bbl Corn, Smooth gun
       taken into service and not returned   O.B. 5, p 124
    2. 1500 cwt Beef   O.B. 5, p 127
    3. 2500 cwt Beef   O.B. 5, p 135
    M.R. 1765-1810 p 169 - Early Wills, p 33

DELONY, Henry, Junr.   Officer

    Captain Mecklenburg Minutemen
    Warrant to George Rawls for transporting Capt. Anderson
    & Capt. Delony's companies of Minutemen from Hampton to
    Portsmouth - 2 Oct. 1776   JCS, Vol. 2, p 183

DELONY, William   Officer Militia

    Recommended as a first Lieutenant in Meck. Co. militia
    9 Sept. 1782   O.B. 5, p 215

DIXON, Sterling   Private Militia

    Muster Roll, Captain Reuben Vaughan's Company - 1779
    Hubard Papers.

DODSON, Edward   Patriot

    For Continental Use   PC April 9, 1782
    1. 350 cwt Beef   O.B. 5, p 126

DODSON, Edward   Officer Militia

    Took oath as an officer in the militia 14 Sept. 1778.
                                             O.B. 4, p 426

DODSON, William   Patriot

    For Continental Use   PC Aug. 12, 1782
    1. 1 Smith's Anvil - value 7 pounds 10 shillings
                                             O.B. 5, p 182

DOGGETT, Benjamin   Patriot

    For Continental Use   PC April 9, 1782
    1. 300 cwt Beef   O.B. 5, p 128

DOGGETT, Benjamin   Soldier

    Private for 3 years in Continental Line BW (E)(G) p 229

DOGGETT, John   Patriot

    For Continental Use   PC April 9, 1782
    1. 650 cwt Beef   O.B. 5, p 128

DORTCH, Abel   Private Militia

    b. 1761 in Meck. Co.   Pen. S-32221
    Drafted 1779 under Capt. Reuben Vaughan, served 5 mon-
    ths. Drafted in Aug. 1781 under Capt. William Drum-
    right and marched to Little York. Detached for commis-
    sary duty after the surrender of Lord Cornwallis.
    Moved to Tennessee and then to Franklin Co. Illinois.

DORTCH, David (Senr.)   Patriot

    For Continental Use   PC May 14, 1782
    1. 650 cwt Beef   O.B. 5, p 147

DORTCH, David (Junr.)   Private Militia

    Muster Roll, Captain Reuben Vaughan's Company - 1779
    Hubard Papers.

DORTCH, Anne   (Widow of Noah Dortch)   Patriot

    For Continental Use   PC May 14, 1782
    1. 575 cwt Beef, 98 cwt Bacon   O.B. 5, p 147

DORTCH, Noah   Officer Militia

Recommended as second Lieutenant in second Battalion of
Meck. Co. militia 8 Sept. 1777   O.B. 4, p 371
Took oath as a militia officer 8 Dec. 1777
                                     O.B. 4, p 382
Took oath as Deputy Clerk of the Meck. Co. Court 14th
Aug. 1775.   O.B. 4, p 316

DOUGLAS, John   Patriot

Appointed overseer of road from Black's Ferry road to
to Fox' Ferry in place of Peter Thomas 13 Sept. 1778.
                                     O.B. 4, p 518

DRAPER, Joshua   Patriot

For Continental Use   PC May 14, 1782
Use of Blacksmith shop, tools and coal for Continental
work.   O.B. 5, p 150

DRAPER, Solomon   Patriot

Public service - Served as Grand Juror 8 May 1780, 12
Nov. 1781, 13 May 1782, 8 July 1782 and 13 May 1783.
                   O.B. 5, pp 34-109-142-172-347

DRAPER, Sol   (Solomon, Jr.)   Private Militia

b. Amelia Co. 1756. Enlisted 2 Sept. 1780. Planter.
Meck. Co. militia - 5ft 10 in, brown hair, hazel eyes,
fair complexion. Service 8 months.   CS(E), p 4

DRAPER, William   Patriot

For Continental Use   PC May 14, 1782
1. 16 days service, himself, for Continental establish-
    ment.   O.B. 5, p 150

DRUMRIGHT, William   Patriot

For Continental Use   PC April 10, 1782
1 208 cwt Beef - 315 cwt Beef   O.B. 5, p 136

DRUMRIGHT, William   Officer Militia

Recommended as an Ensign in second Battalion of Meck.
Co. militia, under Capt. Samuel Marshall, 13 Oct. 1777
                                     O.B. 4, p 374
Took oath as a militia officer 12 Jan. 1778
                                     O.B. 4, p 389
Second Lieutenant 14 June 1779. Captain Aug. 1781

DUNCAN, George   Patriot

    For Continental Use   PC May 14, 1782
    1. 350 cwt Beef   O.B. 5, p 146
    2. Smooth gun taken into service and not returned.
                                                       O.B. 5, p 150

DUNSTON, Charles   Soldier

    A soldier in the service of the United States 8 May 17-
    80.   O.B. 5, p 34

DURHAM, John   Patriot

    For Continental Use   PC May 14, 1782
    1. Smooth gun taken into service and not returned.
    2. Making horseshoes   O.B. 5, p 147

DURHAM, Samuel   Patriot

    For Continental Use   PC May 14, 1782
    1. 400 cwt Beef   O.B. 5, p 146

DURHAM, Samuel   Private Militia

    b. 1752 Fauquier Co. d. 1838 Green Co., Ky. Pen. R-3135
    Enlisted in Meck. Co. Sept. 1776 under Capt. William
    Lucas.

DURHAM, Thomas   Patriot

    For Continental Use.
    1. 575 cwt Beef   Meck. Book Lists, p 10

EASTER, Enos   Patriot

    Public service - Served as a Juror 10 Sept. 1782, 10
    Dec. 1782, 13 May 1783 and 12 Aug. 1783
                                        O.B. 5, pp 227-259-348-415

EASTER, John   Patriot

    John Easter, Methodist Minister, was drafted in Meck.
    Co. militia, but hired Edward Bevill as a substitute to
    serve for him in 1781   Bevill Pen. S-16638

EASTER, Richard   Patriot

    Public service - Served as a Juror 10 Dec. 1782.
                                                       O.B. 5, p 259

EASTLAND, Sarah   <u>Patriot</u>

    For Continental Use   PC May 14, 1782
    1. Attending and accomodating at her house 3 sick sol-
        diers for 21 days. 10 bu. Oats   <u>O.B. 5, p 149</u>

EASTLAND, William   <u>Patriot</u>

    For Continental Use   PC May 14, 1782
    1. Wheatstraw sufficient for bottom of 13 tents, 3 bbl.
        of Corn, pasturage for 11 horses   <u>O.B. 5, p 150</u>

EASTLAND, William   <u>Officer Militia</u>

    Recommended as a second Lieutenant in second Battalion
    of Meck. Co. militia 13 Oct. 1777   <u>O.B. 4, p 374</u>
    Took oath as a militia officer 13 July 1778
                              <u>O.B. 4, p 421</u>

EDMONDSON, Samuel   <u>Patriot</u>

    For Continental Use   PC April 9, 1782
    1. 175 cwt Beef   <u>O.B. 5, p 125</u>

EDMUNDSON, Benjamin   <u>Private Militia</u>

    Received pay for service in the militia. Aud. Acct
    Book 22, page 19.

EDWARDS, Isaac   <u>Private Militia</u>

    Received pay for militia service. Aud. Acct Book 22,
    page 18.

EDWARDS, John   <u>Patriot</u>

    For Continental Use   PC April 9, 1782
    1. 600 cwt Beef   <u>O.B. 5, p 128</u>

ELAM, Alexander   <u>Patriot</u>

    For Continental Use   PC April 10, 1782
    1. 325 cwt Beef, 71 cwt Bacon   <u>O.B. 5, p 138</u>

ELAM, Alexander   <u>Soldier</u>

    b. 1762 Meck. Co. - d. 1799   BW 8723-100
    Private in 2nd Va. State Reg. for three years.
                           <u>Burgess, Vol. I, p 182</u>
    Enlisted 19 March 1777, discharged 1 May 1780.
            <u>Dep. 22 Feb. 1794</u> Leg. Pet., Meck. Co.

ELAM, Joel   Patriot

    For Continental Use   PC April 9, 1782
    1. 325 cwt Beef, 6½ bu. Wheat   O.B. 5, p 129

ELLIS, Stephen   Private Militia

    b. Prince George Co. 19 Oct. 1764   Pen. R-3322
    d. Brunswick Co. 11 Dec. 1834 - Res. Meck. Co. during
    Rev. War. Enlisted in Meck. Co. in 1781 for 3 months
    under Capt. Asa Oliver and Major Binns Jones. Serving
    in Gloucestor under Capt. Stephen Mabry and Col. Lewis
    Burwell when Cornwallis surrendered.

EPPERSON, Richard   Officer Militia

    Recommended as first Lieutenant in first Battaliom of
    Meck. Co. militia, under Capt. Charles Clay, 13 Oct.
    1777.   O.B. 4, p 374
    Took oath as a militia officer 8 Dec. 1777   4, p 382
    Recommended as Captain in militia 12 Dec. 1780
                                                    O.B. 5, p 90
    One of commissioners appointed for carrying out Act of
    Assembly in laying a tax payable in certain enumerated
    commodities.   O.B. 5, p 100

EPPS, John   Patriot

    For Continental Use   PC May 14, 1782
    1. 300 cwt Beef   O.B. 5, p 151

EPPS, William   Private Militia

    Muster Roll, Captain Reuben Vaughan's Company - 1779
    Hubard Papers.

ERSKINE, Thomas   Patriot

    Gentleman Justice 12 May 1777 - Took oath of fidelity
    as Sheriff 12 May 1777   O.B. 4, p 338

EVANS, Anthony   Patriot

    For Continental Use   PC April 9, 1782
    1. 275 cwt Beef, 16 cwt Bacon   O.B. 5, p 128

EVANS, Charles   Soldier

    b. 1762 Petersburg, Va. Farmer - black hair and eyes.
    Enlisted Meck. Co. 2 Oct. 1780 for 18 months. (E) p 260

EVANS, Charles   Patriot

    For Continental Use   PC April 9, 1782
    1. 275 cwt Beef   O.B. 5, p 124

EVANS, Dick   (Richard)   Private Militia

    Muster Roll, Captain Reuben Vaughan's Company - 1779
    Hubard Papers.

EVANS, Godfrey   Private Militia
    Muster Roll, Captain Reuben Vaughan's Company - 1779
    Hubard Papers.

EVANS, John   Patriot

    Public service - Served as Juror 10 Sept. 1782
                             O.B. 5, p 219

EVANS, Ludwell   Patriot

    For Continental Use   PC April 9, 1782
    1. Sorrel stallion - value 175 pounds   O.B. 5, p 131
    2. 750 cwt Beef - Certified at Court 10 May 1784
                                O.B. 6, p. 12

EVANS, Mark   Private Militia

    Muster Roll, Captain Reuben Vaughan's Company - 1779
    Hubard Papers.

EVANS, Major   Patriot

    For Continental Use   PC April 9, 1782
    1. 225 cwt Beef   O.B. 5, p 127

EVANS, Stephen, Junr.   Patriot

    For Continental Use   PC April 9, 1782
    1. 750 cwt Beef   O.B. 5, p 127

EVANS, Thomas (Free Negro)   Soldier

    "A Revolutionary soldier from Mecklenburg County, but
    living in Lunenburg in 1819. He enlisted in the comp-
    any of Capt. Henry Dudley in the 2nd Va. Regiment com-
    manded by Col. Brent, and was in care of the Col's lug-
    gage while the Battle of Monmouth was being fought, and
    was with Gen. Muhlenburg's Brigade in charge of luggage
    at the Battle of Stony Point".
              Bell: The Old Free State, Vol. 1, p. 269

EVANS, Thomas   Patriot

    For Continental Use   PC April 10, 1782
    1. 225 cwt Beef   O.B. 5, p 134

EVANS, William   Patriot

    Public Service - Served as a Juror 11 Nov. 1776
                    O.B. 4, p 344

EVANS, William   Soldier

    b. 26 Dec. 1746 - d. 1806 Wilkes Co. Ga.
    Received bounty land in Washington County, Georgia, for
    Revolutionary War services.

EZELL, Balaam   Soldier

    b. 7 Oct. 1756 in Sussex Co.   Pen. S-31016
    Entered service in Sussex County - served seven months.
    Moved to Brunswick County after Rev. War, then moved to
    Meck. Co. where he lived 14 years. Then moved to Trigg
    Co. Ky.

EZELL, John   Patriot

    For Continental Use   PC April 9, 1782
    1. 285 cwt Beef   O.B. 5, p 127

EZELL, Michael   Patriot

    For Continental Use   PC Feb. 15, 1785
    1. 275 cwt Beef   O.B. 6, p 222

FANN, Willebee (Willoughby)   Patriot

    Public Service - Overseer of road, replaced by Peter
    Thomas, 13 July 1778, when Fann removed from county.
                    O.B. 4, p 415

FANNING, Laughlin   Officer Militia

    Took oath of militia officer 12 Oct. 1778 O.B. 4, p 442

FARRAR, Abel   Soldier

    b. 1763   Decl. for Pen. 1833
    15 July 1833 - Declaration of Abel Farrar for a pension
    ordered to be certified to the War Department
             Meck. Co. Court, Min. Book 1, p 38
  M.R. 1765-1810, p 46

FARRAR, Francis   Private Militia

    b. Meck. Co. 8 April 1764   Pen. S-31672
    Entered service in Sept. 1780 as a substitute for David
    Allen - served 3 months under Capt. John Faulkner.
    Served a second tour under Capt. Robert Smith in Meck.
    Co. militia. Enlisted in Aug. 1781 under Capt. Elijah
    Graves and was stationed in Gloucestor when Cornwallis
    surrendered.

FARRAR, John   Private Militia

    Muster Roll, Captain Reuben Vaughan's Company - 1779
    Hubard Papers.

FARRAR, John   Officer Militia

    Recommended as second Lieutenant in second Battalion
    of Meck. Co. militia, under Capt. Lewis Parham, 13
    Oct. 1777.   O.B. 4, p 374
    Took oath as a militia officer 8 Feb. 1778
                                                   O.B. 4, p 391
    Recommended as a Captain in militia 9.Sept. 1782
                                                   O.B. 5, p 215
    Took oath as Captain in militia 9 June 1783
                                                   O.B. 5, p 375

FARRAR, John   Patriot

    For Continental Use   PC April 9, 1782
    1. 575 cwt Beef   O.B. 5, p 129
    2. 73 days service collecting cattle for the army
                                                   O.B. 5, p 155

FARRAR, Thomas   Patriot

    For Continental Use   PC May 14, 1782
    1. 235 cwt Beef   O.B. 5, p 146
    2. 11 cwt Bacon, 6 bu. Corn, 2 bu Oats   O.B. 5, p 147

FARRAR, William   Patriot

    Public service - Served as a Juror 13 July 1779, 11
    Nov. 1782, 10 Dec. 1782, 14 July 1783
                                          O.B. 5, pp 236-259-390

FEGINS, Henry (Feagan)   Patriot

    For Continental Use   PC Aug. 12, 1782
    1. Gun taken into service and not returned
    Payment made to Jane Newport,   O.B. 5, p 182
    Relict of Henry Fegin   O.B. 5, p 335

FERGUSON, Benjamin   Patriot

        For Continental Use   PC April 9, 1782
        1. 240 cwt Beef   O.B. 5, p 127
        Early Wills, p 36

FERRELL, Benjamin   Officer Militia

        Recommended as a Captain in second Battalion of Meck.
        Co. militia, 13 Oct. 1777   O.B. 4, p 374
        Took oath as a militia officer 9 Feb. 1778
                                                O.B. 4, p 391

FERRELL, Benjamin   Patriot

        For Continental Use   PC April 9, 1782
        1. 450 cwt Beef   O.B. 5, p 126
        2. Bay horse - value 75 pounds   O.B. 5, p 151
        3. Rifle gun taken into service and not returned
                                                 O.B. 5, p 152
        4. Service of wagon, team and driver for 45 days, pro-
           vision found by the public.   O.B. 5, p 154
        M.R. 1765-1810, p 47

FERRELL, James   Officer Militia

        Recommended as first Lieutanant in second Battalion of
        Meck. Co. militia 13 Oct. 1777   O.B. 4, p 374
        Took oath as militia officer 9 Feb. 1778 O.B. 4, p 391

FEILD, Thomas   Soldier

        Soldier in first Battalion of militia 1782
                                                EP, 10 June 1783

FEILD, Thomas   Patriot

        For Continental Use   PC April 9, 1782
        1. 3 bu. Corn, 50 bundles fodder, diets for 12 men, 1
           bbl. Corn, 100 bundles fodder, 2 pole axes, the
           services of a cart with three horses and driver,
           provision found by the public.   O.B. 5, p 130
        2. 73 bbls. Flour   O.B. 5, p 155

FINCH, Adam   Patriot

        For Continental Use
        1. 55 bu. Wheat   Meck. Certificate # 472

FINCH, Edward   Soldier

        Soldier in first Battalion of militia 1782
                                                EP, 10 June 1783

FINCH, Edward, Gent.   Patriot
                        Public Service
     Gentleman Justice 10 April 1783
     Appointed to collect taxes 11 May 1778   O.B. 4, p 402
     Appointed with Benjamin Whitehead and John Brown to
     examine and deface all counterfeit money produced to
     them.
     Served as under (deputy) sheriff 1777 to 1782 under
     John Murray and Reuben Vaughan.

FINCH, Edward   Patriot

     For Continental Use   PC April 10, 1782
     1. 550 cwt Beef   O.B. 5, p 134
     2. Smooth gun taken into service and not returned
                                           O.B. 5, p 149

FINCH, John   Patriot

     Appointed under (deputy) sheriff 14 July 1777 and
     served through 1780.   O.B. 4, p 362
                                           O.B. 5, p 85

FINCH, John   Patriot

     For Continental Use   PC April 10, 1782
     1. 162 gal. West India Rum   O.B. 5, p 135

FINCH, William   Patriot

     For Continental Use   PC April 10, 1782
     1. 350 cwt Beef   O.B. 5, p 134
     2. 250 cwt Beef   O.B. 5, p 151
     M.R. 1765-1810, p. 47 - Early Wills, p. 37

FITZ, Robert W.   Private Militia

     b. 1755 Dinwiddie County   Pen. S-8475
     Entered service March 1776 under Capt. James Anderson,
     Lt. William Baskervill, Lt. John Holmes in Reg. Comm.
     by Col. John Ruffin - served 9 months. Entered ser-
     vice as a substitute from William Baker in 1779 under
     Capt. Reuben Vaughan, Lt. Holmes, Ensign Goode in the
     Reg. commanded by Col. Lewis Burwell - marched to
     South Carolina, in battles at Camden and Stono - serv-
     ed six months. Substituted for Stephen Jones of Hali-
     fax County in company commanded by Capt. Jesse Saund-
     ers, Lt. Bates under Major Long and Col. William Dick
     - served four months. Substituted for William Watkins
     of Halifax County under Capt. Fleming Bates - marched
     to Little York in Aug. 1781, and was there at surren-
     der of Lord Cornwallis. Residing now in Meck. Co.

FITZHUGH, Beverly   Patriot

    Public service - Served as a Juror 13 Aug. 1782
                                        O.B. 5, p 193

FLINN, James (Flynn)   Patriot

    For Continental Use   PC May 14, 1782
    1. Smooth gun taken into service and not returned
                                    O.B. 5, p 147

FLOOD, Burwell   Soldier

    b. Sussex Co. Res. Meck Co. - Trade: Carpenter
    Age 24 April 1780 - black hair, black eyes. Enlisted
    at Williamsburg for duration of war. Rev. Army Vol. 1
    Reg. p 9.
                  Virginia Line - on Capt. Nathan Reid's Com-
    pany Muster Roll, Dec. 7, 1780, under command of Col.
    William Davi(e)s.
                 The New York Historical Society Collections
    Rev. Muster Rolls, 1775-1783   Vol. 2, p. 616

FLOYD, Charles   Patriot

    For Continental Use   PC April 9, 1782
    1. 575 cwt Beef   O.B. 5, p 130
    Early Wills, p. 145

FLOYD, John   Soldier

    b. Meck. Co. 28 Oct. 1758   Pen. W-8817
    Moved with father, while young, to Cumberland County,
    N. C. Entered service in 1776. Returned to Meck. Co.
    in 1780 where he married Nancy Andrews. Moved to New-
    berry Dist., S. C. in 1784. Widow Nancy Floyd allowed
    pension in 1855.

FLOYD, Richard   Patriot

    For Continental Use   PC May 14, 1782
    1. 225 cwt Beef   O.B. 5, p 146

FORD, Calvin   Patriot

    For Continental Use   PC April 9, 1782
    1. 2 year mare - value 45 pounds   O.B. 5, p 130

FOWLER, Alexander   Patriot

    For Continental Use   PC April 9, 1782
    1. 185 cwt Beef   O.B. 5, p 125

FOWLER, Thomas   Patriot

    For Continental Use   PC April 9, 1782
    1. 250 cwt Beef   O.B. 5, p 125

FOWLKES, Thompson   Officer Militia

    Took oath as a lieutenant in the militia 11 Oct. 1779
                           O.B. 4, p 522
    Captain in militia in 1781 under Major Henry Walker and
    Col. Lewis Burwell (Joseph Butler - Pen. W-3384)

FOWLKES, Thompson   Patriot

    For Continental Use   PC April 9, 1782
    1. 475 cwt Beef   O.B. 5, p 125
    Public Service
    Gentleman Justice 10 April 1783
    Appointed to take annual list of tithables in Upper
    District 12 May 1783   O.B. 5, p 291

FOX, Arthur   Officer Militia

    Recommended as an Ensign in Meck. Co. militia 11 Aug.
    1780.   O.B. 5, p 72
    Early Wills, p. 37

FOX, Jacob   Patriot

    For Continental Use   PC April 9, 1782
    1. 400 cwt Beef   O.B. 5, p 124
    2. Service of cart and 2 horses, provision found by the
       public.   O.B. 5, p 154
    Early Wills, p. 37

FOX, Richard   Patriot

    For Continental Use   PC May 14, 1782
    1. 1025 cwt Beef   O.B. 5, p 151
    Early Wills, p. 37

FOX, William   Patriot

    For Continental Use   PC April 9, 1782
    1. 700 cwt Beef   O.B. 5, p 134
    2. 7½ pts Brandy, 30 cwt Mutton   O.B. 5, p 160
    Early Wills, p 37

FOX, William (Junr)   Soldier

    Soldier in militia 1782   EP, 10 June 1783
    2 Va State Reg. (G) p. 285

FRANKLIN, Hugh   Patriot

    For Continental Use   PC April 9, 1782
    1. 575 cwt Beef   O.B. 5, p 129
    2. Horse - valued at 40 pounds   O.B. 5, p 137

FRANKLIN, Owen   Patriot

    For Continental Use   PC April 9, 1782

    1. 59 cwt Bacon   O.B. 5, p 131

FREEMAN, George (Sr.)   Patriot

    For Continental Use   PC April 9, 1782
    1. 385 cwt Beef   O.B. 5, p 129

FREEMAN, George (Jr.)   Officer Militia

    Recommended as an Ensign in second Battalion of Meck.
    Co. militia, under James Lewis, Captain, 13)ct. 1777.
                                   O.B. 4, p 374

FREEMAN, Holman   Patriot

    Public service - Appointed under (deputy) sheriff and
    took oath of fidelity 11 Dec. 1780   O.B. 5, p 85

GARNER, James   Patriot

    For Continental Use   PC April 9, 1782
    1. 235 cwt Beef   O.B. 5, p 128

GARNER, James (Junr)   Private Militia

    b. Meck. Co. Res Meck. Co. - Age 18 in 1780
    Enlisted 12 Oct. 1780 for eighteen months - Farmer, Ht
    5ft 8 in, dark brown hair, hazel eyes, dark complexion
    M.R. 1765-1810, p 49   CS(E), p. 72

GILES, Edward   Private Militia

    Muster Roll, Captain Reuben Vaughan's Company - 1779
    Hubard Papers.

GILL, William (Junr)   Soldier

    Recommended as lieutenant in Meck. Co. militia 8 Sept.
    1777. Subsequently removed to Granville Co., N. C.
    Served in Granville militia.   O.B. 4, p 371
    M.R. 1765-1810, p 51 - Early Wills, p 38

GLASPY, Martin   Patriot

    Public Service - Served as Juror 8 July 1782
                                        O.B. 5, p 172

GLASS, Josiah   Patriot

    Public Service - Served as Juror 13 July 1779
                                        O.B. 4, p 490

GLASSCOCK, Robert   Soldier

    Res. Meck. Co. 1818   BLWt. 90042-160-55 Pen. W-11311
    Enlisted in Chesterfield Co. and served three years.

GLASSCOCK, Zachariah   Patriot

    For Continental Use   PC April 9, 1782
  - 1. 350 cwt Beef   O.B. 5, p 128

GOBOR, John   Patriot

    Public Service - Served as Juror 12 Aug. 1783
                                        O.B. 5, p 415

GODDIN, William   Soldier

    Recruited by Austin Pattilo for Continental Army
                                        O.B. 5, p 298

GOLD, Daniel   Patriot

    For Continental Use   PC May 14, 1782
    1. 450 cwt Beef , 21 cwt Bacon   O.B. 5, p 146

GOMER, John, Senr.   Patriot

    For Continental Use   PC April 9, 1782
    1. 325 cwt Beef   O.B. 5, p 128

GOODE, Bennett   Officer Militia

    Recommended as Colonel in second Battalion of Meck. Co.
    militia 13 Oct. 1777   O.B. 4, p 374
    Took oath of militia officer 8 Dec. 1777 O.B. 4, p 382

GOODE, Bennett   Patriot

    Member of Committee of Safety 8 May 1775
    Gentleman Justice 11 Aug. 1776
    Appointed to take annual list of tithables in Middle
    District 11 May 1778   O.B. 4, p 400

67

GOODE, Bennett   Patriot

    For Continental Use   PC April 9, 1782
    1. 141½ bu. Wheat, 1125 cwt Beef   O.B. 5, p 128
    2. 1 Bay horse - value 100 pounds
    3. 1 Bay horse - value 150 pounds   O.B. 5, p 129
    4. 486 cwt Beef, 480 cwt Beef   O.B. 5, p 133

GOODE, Edward (Junr.)   Officer Militia

    Recommended as secon[d]Lieutenant in first Battalion of
    Meck. Co. militia 13 Oct. 1777   O.B. 4, p 374
    Took oath of militia officer 8 Dec. 1777 O.B. 4, p 382
    Recommended as first Lieutenant in militia 12 Dec.
    1780   O.B. 5, p 90
    Took oath as militia officer 9 July 1781 O.B. 5, p 99

GOODE, Edward   Patriot

    For Continental Use   PC April 9, 1782
    1. 325 cwt Beef, 275 cwt Beef   O.B. 5, p 126
    2. 1 Saddle - Rifle gun taken into service and not re-
       turned   O.B. 5, p 133

GOODE, John (Jack)   Private Militia

    Muster Roll, Captain Reuben Vaughan's Company - 1779
    Hubard Papers.
    Received pay for militia service - Aud. Acct Book 22,
    page 20.

GOODE, John   Patriot

    For Continental Use   PC April 9, 1782
    1. 875 cwt Beef, 586 cwt Bacon   O.B. 5, p 124
    2. 64 Flour barrels   O.B. 5, p 155

GOODE, Richard   Patriot

    For Continental Use   PC May 14, 1782
    1. 1 rifled gun taken into service and not returned
                                              O.B. 5, p 148

GOODE, Samuel   Soldier

    Soldier in the militia 1782   EP, 10 June 1783

GOODE, Samuel, Gent.   Patriot

    Member of Committee of Safety
    Gentleman Justice 13 October 1777   O.B. 4, p 373
    Member of General Assembly 1779
              Reg. Gen. Assembly 1778-1786, p 379

GOODE, Samuel   Patriot

    For Continental Use   PC May 14, 1782
    1. 2150 cwt Beef, 200 cwt Bacon   O.B. 5, p 135
    2. 15 bu. Wheat, 128 bbl. Staves, 107 pieces of heading
       for barrels   O.B. 5, p 152

GOODE, Thomas   Patriot

    For Continental Use   PC April 10, 1782
    1. 8400 bundles fodder, 1 stack tops, pasturage for 40
       horses, pasturage for 41 head cattle, 55 cwt Bacon
                       O.B. 5, p 133

GOODE, Thomas   (Junr ?)   Soldier

    Soldier in militia 1782   EP, 10 June 1783
    Received pay for service in militia - Aud. Acct Book 22
 - page 20.

GOODWIN, Peter   Patriot

    For Continental Use   PC April 10, 1782
    1. 250 cwt Beef   O.B. 5, p 138

GORDON, Thomas   Soldier

    Served as a substitute for Charles Hudson who became
    ill in service and returned home.   Pen. S-8743
    Removed later to North Carolina.

GORDON, William   Soldier

    Enlisted from Meck. Co. for three years. Served in Co.
    of Captain John Stokes, 1st Va. Reg. commanded by Col.
    Richard Parker. He was taken prisoner at the surrender
    of Charleston to Sir Henry Clinton.
       Bounty Land Cert: Sam'l Hogg, 1st Lt., 1st Va. Reg.

GRANT, Daniel   Patriot

    For Continental Use   PC Nov. 11, 1782
    1. Waggon cloth cover - value 5 pounds   O.B. 5, p 241

GRANT, Edward, Junr.   Soldier

    Recommended as a first Lieutenant in militia 6 Feb.
    1781   AC 20 405

GRAVES, Elijah   Officer Militia

    Recommended as an Ensign in first Battalion of militia,
    under Capt. George Tarry, 13 Oct. 1777   O.B. 4, p 374

GRAVES, Elijah   Officer Militia

    Recommended as a Captain in the militia 11 Dec. 1780
                                              O.B. 5, p 90
    Took oath as a militia officer 12 May 1781 O.B. 5, p 96

GRAVES, Elijah   Patriot

    For Continental Use   PC April 9, 1782
    1. Service of a waggon, team and drive for 62 days,
       provision found by the public.   O.B. 5, p 129
    2. Musquet taken into service and not returned.
                                            O.B. 5, p 131
    3. Horse - valued at 46 pounds 10 shillings,
    4. 600 cwt Beef   O.B. 5, p 135

GREEN, Garner   Soldier

    Soldier in 15th Va. Regiment Cert. Ensign Isaac Holmes
                     Va. Gaz. Nov. 28, 1777
GREEN, Matthew   Patriot

    For Continental Use   PC April 9, 1782
    1. 375 cwt Beef   O.B. 5, p 128

GREEN, Matthew   Soldier

    Soldier in first Battalion of militia 1782
                                        EP, 10 June 1783

GREEN, Thomas   Patriot

    Public Service - Served as a Juror 11 Nov. 1776
                                        O.B. 4, p 344

GREEN, Thomas   Soldier

    Received pay for service in militia - Aud. Acct Book 22
    page 18.

GREEN, William   Officer Militia

    Recommended as a Captain in first Battalion of Meck. Co
    militia 13 Oct. 1777   O.B. 4, p 374
    Took oath as a militia officer 8 Dec. 1777
                                            O.B. 4, p 382
    Recommended as a Major in militia 11 Dec. 1780
                                            O.B. 5, p. 90
    Recommended as Lt. Colonel 10 Dec. 1781 O.B. 5, p 115
    Took oath as Lt. Colonel 8 July 1782   O.B. 5, p 159

70

GREEN, William   Patriot

    For Continental Use   PC April 9, 1782
    1. 83 bu Wheat   O.B. 5, p 128
    2. 1200 cwt Beef   O.B. 5, p 129
    3. Wagon, team and driver for 43 days, provision found
       by the public. 200 cwt fodder   O.B. 5, p 132
    4. Musquet taken into service and not returned
                                                O.B. 5, p 154

GREEN, William Wills   Officer Militia

    Recommended as a Colonel in militia 12 Aug. 1782
                                                O.B. 5, p 181
    Took oath as Colonel in militia 13 Jan. 1783
                                                O.B. 5, p 262

GRINAGE, James   Patriot

    For Continental Use
    1. 550 cwt Beef   Meck. Book Lists, p. 16

GRINAGE, Joshua   Soldier

    Soldier in 6th Va. Regiment Jan. 1778. Discharged Feb.
    19, 1778 at Valley Forge.
                    Bell: The Old Free State, Vol. 1, p. 226
                                           Eckenrode, p. 326

GRINAGE, Joshua   Patriot

    For Continental Use   PC May 14, 1782
    1. 500 cwt Beef   O.B. 5, p 146

GREENWOOD, James   Patriot

    Wagon hire with Mecklenburg County militia 1777
                         Va. Mag. Hist., Vol. 8, p. 308
    Early Wills, p 40

GREENWOOD, Thomas   Officer Militia

    Recommended as first Lieutenant in first Battalion of
    Meck. Co. militia, under Capt. Howell Taylor, 13 Oct.
    1777   O.B. 4, p 374
    Took oath as a militia officer 12 Jan. 1778
                                                O.B. 4, p 388
    Recommended as a Captain 12 Aug. 1782   O.B. 5, p 181
    Took Oath as Captain in militia 10 March 1783
                                                O.B. 5, p 276

GREENWOOD, Thomas   Patriot

    For Continental Use   PC April 9, 1782
    1. 600 cwt Beef   O.B. 5, p 128
    2. Horse - valued at 100 pounds   O.B. 5, p 131

GREGORY, Joseph   Patriot

    For Continental Use   PC May 14, 1782
    1. Rifle gun taken into service and not returned
                                           O.B. 5, p 149

GREGORY, Richard   Patriot

    For Continental Use   PC April 9, 1782
    1. 300 cwt Beef   O.B. 5, p 128
    2. 53 cwt Bacon   O.B. 5, p 138

GREGORY, Roger (Senr)   Patriot

    For Continental Use   PC April 9, 1782
    1. 550 cwt Beef   O.B. 5, p 128

GRIFFIN, Elijah   Soldier

    b. 1761 in Halifax Co. - Res. Meck. Co. 1836 Pen. R-4307
    Entered service in Halifax Co. Feb. 1781. Served under
    Capt. Stanfield and Capt. Rogers. At Yorktown under
    Capt. Ralph Faulkner. Discharged after surrender of
    Lord Cornwallis.

GRIFFIN, James   Patriot

    For Continental Use   PC May 14, 1782
    1. 300 cwt Beef   O.B. 5, p 146

GWALTNEY, Michael   Soldier

    b. 11 July 1758 in Brunswick Co.   Pen. S-8637
    Volunteered at Brunswick Courthouse. Served under Capt.
    Joseph Peebles, Col. Frederick Maclin in first tour of
    duty. Served subsequently under Capt. John Willis,
    Capt. Turner Bynum. Drafted under Capt. James Marshall
    in regiment commended by Col. Richard Elliott, marched
    to Little York, and was present at the surrender of
    Lord Cornwallis.

GUY, Christopher   Private Militia

    Muster Roll, Captain Reuben Vaughan's Company 1779 -
    Hubard Papers.

GUY, John   Private Militia

    Muster Roll, Captain Reuben Vaughan's Company 1779 -
Hubard Papers.

GUY, William   Private Militia

    Muster Roll, Captain Reuben Vaughan's Company 1779 -
Hubard Papers.
b. Brunswick Co. 1762   d. 30 Jan. 1837   Pen. S-17969
Drafted 1781 in Meck. Co. under Capt. Stephen Mabry,
Lt. Edward Pennington in regiment commanded by Colonel
Lewis Burwell. Marched to siege of York, but was stat-
ioned across river in Gloucestor when Cornwallis sur-
rendered. Moved to Granville Co. N. C. after war.

HAILEY, Thomas   Patriot

  - Public Service - Appointed surveyor of road in room of
William Culbreath, Junr., deceased, 11 Nov. 1782.
                                     O.B. 5, p 237

HAILEY, William   Soldier

    b. 1748   d. 1830 in Georgia
Drew land in Wilkes County, Ga. for service in Contin-
ental Line. Married in 1771 Mary Tureman, daughter of
Martin and Ann Tureman of Mecklenburg Co. Listed in
Census of 1782 for Meck. Co. Living in Elbert Co. Ga.
in 1792.

HAILE, John   Patriot

    For Continental Use   PC May 14, 1782
    1. Sorrel horse - value 100 pounds   O.B. 5, p 148

HAILE, Thomas   Patriot

    For Continental Use   PC May 14, 1782
    1. 215 cwt Beef   O.B. 5, p 146

HALL, John   Private Militia

    Muster Roll, Captain Reuben Vaughan's Company 1779 -
Hubard Papers.

HALL, James   Officer Militia

    Recommended as a Captain in first Battalion of Meck.
Co. militia 13 Oct. 1777   O.B. 4, p 374
Took oath as militia officer 8 Dec. 1777 O.B. 4, p 382

HALL, James   Patriot

    For Continental Use   PC May 14, 1782
    1. 600 cwt Beef, 24½ cwt Bacon, 250 bundles fodder, 3
        barrells Corn   O.B. 5, p 148

HALL, Miles   Officer Militia

    Recommended as an Ensign in Meck. Co. militia 12 May
    1781   O.B. 5, p 95
    Took oath as a militia officer 11 Nov. 1782
                                                 O.B. 5, p 237
    Recommended as a first Lieutenant in Meck. Co. militia
    9 June 1783   O.B. 5, p 360

HAMBLIN, Thomas (Hamlin)   Patriot

    For Continental Use   PC May 14, 1782
    1. 375 cwt Beef, 33 cwt Bacon   O.B. 5, p 146

HAMILTON, John   Soldier

    Court 8 Sept. 1777
    "Ordered that Francis Ruffin, Gent, supply Judith Ham-
    ilton, wife of John Hamilton, a poor soldier in the ser-
    vice of this state with such necessaries as she may want
    for the support of herself and children, and return his
    account to the Court".
                                         O.B. 4, pp. 369-370

HAMNER, James   Patriot

    Public Service - Appointed surveyor of road in room of
    John Farrar, discharged, 13 Nov. 1775   O.B. 4, p 327
    Early Wills, p 41

HAMNER, John   Soldier

    b. Meck. Co. 1761   Pen. W-10081
    Volunteered in 1779 as guard at military magazine.
    Enlisted in Meck. Co. under Capt. Stephen Mabry in Col.
    Lews Burwell's regiment. Moved to Mercer Co., Indiana,
    in 1801 and to Johnson Co., Indiana, in 1823

HANDSERD, Richard (Hanserd)   Patriot

    For Continental Use   PC April 9, 1782
    1. 600 cwt Beef, 276 cwt Bacon, 2 bu. Wheat,
        Sorrel horse - value 50 pounds   O.B. 5, p 127

HARDY, John   Patriot

For Continental Use   PC April 9, 1782
1. 325 cwt Beef   O.B. 5, p 129

HARGROVE, Howell   Private Militia

Muster Roll, Captain Reuben Vaughan's Company 1779 -
Hubard Papers.

HARPER, John   Patriot

For Continental Use   PC April 10, 1782
1. Gun taken into service and not returned, 2 bu. Corn
   40 bundles fodder, 9 diets   O.B. 5, p 137
Early Wills, p 41

HARRIS, Benjamin   Patriot

For Continental Use   PC May 14, 1782
1. 600 cwt Beef   O.B. 5, p 152

HARRIS, Judith   Patriot

For Continental Use   PC April 10, 1782
1. 375 cwt Beef   O.B. 5, p 136

HARRIS, Philip   Patriot

For Continental Use   PC April 9, 1782
1. 250 cwt Beef   O.B. 5, p 125

HARRISON, James   Soldier

b. Calvert Co. Md. 1742   Pen. S-4300
Moved to Meck. Co. at age 20. Entered service in 1780
under Capt. Richard Epperson - served three months.
Enlisted again under Capt. Robert Smith. Moved to
Tennessee in 1805. Lived in Overton Co., Tenn. Died
12 Dec. 1839.

HARRISON, William   Soldier

Enlisted in Meck. Co.   Pen. W-4481
Served five years. Captured at Charleston, S. C., but
escaped. In battles at Brandywine, Germantown, Stony
Point, Monmouth, Guilford, Pee Dee and Charleston.

HASTY, Henry   Patriot

For Continental Use
1. 250 cwt Beef   Meck. Book Lists, p. 12

HASTY, James   <u>Soldier</u>

    Received pay for service in militia - Aud. Acct Book 22,
    page 20.

HASTY, Thomas   <u>Patriot</u>

    For Continental Use
    1. 215 cwt Beef   <u>Meck. Book Lists, p. 12</u>

HATCHELL, William   <u>Private Militia</u>

    Muster Roll, Captain Reuben Vaughan's Company 1779 -
    Hubard Papers.

HATCHELL, Willis   <u>Private Militia</u>

    Muster Roll, Captain Reuben Vaughan's Company 1779 -
    Hubard Papers.

HATSELL, John   <u>Patriot</u>

    Public Service - Served on Grand Jury 12 May 1781, 12
    Aug. 1783.   <u>O.B. 5, pp 95-415</u>

HATSELL, William   <u>Patriot</u>

    For Continental Use   PC April 9, 1782
    1. 325 cwt Beef   <u>O.B. 5, p 126</u>

HAWKINS, Matthew   <u>Patriot</u>

    For Continental Use   PC May 14, 1782
    1. 81½ bu. Corn   <u>O.B. 5, p 149</u>

HAYES, John   <u>Patriot</u>

    For Continental Use   April 9, 1782
    1. 275 cwt Beef, 24 3/4 cwt Bacon   <u>O.B. 5, p 131</u>

HAYES, John   (Estate)   <u>Patriot</u>

    For Continental Use
    1. 275 cwt Beef   <u>Meck. Book Lists, p. 12</u>
    Early Wills, p 43

HAYES, Winkfield   <u>Patriot</u>

    Public Service - Served as Juror 11 Oct. 1779
                                         <u>O.B. 4, p 527</u>

HAZELWOOD, Daniel   Patriot

    For Continental Use   PC April 9, 1782
    1. 550 cwt Beef, 2 bu. Wheat   O.B. 5, p 127

HEPBURN, Dr. William   Military Surgeon

    Hepburn, Wm., Surgeon - Eckenrode, p. 371
    "The claim of Dr. Hepburn for medicine for and attend-
    ance on John Hudson, a soldier of Col. White's Regiment
    of Horse at the request of Lieut. Yarbough, for 16
    pounds 15 shillings against Continental is allowed and
    ordered to be certified".   O.B. 5, p 262
                   Meck. Co. Court, 13 Jan. 1783

HESTER, Abram   Patriot

    Public Service - Appointed as surveyor of bridge, May 8
    1775.   O.B. 4, p 309
    Early Wills, p 43

HESTER, Ann   Patriot

    For Continental   PC April 9, 1782
    1. 300 cwt Beef   O.B. 5, p 132

HESTER, Barbara   Patriot

    For Continental Use   PC April 9, 1782
    1. 675 cwt Beef   O.B. 5, p 132

HESTER, Francis   Patriot

    For Continental Use   PC April 9, 1782
    1. 600 cwt Beef   O.B. 5, p 125
    2. Rifle gun taken into service and not returned
                                   O.B. 5, p 132

HESTER, Henry   Patriot

    For Continental Use   PC April 9, 1782
    1. 225 cwt Beef   O.B. 5, p 127

HESTER, James   Officer Militia

    Recommended as a Captain in first Battalion of Meck.
    Co. militia 13 Oct. 1777   O.B. 4, p 374
    Took oath as a militia officer 12 Jan. 1778
                                 O.B. 4, p 389

HESTER, James   Patriot

    For Continental Use   PC April 9, 1782
    1. 325 cwt Beef, 7 bu. Corn, 12 cwt Beef, 12 cwt Flour
                                                      O.B. 5, p 132

HICKS, Amos   (Hix)   Patriot

    For Continental Use   PC April 10, 1782
    1. Diets for 4 men 5 days, pasturage for 12 head cattle
       4¼ bu. Corn, 140 bundles fodder, 57 cwt Bacon
                                                     O.B. 5, p 136

HICKS, Daniel, Senr.   Soldier

    b. 1761   Pen. S-5533
    Served in S. C. militia - Placed on Pension Roll 1833
    Richmond Inquirer: Death Notices of Revolutionary Sol-
    diers - Daniel Hicks, Mecklenburg County, 29 Dec. 1857.

HICKS, Isaac   Patriot

    For Continental Use   PC July 8, 1782
    1. 3 Dutch ovens, 4 pots and 1 griddle   O.B. 5, p 160

HICKS, James   Private Militia

    Muster Roll, Captain Reuben Vaughan's Company 1779 -
    Hubard Papers.

HICKS, James   (Senr)   Patriot

    For Continental Use   PC April 9, 1782
    1. 350 cwt Beef   O.B. 5, p 127
    2. 59 days collecting beef for the public O.B. 5, p 154

HILL, Matthew   Patriot

    For Continental Use
    1. 250 cwt Beef   Meck. Book Lists, p. 12

HILL, William   Patriot

    For Continental Use   PC April 10, 1782
    1. 350 cwt Beef   O.B. 5, p 134

HINTON, Francis   Private Militia

    Muster Roll, Captain Reuben Vaughan's Company 1779 -
    Hubard Papers.

HOGAN, Edward   Patriot

    For Continental Use   PC April 10, 1782
    1. 650 cwt Beef   O.B. 5, p 138

HOLLOWAY, Bennett   Patriot

    For Continental Use   PC May 14, 1782
    1. 250 cwt Beef   O.B. 5, p 146

HOLLOWAY, Edward   Patriot

    For Continental Use   PC April 10, 1782
    1. Horse - value 50 pounds, 60 cwt fodder, 6 bu. Corn
                                              O.B. 5, p 138

HOLLOWAY, John   Private Militia

  - Muster Roll, Captain Reuben Vaughan's Company 1779 -
    Hubard Papers.

HOLLOWAY, William, Senr.   Patriot

    For Continental Use   PC May 14, 1782
    1. 275 cwt Beef   O.B. 5, p 147

HOLLOWAY, William (Junr)   Sergeant Militia

    Muster Roll, Captain Reuben Vaughan's Company 1779 -
    Hubard Papers.
    Received pay for service in militia - Aud. Acct Book 22
    page 19.

HOLMES, Isaac   Soldier

    Clerk, Mecklenburg County Committee of Safety, 8 May
    1775.
    Ensign in 15th Va. Regiment, Williamsburg 19 Sept. 1777
                                  Virginia Gazette, Oct. 3, 1777

HOLMES, John   Officer Militia

    Recommended as a second Lieutenant in second Battalion
    of Meck. Co. militia 13 Oct. 1777   O.B. 4, p 374
    Took oath as militia officer 8 Dec. 1777 O.B.4, p 382

HOLMES, John   Patriot

    For Continental Use   PC May 14, 1782
    1. 225 cwt Beef   O.B. 5, p 151

HOLMES, Lucy   Patriot

    For Continental Use   PC May 14, 1782
    1. 275 cwt Beef   O.B. 5, p 151

HOLMES, Pennington   Patriot

    For Continental Use   PC June 10, 1782
    1. 83 days collecting beef for the service
                                                O.B. 5, p 155

HOLMES, Samuel (Senr)   Patriot

    For Continental Use   PC Apr. 10, 1782
    1. 625 cwt Beef   O.B. 5, p 124
    2. 32 diets, 5 bu. Wheat, 4 bu. Corn   O.B. 5, p 135
    3. 490 cwt Beef   O.B. 5, p 151

HOLMES, Samuel, Jr.   Officer Militia

    Recommended as a first Lieutenant in second Battalion
    of Meck. Co. Militia, under Capt. Lewis Parham, 13 Oct.
    1777.   O.B. 4, p 374

HOLMES, Samuel   Officer Militia

    Recommended as an Ensign in militia 14 Feb. 1780
                                                O.B. 5, p. 32
    Recommended as a first Lieutenant 12 May 1781
                                                O.B. 5, p. 95

HOLMES, William   Patriot

    For Continental Use   PC April 9, 1782
    1. 625 cwt Beef   O.B. 5, p 124
    2. 26 diets, 37 cwt Bacon, 6½ bu. Corn   O.B. 5, p 135
    3. Service of cart and 2 horses   O.B. 5, p 154

HOLMES, William, Jr.   Patriot

    For Continental Use   PC June 10, 1782
    Service 61 days collecting beef for public
                                                O.B. 5, p 155

HOMES, John   Soldier

    Received pay for service in militia - Aud. Acct Book 22
    page 18.

HOOBRY, Jacob   (Also Whobry)   Patriot

    Public Service - Served as Juror 12 Aug. 1783
                                                O.B. 5, p 415

HOPKINS, Samuel (Senr)   Patriot

　　For Continental Use
　　1. 375 cwt Beef   Meck. Book Lists, p. 9

HOPKINS, John   Patriot

　　For Continental Use   PC May 14, 1782
　　1. Smooth gun taken into service and not returned
　　　　　　　　　　　　　　　　　　　　　　　O.B. 5, p 152

HOPKINS, Samuel, Junr.   Patriot

　　Member of Committee of Safety 8 May 1775

HOPKINS, Samuel (Junr)   Patriot

　　For Continental Use   PC April 9, 1782
　　1. 575 cwt Beef   O.B. 5, p 124
　　2. 287 cwt Beef   Meck. Book Lists, p. 8

HOPKINS, Samuel (Jr)   Officer Militia

　　Captain, Mecklenburg Militia, on recruiting duty in
　　March 1776.   AB (G) p. 391

HUBBARD, John   Patriot

　　For Continental Use   PC April 10, 1782
　　1. 8 diets, 194 bundles fodder, 10½ bu. Corn
　　　　　　　　　　　　　　　　　　　　　　　O.B. 5, p 137

HUDSON, Charles   Soldier

　　b. Amelia Co. 1751   Pen. S-8743
　　Enlisted March 1776 for 2 years. Served in Continental
　　forces under Capt. James Johnson, Lt. Nicholas Hobson,
　　Lt. Peter Garland, Ensign John Stokes of Lunenburg Co.
　　Taken ill and sent home. Thomas Gordon substituted for
　　him after six months and served rest of enlistment.
　　Moved from Amelia to Lunenburg Co. and then to Meck.
　　Co.

HUDSON, Cuthbert   Soldier

　　b. Va. d. Elbert Co. Ga. 1801. Soldier in Rev. War.
　　　　　　　　　　　　　　　　　　　Ga. DAR Roster, p. 92
　　Early Wills, p 46

HUDSON, Edward   Patriot

　　Served as a Juror 10 Sept. 1782   O.B. 5, p 219

HUDSON, Forrest   Soldier

    Drafted in Mecklenburg County militia.
                                                O.B. 4, p 395

HUDSON, James   Soldier

    Soldier in 15th Va. State Regiment. Isaac Holmes,
    Ensign.   Va. Gazette, Oct. 3, 1777

HUDSON, John, Sr.   Patriot

    For Continental Use   PC April 9, 1782
    1. 675 cwt Beef   O.B. 5, p 126
    2. Smooth gun taken into service and not returned
                                        O.B. 5, p 132

HUDSON, John   Officer Militia

    Recommended as second Lieutenant in first Battalion of
    Meck. Co. militia, under Capt. James Hall, 13 Oct. 17-
    77.   O.B. 4, p 374
    Took oath as militia officer 8 Dec. 1777 O.B. 4, p 382
    Recommended as first Lieutenant in militia 12 May 1781
                                        O.B. 5, p. 95

HUDSON, John   Soldier

    Soldier in Col. White's regiment of horse
                                        O.B. 5, p 262

HUDSON, Robert   Patriot

    For Continental Use   PC April 9, 1782
    1. 350 cwt Beef   O.B. 5, p 129
    2. Hire of a horse impressed 137 days for militia ord-
       ered to South Carolina. Aud. Acct Book 1780/81 -
       page 162.

HUDSON, Stephen   Soldier

    Soldier in 15th Va. State Reg. under Capt. Mason
                                   Va. Gazette, Nov. 28, 1777

HUDSON, Thomas   Patriot

    For Continental Use   PC April 9, 1782
    1. 275 cwt Beef   O.B. 5, p 129

HUDSON, William   Private Militia

    Muster Roll, Captain Reuben Vaughan's Company 1779 -
    Hubard Papers.

HUDSON, William   Patriot

    For Continental Use   PC April 10, 1782
    1. 350 cwt Beef   O.B. 5, p 134
    2. 225 cwt Beef   O.B. 5, p 135

HUDSON, William   Soldier

    Soldier in first Battalion of militia 1782
                             EP, 10 June 1783

HUDSON, William   Patriot

    For Continental Use   PC April 9, 1782
    1. 7 cwt Beef, 7 cwt Flour, 4½ bu. Corn O.B. 5, p 126

HUDSON, William   Patriot

    Public Service - Overseer of road 9 Nov. 1778
                             O.B. 4, p 446

HUDSON, William   Patriot

    Public Service - Served as Juror 13 May 1782
                           O.B. 5, p 142

    Note: The Census of 1782 lists four William Hudsons as
           heads of families residing in the county.

HUGHES, Elizabeth   Patriot

    For Continental Use   PC April 10, 1782
    1. 6½ bu. Corn, 11½ cwt Bacon   O.B. 5, p 135

HUGHES, James   Patriot

    For Continental Use   PC April 10, 1782
    1. 10 bu. Oats, 90 bundles fodder, 7 diets
                             O.B. 5, p 134

HUMPHRIES, John   Patriot

    For Continental Use   PC April 9, 1782
    1. 15 bu. Wheat, 300 cwt Beef   O.B. 5, p 127

HUNDLEY, William, Gent.   Officer Militia

    Recommended as second Lieutenant in first Battalion of
    militia, under Capt. Howell Taylor, 13 Oct. 1777
                          O.B. 4, p 374
    Recommended as first Lieutenant in militia 12 Aug. 1782
                          O.B. 5, p 181

HUNLEY, William   Officer Militia

    Took oath as an Ensign in lilitia 9 Aug. 1779
                                              O.B. 4, p 493
    Recommended as second Lieutenant in militia
    12 Dec. 1780   O.B. 5, p 90
    Took oath as militia officer 12 May 1781 O.B. 5, p 96

HUNT, Berry   Soldier

    Soldier in Mecklenburg militia   (E)(G), p. 404

HUNT, James   Officer Militia

    Took oath of militia officer 12 May 1781 O.B. 5, p 96
    b. 1756 d. 1811 Meck. Co.

HUNT, Presley   Patriot

    For Continental Use   PC May 14, 1782
    1. Cock pin for gun   O.B. 5, p 151

HUNT, William   Patriot

    For Continental Use   PC April 9, 1782
    1. 375 cwt Beef   O.B. 5, p 126
    2. 125 gal. Brandy   O.B. 5, p 151

HUNT, William, Jr.   Officer Militia

    Took oath as an Ensign in militia 13 Sept. 1779
                                              O.B. 4, p 517

HUNT, William, Junr.   Patriot

    For Continental Use   Meck. Book Lists, p. 10
    275 cwt Beef

HURDON, Reuben   Soldier

    b. Amelia Co. 1760. Resided in Meck. Co.
    Enlisted May 1779 for 18 months in second Regiment
    Planter, 5ft 9½ in, brown hair, grey eyes, dark com-
    plexion   CS(E), p. 8

HURT, Philemon   Patriot

    For Continental Use   PC April 9, 1782
    1. 300 cwt Beef   O.B. 5, p 127

HUTCHESON, Charles   Patriot

For Continental Use   Meck. Book Lists, p. 15
1. 775 cwt Beef

HUTCHESON, Charles   Officer Militia

Recommended as second Lieutenant in second Battalion
militia, under Capt. Reuben Vaughan, 13 Oct. 1777
                                                O.B. 4, p 374
Took oath as militia officer 8 Dec. 1777 O.B. 4, p 382

HUTCHESON, John   Patriot

For Continental Use   PC April 9, 1782
1. 575 cwt Beef   O.B. 4, p 130

HUTCHESON, John   Officer Militia

Recommended as an Ensign in lilitia 12 May 1783
                                                O.B. 5, p 299

HUTCHESON, Peter   Patriot

For Continental Use   PC April 9, 1782
1. 450 cwt Beef   O.B. 5, p 132

HUTCHESON, Richard   Officer Militia

Recommended as an Ensign in second Battalion of mili-
tia, under Capt. Reuben Vaughan, 13 Oct. 1777
                                                O.B. 4, p 374
Took oath as militia officer 8 Dec. 1777 O.B. 4, p 382
Recommended as Captain in militia 10 Dec. 1781
                                                O.B. 5, p 113
Took oath as Captain 11 Nov. 1782   O.B. 5, p 237

HUTCHESON, Richard   Patriot

For Continental Use   PC April 9, 1782
1. 325 cwt Beef   O.B. 5, p 130
2. One saddle   O.B. 5, p 133

HUTT, Charles   Patriot

For Continental Use   PC April 9, 1782
1. 775 cwt Beef   O.B. 5, p 127

HUTT, Daniel   Patriot

Clerk, Committee of Safety   CJV, Vol. 2, p. 210
Took oath as Constable 9 March 1178   O.B. 4, p 395

85

HYDE, James   Patriot

    Public Service - Appointed surveyor of road from Runa-
way Castle to Butcher's Creek 11 June 1781
                                O.B. 5, p. 98

HYDE, John   Patriot

    For Continental Use   PC April 9, 1782
    1. 2 Muttons, 20 cwt Bacon   O.B. 5, p 131

HYDE, Robert   Patriot

    For Continental Use   PC April 9, 1782
    1. Sorrel horse - value 120 pounds   O.B. 5, p 130
    2. Service of horse, provision found by public
                               O.B. 5, p 131
    3. Service of waggon, team and driver, provision
       found by the public   O.B. 5, p 154

HYDE, Robert   Soldier

    Soldier in first Battalion of militia 1782
                             EP, 10 June 1783

INSCO, James   Soldier

    Received pay as soldier in militia - Aud. Acct Book 22
page 20.

INSCO, William   Soldier

    b. Essex Co. 10 April 1756   Pen. S-11363
Moved to Meck. Co. Entered service in 1777 as a substitute for his father, James Insco, under Capt. John
Burton. Entered service in 1778 as a substitute for
his brother, James Insco, under Capt. Benjamin Marshall. Entered service in 1781 under Capt Richard Witton

JACKSON, Jonathon   Soldier

    b. 1753 - Placed on Pension Roll 1831
    3 CL - Mecklenburg Pensioner   (G) p. 411
    Served as private in Continental Line.

JACKSON, Matthew   Soldier

    Soldier in second division of Mecklenburg militia at
Portsmouth Sept. 1777
              Va. Gazette, Sept. 19, 1777

JAMES, Joshua   Soldier

    b. 1751 Soldier in Va. State Line. Placed on Pension
    Roll 1831   Meck. Pensioner, (G), p. 413

JEFFRIES, Achilles   Officer Militia

    Recommended as an Ensign in Captain (Charles) Clay's
    Co. of militia 10 July 1780   O.B. 5, p 81
    Recommended as second Lieutenant 12 Dec. 1780
                              O.B. 5, p 90
    Recommended as a Captain 10 Dec. 1781   O.B. 5, p 113

JEFFRIES, John, Sr.   Patriot

    b. Henrico Co. 5 Sept. 1707. d. Meck. Co. 8 Feb. 1792
    For Continental Use   PC April 9, 1782
    1. 1275 cwt Beef   O.B. 5, p 129
    2. Bay horse - value 80 pounds   O.B. 5, p 131
    Early Wills, p 47

JEFFRIES, Swepson   Patriot

    For Continental Use   PC May 12, 1782
    1. 225 cwt Beef   O.B. 5, p 147
    M.R. 1765-1810, p 72 - Early Wills, p 47

JETER, William   Patriot

    Public Service - Served as Juror 13 May 1783
                             O.B. 5, p 348
    Early Wills, pp 68-125-165

JOHNS, John   Patriot

    For Continental Use   PC May 14, 1782
    1. 200 cwt Beef   O.B. 5, p 148

JOHNSON, Caleb   Private Militia

    Recommended as an Ensign in first Battalion of Meck.
    Co. militia, under Capt. James Hester, 13 Oct. 1777
                           O.B. 4, p 374
    Took oath as militia officer 12 Jan. 1778
                           O.B. 4, p 389

JOHNSON, Caleb   Patriot

    For Continental Use   PC April 9, 1782
    1. 325 cwt Beef   O.B. 5, p 125
    2. Service of waggon, team and driver, provision
       found by public
    3. Pasturage for 283 hogs for 12 days   O.B. 5, p 148

JOHNSON, Ellis   Soldier

    Soldier in 2nd Va. State Regiment   (G), p. 420
    Isaac Holmes, Lt. of the Regiment, certified 17 June
    1789 that Ellis Johnson was a soldier in 2nd Va. State
    Regiment and served three years.
                             Meck. Co. Leg. Pet.

JOHNSON, Isaac   Officer Militia

    Recommended as first Lieutenant in second Battalion of
    Meck. Co. militia, under Capt. Samuel Marshall, 13 Oct.
    1777   O.B. 4, p 374
    Took oath as militia officer 12 Jan. 1778 O.B. 4, p 389

JOHNSON, Isaac   Patriot

    For Continental Use   PC April 9, 1782
    1. 340 cwt Beef   O.B. 5, p 127

JOHNSON, James   Patriot

    For Continental Use   PC April 9, 1782
    1. 225 cwt Beef   O.B. 5, p 129

JOHNSON, James (Junr)   Soldier

    Received pay for service in militia - Aud. Acct Book 22
    page 18.

JOHNSON, John   Patriot

    For Continental Use   PC May 14, 1782
    1. 400 cwt Beef   O.B. 5, p 146

JOHNSON, John, Senr.   Patriot

    Public Service - Appointed surveyor of road in room of
    Thomas Reives 13 Oct. 1783   O.B. 5, p 435

JOHNSON, John   Patriot

    Public Service - Appointed surveyor of road from
    Buckhorn Creek to Saffold's Ford in room of Jeffrey
    Russell 8 July 1782   O.B. 5, p 176

JOHNSON, Mary   Patriot

    For Continental Use   PC April 9, 1782
    1. 750 cwt Beef   O.B. 5, p 128
    Early Wills, p 48

JOHNSON, William   Patriot

    Gentleman Justice 12 Nov. 1781
    Appointed to take the annual list of tithables in the
    Middle District 13 May 1782   O.B. 5, p 144
    Appointed to take a list of the number of people, both
    white and black, in the 5th Precinct 9 Sept. 1782
    (Census of 1782)   O.B. 5, p 209

JOHNSON, William   Patriot

    For Continental Use   PC April 9, 1782
    1. 275 cwt Beef   O.B. 5, p 126
    2. Dark bay horse - value 47 pounds   D.B. 5, p 127

JOHNSON, William, Junr.   Soldier

  - Recommended as a first Lieutenant in militia 10 March
    1783   O.B. 5, p 276

JOHNSON, Zachariah   Soldier

    Received pay for service in militia - Aud. Acct Book
    22, page 19.

JOHNSTON, Howell   Soldier

    Received pay for service in militia - Aud. Acct Book
    22, page 19.

JOHNSTON, Philip   Soldier

    Received pay for service in militia - Aud. Acct Book
    22, page 19.

JONES, Adam   Soldier

    "Late of Capt. Ballard's Company of Minute Men from
    Mecklenburg Co. -"   Samuel Cobb,Lt.
                     Va. Gazette, Feb. 21 ,1777

JONES, Balaam   Patriot

    For Continental Use
    1. 285 cwt Beef   Meck. Book Lists, p. 13

JONES, Benjamin   Patriot

    For Continental Use   PC April 10, 1782
    1. 285 cwt Beef   O.B. 5, p 135
    2. 275 cwt Beef   O.B. 5, p 146

JONES, Carroll   Soldier

    Served two tours of duty in Meck. Co. militia under
    Capt. Asa Oliver and Capt. Stephen Mabry.
    Statement in pension application of Joseph Bennett
                               Pen. S-1495

JONES, Daniel   Patriot

    For Continental Use   PC April 9, 1782
    1. 325 cwt Beef   O.B. 5, p 129

JONES, Daniel (Estate)   Patriot

    For Continental Use   PC April 10, 1782
    1. 10 bbls. Corn   O.B. 5, p 138
    2. 1350 cwt Beef   Meck. Book Lists, p. 9

JONES, Harold   Soldier

    James Clark went as a substitute for Harold Jones into
    service in 1781   Pen. S-30941

JONES, James   Soldier

    Took oath as an Ensign in militia 12 June 1780
                               O.B. 5, p 54

JONES, James (Senr)   Patriot

    For Continental Use   PC May 14, 1782
    1. 350 cwt Beef   O.B. 5, p 146

JONES, John   Patriot

    Member of Committee of Safety 8 May 1775
    Early Wills, p 49

JONES, John   Patriot

    For Continental Use   PC April 9, 1782
    1. 550 cwt Beef   O.B. 5, p 124

JONES, John   Soldier

    b. Meck. Co.   Pen. R-5716
    Enlisted in service from Meck. Co. Living in 1835.

JONES, Peter   Patriot

    For Continental Use   PC April 9, 1782
    1. 1110 cwt Beef   O.B. 5, p 131

JONES, Richard   Patriot

    Public Service - Appointed syrveyor of road from But-
    cher's Creek to the old Courthouse 13 March 1780
                                            O.B. 5, p 16

JONES, Richard   Patriot

    For Continental Use   PC April 9, 1782
    1. 225 cwt Beef, 10½ bu. Corn   O.B. 5, p 126

JONES, Robert   Soldier

    Recommended as a Lieutenant in militia 12 May 1781
                                            O.B. 5, p 95

JONES, Robert   Patriot

  _ Recommended for appointment as a Justice for Meck. Co.
    15 April 1783   O.B. 5, p 289

JONES, Stephen   Patriot

    For Continental Use   PC April 9, 1782
    1. 33 gallons Vinegar   O.B. 5, p 125
    2. 350 cwt Beef   O.B. 5, p 155

JONES, Tabitha   Patriot

    For Continental Use   PC April 9, 1782
    1. 325 cwt Beef   O.B. 5, p 127

JONES, Thomas (Senr)   Patriot

    Public Service - Appointed surveyor of road from
    Little Buffalo Creek to Royster's Ferry 10 Nov. 1777
                                            O.B. 4, p 381
    Note: d. 1782 - Formerly of Chesterfield County
    Early Wills, p 51

JONES, Thomas, Junr.   Officer Militia

    Recommended as a second Lieutenant in first Battalion
    of militia, under Capt. Henry Walker, 13 Oct. 1777
                                            O.B. 4, p 374
    Took oath as a militia officer 8 Dec. 1777
                                            O.B. 5, p 382
    Recommended as a Capt. in militia 12 Dec. 1780
                                            O.B. 5, p 90

JONES, Tignal, Junr.   Officer Militia

Recommended as a first Lieutenant in second Battalion
of militia, under Capt. Richard Swepson, 13 Oct. 1777
                                            O.B. 4, p 374
Took oath of militia officer 13 July 1778
Early Wills, p 51   O.B. 4, p 421

JONES, Tignal, Senr.   Patriot

    For Continental Use   PC May 14, 1782
    1. Pasturage for 20 horses   O.B. 5, p 149
    2. Empty casks   O.B. 5, p 150

JONES, William   Patriot

    For Continental Use   PC April 10, 1782
    1. 375 cwt Beef   O.B. 5, p 155

JONES, William   Officer Militia

Recommended as an Ensign in second Battalion of Meck.
Co. militia, under Capt. John Brown, 13 Oct. 1777
                                            O.B. 4, p 374
Took oath as a militia officer 12 Jan. 1778
                                            O.B. 5, p 389

KEETON, Joseph   Patriot

    For Continental Use   PC May 13, 1782
    1. Horse - valued at 60 pounds   O.B. 5, p 143

KEETON, Joseph   Soldier

Received pay for service in militia - Aud. Acct Book
22, page 19.

KELLY, Charles   Soldier

Muster Roll, Captain Reuben Vaughan's Company 1779 -
Hubard Papers.

KELLY, James   Soldier

Received pay for service in militia - Aud. Acct Book
22, page 18.

KENDRICK, James   Patriot

    For Continental Use   Claim Oct. 10, 1783
    For Beef furnished   Comm. Book IV, p. 64

KENDRICK, John   <u>Officer Militia</u>

    Recommended as a first Lieutenant in the secon^d Battal-
ion of Meck. Co. militia, under Capt. James Lewis, 13
Oct. 1777.   <u>O.B. 4, p 374</u>
Took oath of militia officer 11 May 1778 <u>O.B. 4, p 403</u>

KENDRICK, John   <u>Patriot</u>

    For Continental Use   PC April 9, 1782
1. 300 cwt Beef   <u>O.B. 5, p 128</u>

KENDRICK, John   <u>Soldier</u>

    Received pay for service in militia - Aud. Acct Book
22, page 19.

KENNON, John   <u>Patriot</u>

    For Continental Use   PC May 14, 1782
1. Pasturage for 460 beeves, 12 bu. Corn, $13\frac{1}{2}$ bu. Oats
   200 bundles fodder, 20 diets   <u>O.B. 5, p 150</u>

KENNON, Richard   <u>Captain Cont. Line</u>

    2nd Lieut. 5 CL March 1, 1776; 1st Lieut. Dec. 17,
1776; Captain at White Plains in Aug. 1778.
                                                       <u>Gwathmey</u>

KIDD, James H.   <u>Soldier</u>

    b. Meck. Co. 16 Dec. 1763   Pen. S-31796
Muster Roll, Captain Reuben Vaughan's Company 1779 -
Hubard Papers. Entered service in 1780 under Capt.
John Kendrick as substitute for his father James Kidd.
Served under Capt. Benjamin Ferrell and Capt. John
Brown.

KIDD, James   <u>Patriot</u>

    For Continental Use   PC April 9, 1782
1. 350 cwt Beef   <u>O.B. 5, p 125</u>

KIDD, William   <u>Soldier</u>

    Received pay for service in militia - Aud. Acct Book
22, page 18.

KING, Charles   <u>Patriot</u>

    For Continental Use   PC April 9, 1782
1. 400 cwt Beef   <u>O.B. 5, p 124</u>

KING, James   Patriot

    For Continental Use   PC April 9, 1782
    1. Service of a horse 21 day, provision found by the
       public.   O.B. 5, p 132

KING, William   Soldier

    Received pay for service in militia - Aud. Acct Book
    22, page 18.

LADD, Garrard   Patriot

    For Continental Use   PC April 9, 1782
    1. 225 cwt Beef   O.B. 5, p 125

LADD, James   Sergeant Militia

    Muster Roll, Captain Reuben Vaughan's Company 1779 -
    Hubard Papers.

LADD, Ursley   Patriot

    For Continental Use   PC April 9, 1782
    1. 225 cwt Beef   O.B. 5, p 125
    Early Wills, p 53

LADD, William (Junr)   Soldier

    Received pay for service in militia - Aud. Acct Book
    22, page 18.
    Early Wills, p 53

LAMBERT, Hugh   Patriot

    For Continental Use   PC April 9, 1782
    1. 400 cwt Beef   O.B. 5, p 124
    Early Wills, p 53

LAMBERT, Jervis   Patriot

    For Continental Use   PC April 9, 1782
    1. 250 cwt Beef   O.B. 5, p 130

LAMBERT, John   Patriot

    For Continental Use   PC April 9, 1782
    1. 475 cwt Beef, 30 bu. Wheat   O.B. 5, p 124

LAMBERT, Joseph   Soldier

    Received pay for service in militia - Aud. Acct Book
    22, page 18.

LAMBERT, Joseph   <u>Patriot</u>

    For Continental Use   PC April 9, 1782
    1. 375 cwt Beef   <u>O.B. 5, p 130</u>

LAMBERT, Lewis   <u>Patriot</u>

    For Continental Use   PC April 10, 1782
    1. 425 cwt Beef, 406 cwt fodder, 33 bbls Corn
                                         <u>O.B. 5, p 136</u>

LAMPKIN, Jeremiah (Lamkin)   <u>Patriot</u>

    For Continental Use   PC April 9, 1782
    1. 375 cwt Beef   <u>O.B. 5, p 128</u>
    2. Service of wagon, team and driver 12 days, provis-
       ion found by the public.   <u>O.B. 5, p 130</u>
    3. Service of himself and horse 10 days, provision
       found by the public.   <u>O.B. 5, p 137</u>

LAMPKIN, James   <u>Patriot</u>

    Public Service - Took oath as required by law for
    Constable 14 Oct. 1776.   <u>O.B. 4, p 343</u>

LAMPKIN, Sampson   <u>Patriot</u>

    Public Service - Served as Juror 12 May 1781, 13 May
    1782, 10 Dec. 1782   <u>O.B. 5, pp. 95-142-259</u>

LANGLEY, Thomas   <u>Patriot</u>

    For Continental Use   PC April 9, 1782
    1. 375 cwt Beef   <u>O.B. 5, p 129</u>
    M.R. 1765-1810 p 79 - Early Wills, pp 54-<u>133</u>

LARK, Robert   <u>Patriot</u>

    For Continental Use   PC April 9, 1782
    1. 3600 cwt Beef, 438 cwt Beef, 62 cwt Bacon
                                        <u>O.B. 5, p 128</u>
    2. Smooth gun taken into service and not returned
                                        <u>O.B. 5, p 147</u>

LARK, Samuel   <u>Soldier</u>

    Sergeant Major - Muster Roll, Captain Reuben Vaughan's
    Company 1779 - Hubard Papers.

LARK, Samuel   <u>Soldier</u>

    Quartermaster - Soldiers in militia 1782
    Early Wills, p 55   <u>EP, 10 June 1783</u>

LEIGH, Walter   Patriot

    For Continental Use - Service collecting beef for army
                                    Comm. Book 4, p. 64

LEIGH, William   Patriot

    Member of the Committee of Safety 8 May 1775

LEIGH, William   Officer Militia

    Recommended as a Captain in second Battalion of Meck.
    Co. militia 13 Oct. 1777   O.B. 4, p 374
    Took oath as a militia officer 8 Dec. 1777
                                        O.B. 4, p 382

LESTER, Henry   (Baptist Minister)   Patriot

    For Continental Use   PC April 9, 1782
    1. 275 cwt Beef   O.B. 5, p 124

LETT, Joseph   Patriot

    Public Service - Appointed surveyor of road in place
    of Edward Waller 10 April 1783   O.B. 5, p 282

LEWIS, Charles   Patriot

    For Continental Use   PC April 10, 1782
    1. 82½ bu. Corn, 30 bundles fodder   O.B. 5, p 154

LEWIS, Charles   Soldier

    Soldier in militia 1782
                                    EP, 10 June 1783

LEWIS, Edward   Patriot

    Public Service - Served as Juror 11 May 1778, 14 Sept.
    1778, 8 May 1780   O.B. 4, pp 402,426 - O.B. 5, p 33
    Early Wills, p 55

LEWIS, Edward   Patriot

    For Continental Use   PC April 10, 1782
    1. Smooth gun taken into service and not returned
                                        O.B. 5, p 133

LEWIS, James   Officer Militia

    Recommended as Captain in militia 13 Oct. 1777
                                        O.B. 4, p 374

LEWIS, John   Soldier

    b. 1760 in Meck. Co. Living in 1840.
In service in 1779 under Capt. Charles Clay in
Southern Campaign. Affidavit to pension application
of Clement Blackbourn.   Pen. S-10388

LEWIS, Mary   Patriot

    For Continental Use   PC April 9, 1782
1. 525 cwt Beef   O.B. 5, p 128
Early Wills, p 55

LEWIS, Richard   Private Militia

    Muster Roll, Captain Reuben Vaughan's Company 1779 -
Hubard Papers.

LEWIS, Thomas   Soldier

    Soldier in Meck. Co. militia   (E)(G), p. 473

LIGHTFOOT, Francis   Patriot

    For Continental Use   PC April 9, 1782
1. 225 cwt Beef   O.B. 5, p 125

LIPFORD, John   Patriot

    Public Service - Served as Juror 10 Sept. 1782
                              O.B. 5, pp. 219,227,228

LIPFORD, Scruggs   Soldier

    Received pay for militia service - Aud. Acct Book 22,
page 19.

LIPTROT, John   Patriot

    For Continental Use   PC May 12, 1782
1. Smooth gun taken into service and not returned
                                       O.B. 5, p 147

LIPTROT, William   Soldier

    b. 1755 in Meck. Co. Res. of Meck. Co.
Enlisted 3 Sept. 1780. Planter: 5ft 9½ in, black hair
and eyes. Served in 2nd regiment.   CS(E), p. 29

LOCKETT, Abner   Patriot

    For Continental Use   PC May 14, 1782

1. 325 cwt Beef, 48 diets, Gun taken into service and
   not returned   O.B 5, p 148

LOCKETT, Abner   Officer Militia

   Recommended as an Ensign in militia 8 March 1779
                                                 O.B. 4, p 457
   Recommended as second Lieutenant in militia 12 May
   1781   O.B. 5, p 95
   Recommended as a Captain in militia 9 June 1783
                                                 O.B. 5, p 360

LOCKETT, Royal   Soldier

   b. 1751 in Cumberland Co. Moved to Meck. Co. 1785
                                                 Pen. S-6799
   Served two years. In 7th Va. Reg. Cont. Forces. In
   battle at Brandywine. Served under Capt. Charles
   Fleming and Lt. William Moseley.

LUCAS, Jeremiah   Soldier

   Muster Roll, Captain Reuben Vaughan's Company 1779 -
   Hubard Papers.

LUCAS, James   Widow: Mary Pen. W-12163

   Militia soldier with Virginia troops in North Carolina
   Treated at Salisbury Hospital by Dr. James McCan.
                                          Meck. Pet. 16 Dec. 1797

LUCAS, William, Gent   Patriot

   Member of the Committee of Safety 8 May 1775.
   Took the oath of a Justice as required by the Ord. of
   Conv., and oath of a Justice of Oyer & Terminer.
   11 May 1778   O.B. 4, p 400

LUCAS, William   Officer Militia

   Recommended as a Lieut. Col. in second Battalion of
   Meck. Co. Militia 13 Oct. 1777   O.B. 4, p 374
   Took oath as a militia officer 12 Jan. 1778
                                                 O.B. 4, p 388

LUCAS, William, Junr.   Officer Militia

   Recommended as an Ensign in second Battalion of Meck.
   Co. militia 13 Oct. 1777   O.B. 4, p 374
   Took oath as a militia officer 9 Feb. 1778
                                                 O.B. 4, p 391

Took oath as a Captain of militia 11 Oct. 1779
O.B. 4, p 522
Recommended as a Major in the militia 12 Aug. 1782
O.B. 5, p 181
Took oath as a Major in the militia 10 March 1783
O.B. 5, p 270

LUCAS, William (Junr)   Patriot

For Continental Use   PC April 9, 1782
1. 600 cwt Beef   O.B. 5, p 128
2. Bay horse - value 70 pounds   O.B. 5, p 129
3. Smooth gun taken into service and not returned, 450
   cwt Fodder, 10 bu. Corn   O.B. 5, p 155

McCAN, Dr. James   Surgeon Militia

Surgeon, Mecklenburg Pet. 1789   (G), p. 513
James McCan, a citizen of Meck. Co., acted as physic-
ian to the militia of this state on their march to So.
Carolina.   Leg. Pet., Dec. 16, 1797

McCARTER, James   Soldier

b. 1758   d. 18 April 1841
Soldier in 2nd Va. State Regiment.
Sept. Court 1841
              James McCarter, a pensioner under Act
7 June 1832, died April 18, 1841, and left a widow
Nancy who is still alive and a resident of this County
Ordered same be certified to the War Department.
                           Minute Book 3, p. 153

McCARTER, John   Soldier

b. 1753 in Meck. Co. Res. Meck. Co.
Enlisted for 8 months 8 Sept. 1780. Planter: 5ft 9in,
black hair, blue eyes, dark complexion.
                                   CS(E), p. 3

McCRAW, Dancy   Patriot

For Continental Use   PC April 9, 1782
1. 350 cwt Beef - 42 cwt Bacon   O.B. 5, p 128

McCRAW, Danny   Soldier

Soldier in the militia 1782   EP, 10 June 1783

McDANIEL, Drury   Patriot

For Continental Use   PC June 10, 1782
1. 68 days collecting beef for the service - Received
   150 pounds paper in part for same Oct. 1781
                                              O.B. 5, p 155

McDANIEL, James   Patriot

   Public Service - Served as Juror 11 Nov. 1776
                                              O.B. 4, p 344

McDANIEL, John   Patriot

   For Continental Use   PC June 10, 1782
   1. 69 days service collecting beef for the service
   Early Wills, p 57   O.B. 5, p 155

McHARG, Ebenezer   Soldier

   Agent for McDonald, merchant in Meck. Co.
   Took oath of allegiance, served in the militia, paid
   his contributions towards raising men whenever there-
   to required, considered a citizen of this Commonwealth
                                              Pet. 10 Nov. 1779

McHARG, Elizabeth   Patriot

   For Continental Use   PC April 9, 1782
   1. 700 cwt Beef   O.B. 5, p 130

McLIN, Frederick (Maclin)   Patriot
   For Continental Use
                                              PC April 10, 1782
   1. 6½ barrels Corn   O.B. 5, p 135

McLIN, John   (Maclin)   Soldier

   Ordered that Reuben Morgan supply Frances Maclin, the
   wife of John Maclin a poor soldier now in the service
   with two barrels of corn.   O.B. 5, p 19

McLIN, Thomas   (Maclin)   Patriot

   For Continental Use   PC April 9, 1782
   1. 325 cwt Beef   O.B. 5, p 125

McLACHLIN, Daniel   Soldier

   Stephen Ashby, Capt. in 8th Va. Reg., certified 22 Oct
   1788 that Daniel McLachlin enlisted in 1776 for two
   years, and in 1777 for duration of the war. He was
   taken prisoner at Charleston, S. C.
                                              Meck. Pet. 24 Nov. 1795

McLACHLIN, John   Soldier

    Enlisted as a soldier in 1777 for three years under
Capt. Lewis Burwell of Meck. Co. in 2nd Va. State Reg.
Discharged at Williamsburg. Signed by Col. William
Blunt, Isaac Holmes, Lt.
                          Meck. Pet. 24 Nov. 1795

McKENNEY, James (Senr)   Patriot

    For Continental Use   PC April 10, 1782
    1. 220 cwt Beef   O.B. 5, p 134
    2. 254 cwt Beef, 200 cwt Bacon
                 Meck. Book Lists, pp. 7,18

McKINNEY, Charles   Soldier

    Soldier in Revolutionary War   Pen. S-3152
    Moved to Limestone Co. Alabama.

                 Alabama DAR Roster

McNEIL, John   Patriot

    For Continental Use   PC April 9, 1782
    1. 375 cwt Beef   O.B. 5, p 127
    Early Wills, p 58

McNEIL, John   Soldier

    Soldier in first Battalion of militia 1782
                   EP, 10 June 1783

McQUIE, John   Patriot

    For Continental Use   PC April 9, 1782
    1. 325 cwt Beef   O.B. 5, p 129

McQUIE, William   Soldier

    b. in Amelia Co. 1758   Pen. S-16952
Residing in Meck. Co. where he entered service under
Capt. James Anderson and served 18 months. Entered
service a second time under Capt. Asa Oliver as a
substitute for William Davis who was drafted. Served
one year. Resided in Meck. Co. until 1790 when he
removed to Kentucky. Moved to Pike County, Missouri
in 1830.

MABRY, Stephen   Officer Militia

    Recommended as a Captain in second Battalion of Meck.
Co. militia 13 Oct. 1777   O.B. 4, p 374
Took oath as militia officer 8 Dec. 1777 O.B. 4, p 382

MABRY, Stephan   Patriot

    For Continental Use   PC June 10, 1782
    1. 275 cwt Beef   O.B. 5, p 155
    2. Gun taken into service and not returned
                                               O.B. 5, p 160

MALLETT, John   Private Militia

    Muster Roll, Captain Reuben Vaughan's Company 1779
    Hubard Papers.

MALLETT, Stephen   Patriot

    For Continental Use   PC April 9, 1782
    1. 350 cwt Beef   O.B. 5, p 129

MALLETT, Stephen (Junr)   Soldier

    Received pay for service in militia - Aud. Acct Book
    22, page 20

MALONE, Benjamin   Officer Militia

    Took oath as Lieutenant in militia 13 Sept. 1779
                                               O.B. 4, p 517

MALONE, Drury   Patriot

    For Continental Use   PC May 14, 1782
    1. 575 cwt Beef   O.B. 5, p 146
    Early Wills, p 59 - M.R. 1765-1810, p 84

MALONE, Isaac   Soldier

    Richmond Inquirer - Death Notices of Rev. Soldiers
    Isaac Malone, born Meck. Co. died 4 July 1850

MALONE, Nathaniel   Officer Militia

    Took oath as an Ensign in militia 13 Sept. 1779
                                               O.B. 4, p 517
    Recommended as second Lieutenant in militia 11 Aug.
    1780   O.B. 5, p 72
    Early Wills, p 59 - M.R. 1765-1810, p 84

MARABLE, Matthew   Patriot

    For Continental Use   PC April 9, 1782
    1. 850 cwt Beef   O.B. 5, p 125
    Early Wills, p 60

MARABLE, William   Patriot

    For Continental Use   PC May 14, 1782
    1. 375 cwt Beef   O.B. 5, p 146

MARROW, Daniel   Officer Militia

    Recommended as an Ensign in first Battalion of Meck.
    Co. militia 13 Oct. 1777   O.B. 4, p 374
    Recommended as second Lieutenant in militia 12 Dec.
    1780   O.B. 5, p 90

MARROW, Daniel   (Senr)   Patriot

    Thomas Culbreath made oath that a certificate given to
    Daniel Marrow for a gun impressed into service Jan.
    1781 was lost. His claim for 6 pounds specie allowed,
    to be charged to Continental   PC March 10, 1783
                                             O.B. 5, p 278

MARSHALL, Benjamin   Officer Militia

    William Insco made affidavit that he served a tour of
    duty under Capt. Benjamin Marshall in 1780.
                                William Insco - Pen. S-11363

MARSHALL, Francis   Patriot

    For Continental Use   PC June 10, 1782
    1. Musquet taken into service and not returned
                                             O.B. 5, p 154

MARSHALL, Francis   Soldier

    BLWt. 31331-160-55   Wife Sarah - Pen. W-6793
    b. Cumberland Co. 8 March 1750 - d. Sumner Co. Tenn.
    23 Jan. 1836 - m. (1) 27 June 1773 Phebe Hatcher, b.
    Cumberland Co. d. 1809 Meck. Co. Moved to Smith Co.
    Tenn. 1810. m (2) 1813 Sarah Jacobs, Smith Co. Tenn.
    Served three enlistments in Va. Forces in Rev. War as
    private. Moved to Meck. Co. after war.

MARSHALL, John   Patriot

    For Continental Use   PC May 14, 1782
    1. 400 cwt Beef   O.B. 5, p 146

MARSHALL, Samuel   Officer Militia

    Recommended as a Captain in second Battalion of Meck.
    Co. militia 13 Oct. 1777   O.B. 4, p 374
      Took oath as officer 12 Jan. 1778   O.B. 4, p 389

MARSHALL, Samuel   Patriot

    For Continental Use   PC April 9, 1782
    1. 300 cwt Beef   O.B. 5, p 127

MARSHALL, William   Patriot

    Public Service - Served as Juror 12 May 1781, 8 Sept
    1783   O.B. 5, pp. 95, 429

MARSHALL William   (Junr ?)   Soldier

    Recommended as an Ensign in Militia 9 June 1783
                                             O.B. 5, p 360

MARTIN, Thomas   Patriot

    For Continental Use
    1. 325 cwt Beef   Meck. Book Lists, p. 7

MASON, William   Private Militia

    Muster Roll, Captain Reuben Vaughan's Company 1779 -
    Hubard Papers.
    Early Wills, p 61

MATTHEWS, Nehemiah   Soldier

    Soldier in 15th Va. State Regiment, Isaac Holmes,
    Ensign.   Va. Gazette, Oct. 3, 1777

MAYES, John   Patriot

    For Continental Use   PC May 10, 1782
    1. Smooth gun taken into service and not returned
                                             O.B. 5, p 147
    2. 200 cwt Beef   Meck. Book Lists, p. 12

MAYNARD, Nicholas   Patriot

    For Continental Use   PC April 9, 1782
    1. 650 cwt Beef   O.B. 5, p 128
    2. 61 cwt Bacon, 3 bu. Corn, 240 cwt Fodder
    Early Wills, p 62   O.B. 5, p 130

MAYNARD, William   Patriot

    For Continental Use   PC July 8, 1782
    1. Gun taken into service and not returned
    Early Wills, p 62   O.B. 5, p 160

104

MAYO, Joseph   Patriot

    For Continental Use
    1. 550 cwt Beef   Meck. Book Lists, p. 14

MEALER, Matthew   Patriot

    For Continental Use   PC April 9, 1782
    1. 325 cwt Beef   O.B. 5, p 128

MEALER, Philip   Patriot

    For Continental Use   PC April 9, 1782
    1. 70 diets, forage, furnished 2 men and two horses
    Early Wills, p 62   O.B. 5, p 132

MEALER, William   Private Militia

    Muster Roll, Captain Reuben Vaughan's Company 1779 -
    Hubard Papers
    M.R. 1765-1810, p 87

MEANLEY, Richard (Manley)   Patriot

    A Gun Smith excused from militia to make guns for the
    public.   Va. Cal. State Papers ,Vol. 2, p. 290

MEARES, Thomas   Private Militia

    Muster Roll, Captain Reuben Vaughan's Company 1779 -
    Hubard Papers.

MELTON, Richard   Soldier

    Soldier in 15th Va. State Regiment, Isaac Holmes,
    Ensign   Va. Gazette, Oct. 3, 1777

MILLER, Hugh   Patriot

    1. 3 cwt Powder, 50 bu. Corn, 1200 bundles Fodder,
       Service of waggon and team for 44 days, provision
       found by the public.   O.B. 5, p 152

MILLENDER, William   Patriot

    Public Service - Served as a Juror 12 Nov. 1781
                                          O.B. 5, p 109

MINOR, William   Soldier

    Mentioned in pension application of David Boswell
                                          Pen. R-645

MITCHELL, Abram   Patriot

    For Continental Use   PC May 14, 1782
    1. 23 diets, 23 gal. Oats, pasturage for 58 horses
                                             O.B. 5, p 150
    2. 11 diets, 14½ gal. Corn, 10 gal. Oats, pasturage and
       lodging for an express rider from 31 Jan. to 5 Oct.
       following   O.B. 5, p 381

MITCHELL, Edward   Patriot

    One of the collector's of the taxes imposed for recruit
    ing this state's quota of troops to serve in American
    army - 14 July 1783   O.B. 5, p 402

MITCHELL, Edward   Soldier

    Soldier in militia in 1782
                                             EP, 10 June 1783
    Received pay for service in militia - Aud. Acct Book 22
    page 19.

MITCHELL, Edward   Patriot

    For Continental Use   PC April 9, 1782
    1. 350 cwt Beef   O.B. 5, p 129

MITCHELL, Elijah   Patriot

    For Continental Use   PC June 9, 1783
    1. Claim for a horse allowed, and ordered certified for
       payment   O.B. 5, p 360

MITCHELL, William   Patriot

    For Continental Use   PC April 10, 1782
    1. Service of waggon, team and driver, provision found
       by the public, 2 bu. Corn, Horse - value 50 pounds
                                             O.B. 5, p 137
    2. Horse - value 25 pounds   O.B. 5, p 431

MIZE, John   Private Militia

    Muster Roll, Captain Reuben Vaughan's Company 1779 -
    Hubard Papers.

MOODY, Francis   Soldier

    Francis Moody, a Revolutionary Soldier, and his wife
    Ann Hester, both born in Mecklenburg County, Virginia.
    He died in Tuscaloosa County, and his wife died in
    Fayette County, Alabama.
                                    Rev. Soldiers in Alabama
    Early Wills, p 63 - M.R. 1765-1810, p 89

MOON, Gideon   <u>Soldier</u>

    Soldier wounded at Hampton while building entrench-
    ments.   <u>Meck. Pet. 10 Oct. 1777</u>

MOORE, Feild   <u>Patriot</u>

    For Continental Use   PC May 14, 1782
    1. Horse - value 20 pounds   <u>O.B. 5, p 147</u>

MOORE, Mark   <u>Patriot</u>

    For Continental Use   PC April 9, 1782
    1. 350 cwt Beef   <u>O.B. 5, p 127</u>

MOORE, Thomas   <u>Patriot</u>

    For Continental Use   PC May 14, 1782
    1. 275 cwt Beef   <u>O.B. 5, p 145</u>
    Early Wills, p 63

MORGAN, John   <u>Soldier</u>

    Received pay for service in militia - Aud. Acct Book
    22, page 18. b. 1758 in Meck. Co.
    Early Wills, p 63 - M.R. 1765-1810, p 90

MORGAN, Reuben   <u>Patriot</u>

    For Continental Use   PC April 9, 1782
    1. 125 cwt Bacon, 900 cwt Beef   <u>O.B. 5, p 130</u>
    Early Wills, p 63

MORGAN, Reuben (Estate)   PC April 9, 1782
    For Continental Use   <u>O.B. 5, p 125</u>
    1. 725 cwt Beef
    2. Bay horse - value 125 pounds   <u>O.B. 5, p 132</u>

MORRISON, Alexander   <u>Soldier</u>

    Soldier in service in Georgia
                                            <u>Will Book 1, p . 255</u>

MORTON, James   <u>Patriot</u>

    For Continental Use   PC April 9, 1782
    1. Horse for use taken to ride express to Petersburg
       to the Baron de Kalb   <u>O.B. 5, p 130</u>

MOSS, Joshua   <u>Patriot</u>

    For Continental Use   PC April 9, 1782
    1. 300 cwt Beef   <u>O.B. 5, p 128</u>

MOSS, Nathaniel   Patriot

    For Continental Use   PC May 14, 1782
    1. 250 cwt Beef   O.B. 5, p 147
    M.R. 1765-1810, p 91

MOSS, Ray   Private Militia

    Muster Roll, Captain Reuben Vaughan's Company 1779 -
    Hubard Papers
    M.R. 1765-1810, p 91

MUNFORD, Col. Robert   Patriot-Soldier

    Member of the Committee of Safety
    Gentleman Justice 8 May 1775   - County Lieutenant
    Appointed to take annual list of tithables in Middle
    District 12 May 1777   O.B. 4, p 356
    Colonel in command of militia at Guilford Courthouse

MUNFORD, Col. Robert   Patriot

    For Continental Use   PC April 9, 1782
    1. 2675 cwt Beef   O.B. 5, p 129
    2. Sorrel horse - value 150 pounds, 1025 cwt Beef,
                                         O.B. 5, p 129
    3. Service of wagon, team and driver 30 days, provis-
       ion found by public, service of wagon and team for
       28 days, provision found by public, 3575 cwt Beef,
       98 cwt Bacon, 80 cwt Meal, 486 bundles of fodder,
       252 bu. Corn   O.B. 5, p 137

MURRAY, John   Officer Militia

    Recommended as a Captain in first Battalion of Meck.
    Co. militia 13 Oct. 1777   O.B. 4, p 374
    Took oath as a militia officer 8 Dec. 1777
                                         O.B. 4, p 382
    Recommended as a Major and took oath 8 March 1779
                                         O.B. 4, p 455
    Recommended as a Colonel in militia 10 Dec. 1781
                                         O.B. 5, p 115
    Took oath as a Colonel 8 July 1782   O.B. 5, p 159

MURRAY, John   Patriot

    For Continental Use   PC April 9, 1782
    1. Sorrel horse - value 90 pounds   O.B. 5, p 132
    2. Waggon, gear and three horses - value 150 pounds
                                         O.B. 5, p 134
    3. 310 cwt Bacon, 66 bu. Corn, 2140 bundles fodder
                                         O.B. 5, p 137

MUSTIAN, John   Patriot

    For Continental Use   PC April 10, 1782
    1. 225 cwt Beef   O.B. 5, p 134

NANCE, Daniel   Patriot

    For Continental Use   PC May 14, 1782
    1. 325 cwt Beef   O.B. 5, p 148

NANCE, Robert   Patriot

    For Continental Use   PC April 9, 1782
    1. 250 cwt Beef   O.B. 5, p 129

NANCE, Thomas   Patriot

  - For Continental Use   PC May 14; 1782
    1. 350 cwt Beef   O.B. 5, p 151

NANNEY, William   Soldier

    Received pay for service in militia - Aud. Acct Book
    22, page 18.

NASH, John   Patriot

    For Continental Use   PC April 9, 1782
    1. 335 cwt Beef   O.B. 5, p 124

NASH, William   Patriot

    For Continental Use   PC May 14, 1782
    1. 525 cwt Beef   O.B. 5, p 146
    Early Wills, p 65

NEAL, John   Patriot

    Public Service - Served as a Juror 15 Sept. 1778, 13
    July 1779   O.B. 4, pp. 439, 490

NEAL, Thomas   Officer Militia

    Recommended as an Ensign in first Battalion of Meck.
    Co. militia, under Capt. John Murray, 13 Oct. 1777
                                               O.B. 4, p 374

NEAL, Thomas   Officer Militia

    Recommended as an Ensign in first Battalion of militia
    under Capt. Asa Oliver 13 Oct. 1777   O.B. 4, p 374

NEAL, Thomas   <u>Soldier</u>

    b. Amelia Co.   Pen. W-5407
    d. Halifax County 10 April 10, 1822.
    Drafted in Amelia Co. 30 Oct. 1779, served 5 months.
    Served two additional enlistments totaling nine months
    Moved to Meck. Co. in 1784. Married in Meck. Co. 1787.
    Subsequently moved to Halifax County.
    M.R. 1765-1810, p 94

NEAL, William   <u>Officer Militia</u>

    Recommended as first Lieutenant in first Battalion of
    militia, under Capt. Henry Walker, 13 Oct. 1777
                                           <u>O.B. 4, p 374</u>
    Took oath as a militia officer 9 March 1778
                                             <u>O.B. 4, p 394</u>

NEAL, William (Senr)   <u>Patriot</u>

    For Continental Use   PC April 9, 1782
    1. 750 cwt Beef   <u>O.B. 5, p 129</u>
    2. 72 diets, pasturage for 28 head cattle
                                             <u>O.B. 5, p 135</u>

NELSON, Major John   <u>Officer</u>

    b. York Co. d. Meck. Co.   Pen. W-5414
    Appointed Captain in First Regiment of Cavalry in 1776
    under Col. Bland. Subsequently appointed Major and
    served until 14 Feb. 1782.
    See - M.R. 1765-1810, pp. 174-186

NEWPORT, Jane   <u>Patriot</u>

    For Continental Use   PC April 9, 1782
    1. 250 cwt Beef   <u>O.B. 5, p 128</u>

NEWPORT, Peter   <u>Patriot</u>

    For Continental Use   PC April 10, 1782
    1. 21 cwt Bacon   <u>O.B. 5, p 135</u>

NEWTON, Robert B.   <u>Patriot</u>

    For Continental Use   PC April 9, 1782
    1. 275 cwt Beef   <u>O.B. 5, p 126</u>
    2. 275 cwt Beef   <u>O.B. 5, p 146</u>

NEWTON, Thomas Jr.   <u>Patriot</u>

    Rifle for Capt. Ballard's Co. of Minutemen
                         <u>Acct Book 75, p.16, Jan. 1776</u>

NICHOLAS, George   Patriot

        For Continental Use   PC April 9, 1782
        1. 275 cwt Beef   O.B. 5, p 126
        Early Wills, p 75

NOBLIN, Thomas   Patriot

        For Continental Use   PC April 9, 1782
        1. 250 cwt Beef   O.B. 5, p 127

NORMENT, William   Patriot

        For Continental Use   PC April 9, 1782
        1. 575 cwt Beef, 82 cwt Bacon   O.B. 5, p 127
        2. Gun taken into service and not returned
        Early Wills, p 141   O.B. 5, p 136

NORTHINGTON, Chavis   Patriot

        For Continental Use
        1. 275 cwt Beef   Meck. Book Lists, p. 8

NORTHINGTON, Jabez   Patriot

        For Continental Use   PC April 9, 1782
        1. 275 cwt Beef   O.B. 5, p 127

NOWELL, Thomas   Patriot

        For Continental Use   PC April 9, 1782
        1. 300 cwt Beef   O.B. 5, p 131

OGBURN, John   Patriot

        Public Service - Served as a Juror 12 May 1783
                                                O.B. 5, p 294

OLIVER, Asa   Officer Militia

        Recommended as a Captain in first Battalion of Meck.
        Co. militia 13 Oct. 1777   O.B. 4, p 374
        Took oath of militia officer 12 Jan. 1778
        Early Wills, p 66   O.B. 4, p 389

OLIVER, John   (Senr)   Patriot

        For Continental Use   PC April 10, 1782
        1. 600 cwt Beef, 125 cwt Pork, 28 bu. Corn, 300 bundl-
           es fodder, 75 cwt Pork, Gun taken into service and
           not returned   O.B. 5, p 137

                         111

OLIVER, John (Junr)   Soldier

    Soldier in militia 1782   EP, 10 June 1783

OSLIN, Jesse   Patriot

    For Continental Use   PC April 9, 1782
    1. 350 cwt Beef   O.B. 5, p 124
    2. Gun taken into service, proven by oath of John
        Saunders, 14 Oct. 1782   O.B. 5, p 234

OVERBY, Drury   Patriot

    For Continental Use   PC May 14, 1782
    1. 325 cwt Beef   O.B. 5, p 146

OVERBY, Jeremiah   Patriot

    For Continental Use   PC April 9, 1782
    1. 575 cwt Beef   O.B. 5, p 129

OVERBY, Peter   Patriot

    For Continental Use   PC May 14, 1782
    1. 475 cwt Beef   O.B. 5, p 146

OVERTON, Moses   Patriot

    Public Service - Served as a Juror 15 Sept. 1778,
                             O.B. 4, p 439
    Served as a Juror 12 May 1781, 10 Sept. 1782
                      O.B. 5, pp. 95, 227

OWEN, John   Patriot

    For Continental Use   PC Nov. 11, 1782
    1. Saddles and sheepskin   O.B. 5, p 241

OWEN, John, Junr.   Patriot

    For Continental Use   PC April 9, 1782
    1. Black mare taken for army   O.B. 5, p 216

OWEN, Thomas   Patriot

    For Continental Use   PC Sept. 9, 1782
    1. Bay mare taken for army   O.B. 5, p 216

PARHAM, Lewis   Officer Militia

    Recommended as a Captain in second Battalion of Meck.
    Co. militia 13 Oct. 1777   O.B. 4, p 374

Took oath as a militia officer 12 Jan. 1778

O.B. 4, p 388

PARHAM, Lewis   Patriot

Member of the Committee of Safety
Gentleman Justice 8 Sept. 1776
Appointed Commissioner, with Henry Speed, to carry into execution an Act of Assembly for laying a tax payable in certain enumerated commodities 11 Oct. 1779

O.B. 4, p 526

Appointed to take the annual list of tithables in the
Lower District 12 May 1781   O.B. 5, p 94
Qualified as Commissioner for equalizing the land tax.
14 April 1783   O.B. 5, p 283

PARHAM, Lewis   Patriot

- For Continental Use   PC May 14, 1782
  1. 625 cwt Beef   O.B. 5, p 147

PARRISH, John   Patriot

For Continental Use   PC May 14, 1782
1. 300 cwt Beef   O.B. 5, p 147

PARRISH, Moses   Soldier

b. 1743 - Resident Meck. Co.   Pen. S-38286
Enlisted March 1776 in Halifax Co. for 4 years. Served
under Capt. Nathaniel Cocke in 7th Va. Regiment. In
battles at Brandywine and Monmouth.
Early Wills, p 67

PARKS, James   Patriot

For Continental Use   PC May 14, 1782
1. 300 cwt Beef, 3 diets, 1 bu. Corn   O.B. 5, p 147
2. 300 cwt Beef   O.B. 5, p 149

PARKS, John   Soldier

Muster Roll, Captain Reuben Vaughan's Company 1779 -
Hubard Papers.

PATILLO, Austin   Patriot

For Continental Use   PC July 8, 1782
1. Rifled gun and Shot bag taken into service and not
   returned.   O.B. 5, p 160

113

PATILLO, Austin   Patriot

    Appointed a recruiting officer for one of the distri-
cts laid off in the County of Meck. pursuant to an Act
of Assembly passed in May 1780 for speedily recruiting
the quota of this State for Continental Army.
                                  O.B. 5, p 298

PATRICK, John   Patriot

    For Continental Use   PC May 14, 1782
    1. 290 cwt Beef   O.B. 5, p 151

PEGRAM, Alice   Army Nurse

    Meck. Co. - Nursing sick soldier. Curing an ulcer on
a soldier in Captain Spencer's Company of Culpeper
Battalion.   CJS, Vol. 1, p. 27

PEGRAM William   Patriot

    For Continental Use   PC May 14, 1782
    1. Horse and saddle   O.B. 5, p 151

PENNINGTON, Benjamin   Patriot

    For Continental Use   PC April 9, 1782
    1. 275 cwt Beef   O.B. 5, p 124
    2. Gun taken into service and not returned
                                   O.B. 5, p 160

PENNINGTON, Edward   Officer Militia

    Recommended as an Ensign in the militia 8 March 1779
                                  O.B. 4, p 457

PENNINGTON, Edward   Soldier

    Soldier in the militia 1782   EP, 10 June 1783

PENNINGTON, Edward (Senr)   Patriot

    For Continental Use   PC April 9, 1782
    1. 300 cwt Beef   O.B. 5, p 129
    2. Gun taken into service and not returned
                                   O.B. 5, p 160

PENNINGTON, Edward   Patriot

    One of the collector's of the taxes imposed for recr-
uiting this State's quota of troops to serve in army,
9 June 1783.   O.B. 5, p 389

PENNINGTON, Henry   <u>Officer Militia</u>

    Recommended as an Ensign to fill vacancy in the mili-
    tia 14 June 1779   <u>O.B. 4, p 476</u>

PENNINGTON, Henry   <u>Soldier</u>

    Received pay for service in militia - Aud. Acct Book
    22, page 18.

PENNINGTON, Howell   <u>Patriot</u>

    For Continental Use   PC April 9, 1782
    1. 375 cwt Beef   <u>O.B. 5, p 124</u>

PENNINGTON, James   <u>Patriot</u>

    For Continental Use   PC April 9, 1782
 - 1. 325 cwt Beef   <u>O.B. 5, p 125</u>
    2. Smooth gun taken into service and not returned
                                         <u>O.B. 5, p 147</u>

PENNINGTON, John George   <u>Patriot</u>

    For Continental Use   PC April 9, 1782
    1. 300 cwt Beef   <u>O.B. 5, p 124</u>

PENNINGTON, Philip   <u>Soldier</u>

    Received pay for service in militia - Aud. Acct Book
    22, page 18.

PERKINS, David   (Purkins)   <u>Patriot</u>

    For Continental Use   PC May 14, 1782
    1. 250 cwt Beef   <u>O.B. 5, p 146</u>
    Early Wills, p 68

PERRY, William   <u>Patriot</u>

    Gun taken by Lt. Davis on southward march, and not re-
    turned - 10 March 1783   <u>O.B. 5, p 278</u>

PETTUS, Samuel   <u>Patriot</u>

    For Continental Use   PC April 9, 1782
    1. 350 cwt Beef   <u>O.B. 5, p 131</u>

PETTUS, Samuel Overton   <u>Lieut. Artillery</u>

    b. 11 March 1751 Lunenburg Co. d. 12 Feb. 1819 in
    Chase City, Meck. Co.

m. 1783 Hannah Minor b. March 1755 d. 1829. Will of
Samuel Overton Pettus dated 9 Feb. 1819 recorded 8th
June 1819 Will Book 9, page 9.
Lieutenant in Artillery - Revolutionary War

Tenn. DAR Roster, p. 127

PETTUS, Thomas   Patriot

    For Continental Use   PC April 9, 1782
    1. 620 cwt Beef   O.B. 5, p 125

PETTUS, Thomas, Junr.   Officer Militia

    Recommended as an Ensign in first Battalion of Meck.
    Co. militia, under Capt. William Green, 13 Oct. 1777
                                           O.B. 4, p 374
    Took oath as militia officer 11 May 1778 O.B. 4, p 403
    Recommended as second Lieutenant in militia 12 Dec.
    1780   O.B. 5, p 90
    Took oath as a militia officer 12 May 1781
                                            O.B. 5, p 96
    Recommended as first Lieutenant 10 Dec. 1781
                                         O.B. 5, p 113

PHILLIPS, Dabney   Patriot

    For Continental Use   PC May 14, 1782
    1. 415 cwt Beef   O.B. 5, p 147

PHILLIPS, Dabney   Soldier

    Soldier in militia 1782   EP, 10 June 1783

PHILLIPS, Martin   Patriot

    For Continental Use   PC April 9, 1782
    1. 102 cwt Bacon   O.B. 5, p 123
    2. 625 cwt Beef   O.B. 5, p 147

PHILLIPS, Pettus   Patriot

    Public Service - Served as Juror 10 Sept. 1782, 10 Dec
    1782   O.B. 5, pp. 227, 259
    Early Wills, p 68

PHILLIPS, Thomas   Soldier

    b. 19 April 1761 Meck. Co.   Pen. W-2848
    d. 18 Feb. 1818 Green Co. Ky. m. 31 May 1792 Sarah
    Parson of Charlotte Co. Moved to Green Co. Ky. 1805
    Enlisted Meck. Co. 1776 for two years, served under
    Cant. Robert Ballard. In battles at Trenton and Brandy
    -wine. In 1781 at Guilford Court House.

PINSON, Thomas   Patriot

    For Continental Use   PC May 14, 1782
    1. 350 cwt Beef   O.B. 5, p 146

PISTOLE, Charles   Patriot

    For Continental Use   PC April 9, 1782
    1. 450 cwt Beef   O.B. 5, p 129

POINDEXTER, Philip   Patriot

    For Continental Use   PC April 9, 1782
    1. 335 cwt Beef   O.B. 5, p 131

POINDEXTER, Philip, Junr.   Patriot

    For Continental Use
    1. 285 cwt Beef   Meck. Book Lists, p. 14

POOL, James   Soldier

    b. Brunswick Co. 1756   Pen. W-9233
    Living in Meck. Co. when he entered war. Enlisted in
    1776 as a substitute for John Thompson. Later drafted.
    Entered service again as a substitute for James Allen
    of Charlotte Co. Moved to Craven Co. S. C. in 1790's.
    Living in Laurens Dist., S. C. in 1832. Wife Ursula
    was pensioner.

POOL, Walter   Officer Militia

    Recommended as an Ensign in militia 12 May 1781.
    Early Wills, p 69   O.B. 5, p 95

POOL, William   Patriot

    For Continental Use   PC April 9, 1782
    1. 375 cwt Beef   O.B. 5, p 125
    Early Wills, p 69

POOLE, Thomas   Patriot

    For Continental Use   PC Nov. 11, 1782
    1. Black horse taken for army   O.B. 5, p 241

PORTCH, Joshua (Poarch)   Soldier

    Soldier in militia stationed at Cabin Point.
                   Ex. Comm., 23 Feb. 1781

POTTER, John   Patriot

    For Continental Use   PC May 14, 1782
    1. Service of waggon, team and driver, provision
       found by public, 2 waggon loads wheat straw, 1 bbl.
       corn meal, 16 bu. corn.   O.B. 5, p 149

POWELL, Thomas   Patriot

    Civil Officer of Meck. Co. Signed Public Service
    Claims for county.

POWERS, Joseph   Patriot

    For Continental Use   PC May 14, 1782
    1. Gun taken into service and not returned.
                            O.B. 5, p 147

POWERS, William   Patriot

    Public Service - Served as a Juror 10 Sept. 1782
                              O.B. 5, p 219

PRICE, William   Patriot

    For Continental Use   PC April 9, 1782
    1. 525 cwt Beef   O.B. 5, p 129

PUCKETT, Page   Soldier

    Soldier in 15th Va. State Regiment, Isaac Holmes,
    Ensign.   Va. Gazette, Oct. 3, 1777

PULLIAM, Benjamin   Patriot

    For Continental Use   PC April 9, 1782
    1. 500 cwt Beef, 1 bbl. Corn   O.B. 5, p 129
    Early Wills, p 69

PULLIAM, James   Patriot

    For Continental Use   PC May 14, 1782
    1. 225 cwt Beef   O.B. 5, p 146

PULLIAM, John   Patriot

    For Continental Use   PC May 14, 1782
    1. Smooth gun taken into service and not returned
    Early Wills, p 69   O.B. 5, p 147

PULLY, Spettle   Patriot

Public Service - Overseer of road 9 Nov. 1778.

O.B. 4, p. 446

PULLY, William   Soldier

Private in Va. State Line. BLWt. Warrant No. 3241 for
100 acres of land for his service as a private for
three years.   Burgess, Vol. 3, p. 1338

PURYEAR, John   Patriot

For Continental Use   PC April 9, 1782
1. 1025 cwt Beef   O.B. 5, p 127
2. Sorrel horse - value 175 pounds   O.B. 5, p 129
3. Service of a waggon, team and driver for 29 days,
   provision found by the public   O.B. 5, p 132
4. Service of a waggon, team and driver for 76 days,
   provision found by the public   O.B. 5, p 154
Early Wills, p 70

PURYEAR, John (Roanoke)   Patriot

For Continental Use   PC April 9, 1782
1. 675 cwt Beef   O.B. 5, p 128

PURYEAR, Obadiah   Soldier

Soldier in militia 1782   EP, 10 June 1783

PURYEAR, Samuel   Soldier

Soldier in militia 1782   EP, 10 June 1783

PURYEAR, Samuel (Senr)   Patriot

For Continental Use   PC April 9, 1782
1. 325 cwt Beef   O.B. 5, p 129

PURYEAR, Sarah   Patriot

For Continental Use   PC April 9, 1782
1. 350 cwt Beef   O.B. 5, p 125
Note: Widow of John Puryear, Jr.
Early Wills, p 70

PURYEAR, Seymour   Patriot

For Continental Use   PC April 9, 1782
1. 300 cwt Beef   O.B. 5, p 125
Early Wills, p 70

RAGSDALE, David   Patriot

```
        For Continental Use                    PC April 9, 1782
        1. 11 cwt Bacon                         O.B. 5, p 131

RAGSDALE, John                                          Patriot

        Public Service - Served as a Juror 8 Sept. 1783
        Early Wills, p 71                       O.B. 5, p 429

RAGSDALE, Peter                                         Soldier

        Enlisted 3 Sept. 1780 for two years, in 2nd Va. Reg.
                                                CS (E), p. 30

RAGSDALE, Peter   (Senr)                               Patriot

        Public Service - Appointed overseer of road 8 Nov.
        1779                                    O.B. 5, p. 5
        Early Wills, p 71

RAGSDALE, Richard                                      Patriot

        For Continental Use                    PC April 9, 1782
        1. 650 cwt Beef                         O.B. 5, p 130
        2. Horse - value 100 pounds             O.B. 5, p 131
        Early Wills, p 71

RAGSDALE, William                                     Patriot

        For Continental Use                    PC April 10, 1782
        1. 21 cwt Bacon                         O.B. 5, p 138
        Early Wills, p 71

RAIBORNE, George                                       Soldier

        Res. Meck. Co.  Enlisted 16 March 1778 as a Fifer in
        Company of Capt. John. Faulkner to serve in 5th Va.
        Reg.  Served in 2nd Va. Reg.  Taken prisoner at
        Charleston for nine months, escaped.
                                        Meck. Pet, 12 Dec. 1797

RAINEY, Buckner                                        Soldier

        Served in militia under Capt. Stephen Mabry and Col.
        Lewis Burwell. Pension application of William Guy.
                                        Nat. Archives, Pen. S-17969

RAINEY, Francis                                        Patriot

        For Continental Use                    PC April 9, 1782
        1. 400 cwt Beef                         O.B. 5, p 124
```

RAINEY, Williamson   Soldier

    b. Meck. Co. 2 Nov. 1760   Pen. R-8563
    Entered service in 1777, served under Capt. John Bur-
    ton, Major James Anderson, Col. Frederick Maclin.
    Drafted 1799 and served under Capt. Benjamin Marshall.
    Drafted in 1781 under Capt. Richard Witton. Served
    with William Insco and William Coleman of Meck. Co.

RAMEY, James   (Reamey)   Private Militia

    Muster Roll, Captain Reuben Vaughan's Company 1779 -
    Hubard Papers.

RANDOLPH, Joseph   Soldier

    b. Spottsyylvania Co. Res. Meck. Co. Died in S. C.
    Enlisted from Meck. Co. Planter: 5ft 6in, black hair,
    hazel eyes, fair complexion.
                                            CS(E), p. 17

RANDOLPH, William   Officer Militia

    Recommended as a Major in militia 10 Dec. 1781
                                           O.B. 5, p 115
    Took oath as a Major in militia 8 July 1782
                                           O.B. 5, p 159
    Recommended as a Lieut. Col. 12 Aug. 1782
                                           O.B. 5, p 181
    Took oath as Lieut. Col. 13 Jan. 1783 O.B. 5, p 262

RANDOLPH, William   Patriot

    Gentleman Justice 12 Nov. 1781
    Appointed to take a list of the number of people, both
    white and black, in the 6th Precinct 9 Sept. 1782.
    Meck. Co. Census 1782.   O.B. 5, p. 209

RAYNOR, John   Patriot

    Civil Officer - Issued receipts for public supplies.
    Signature appears on   Meck. Co. Public Claims

REES, (John)   (Reese)   Soldier

    The father of Eton and John Rees is a prisoner of war
    in Charleston. 12 Feb. 1781   O.B. 5, p. 89

REIVES, Thomas   (Rives)   Patriot

    For Continental Use   PC April 9, 1782
    1. 335 cwt Beef   O.B. 5, p 130

RICHARDSON, Thomas   Patriot

```
                   For Continental Use                    PC May 14, 1782
                   1. Rifle gun taken into service and not returned
                                                          O.B. 5, p 152
                   2. 340 cwt Beef              Meck. Book Lists, p. 8

RIX, Philip  (Reekes)                                   Officer Militia

       Recommended as a first Lieutenant in militia 10 Dec.
       1781                                              O.B. 5, p 115

ROADS, John   (Rhodes)                                        Patriot

       For Continental Use                      PC April 9, 1782
       1. 230 cwt Beef                          O.B. 5, p 128

ROBERTS, Thomas                                               Soldier

       Received pay for services in militia - Aud. Acct Book
       22, page 19.

ROBERTS, William                                        Private Militia

       Muster Roll, Captain Reuben Vaughan's Company 1779 -
       Hubard Papers.

ROBERTS, William                                              Patriot

       For Continental Use                      PC April 9, 1782
       1. 2 cwt Beef, 2 cwt Flour, 1/2 bu. Corn O.B. 5, p 126

ROBERTS, William S.                                     Private Militia

       Muster Roll, Captain Reuben Vaughan's Company 1779 -
       Hubard Papers.

ROBERTSON, James                                             Soldier

       Received pay for service in militia - Aud. Acct Book
       22, page 20.

ROBERTSON, John                                             Soldier

       Res. Meck. Co.  Enlisted 2 Sept. 1780 for eight months
       b. Chesterfield Co. Planter: 5ft 9in, brown hair, blue
       eyes, dark complexion.                   CS(E), p. 17

ROBERTSON, William                                           Patriot

       For Continental Use                      PC April 10, 1782
       1. 62 cwt Bacon                          O.B. 5, p 138
```

ROBINSON, Benjamin   Patriot

    For Continental Use   PC April 10, 1782
    1. Horse - valued at 15 pounds 10 shillings specie
                                           O.B. 5, p 135

ROBINSON, William   Patriot

    For Continental Use   PC April 9, 1782
    1. 575 cwt Beef   O.B. 5, p 128

ROFFE, William   Patriot

    For Continental Use   PC April 10, 1782
    1. 325 cwt Beef   O.B. 5, p 135
    2. 20 bu. Oats, 6 bu. Corn, 9 diets   O.B. 5, p 136

ROFFE, William, Junr.   Officer Militia

    Recommended as a first Lieutenant in second Battalion
    of Meck. Co. militia, under Capt. William Leigh, Oct.
    13, 1777   O.B. 4, p 374
    Took oath as a militia officer 8 Dec. 1777
                                           O.B. 4, p 382
    Recommended as a Captain in room of William Leigh
    removed from county.   O.B. 4, p 457
    Took oath as a Captain 12 May 1781   O.B. 5, p 96

ROSS, David   Patriot

    For Continental Use   PC April 9, 1782
    1. 3 bu. Alum salt   O.B. 5, p 125
    2. 1050 cwt Beef   O.B. 5, p 131
    3. 800 bundles of fodder   O.B. 5, p 133

ROTTENBERRY, Samuel   Patriot

    For Continental Use   PC May 14, 1782
    1. Saddle for army use   O.B. 5, p 152

ROWLETT, William   Patriot

    For Continental Use   PC May 14, 1782
    1. Rifled gun taken into service and not returned
                                           O.B. 5, p 148

ROYSTER, Charles   Patriot

    For Continental Use   PC April 9, 1782
    1. Bay horse - value 150 pounds, 375 cwt Beef
                                           O.B. 5, p 148

ROYSTER, Charles   Officer Militia

    Recommended as a first Lieutenant in first Battalion
    of Meck. Co. militia, under Capt. James Hall, 13 Oct.
    1777   O.B. 4, p 374
    Took oath of a militia officer 8 Dec. 1777
                                                 O.B. 4, p 382
    Recommended as a Captain 12 May 1781   O.B. 5, p. 95

ROYSTER, David   Officer Militia

    Recommended as a second Lieutenant in militia 12 Dec.
    1781   O.B. 5, p. 90

ROYSTER, Jacob   Patriot

    For Continental Use   PC May 14, 1782
    1. 500 cwt Beef   O.B. 5, p 146

ROYSTER, Jacob   Patriot

    Appointed to take the annual list of tithables in the
    district on south side of Roanoke River 8 April, 1776
                                                 O.B. 4, p 334
    Gentleman Justice 12 Aug. 1776

ROYSTER, Joseph   Patriot

    For Continental Use   PC May 14, 1782
    1. 275 cwt Beef, 6 bu. Corn, 214 bundles fodder
                                                 O.B. 5, p 150

ROYSTER, Joseph (Junr)   Officer Militia

    Took oath as a second Lieutenant in militia 8 Sept.
    1777   O.B. 4, p 369
    Recommended as first Lieutenant in the first Battalion
    of Meck. Co. militia 13 Oct. 1777   O.B. 4, p 374

ROYSTER, William   Patriot

    For Continental Use   PC April 9, 1782
    1. 750 cwt Beef   O.B. 5, p 128
    2. 128 diets, 12 bu. Corn, pasturage for 46 head
       cattle   O.B. 5, p 131

RUDD, Feild   Patriot

    Public Service - Served as a Juror 12 Oct. 1777
                                                 O.B. 4, p 536

RUDD, Joseph   Patriot

For Continental Use
1. Gun furnished Virginia Militia on Cert. of Captain
   James Anderson   VMH. Vol. 12, p. 312

RUFFIN, Francis, Esq.   Patriot

Member of the Committee of Safety 8 May 1775
Gentleman Justice 11 Aug. 1777

RUFFIN, Francis   Patriot

For Continental Use   PC April 9, 1782
1. 575 cwt Beef, 91½ bu. Corn   O.B. 5, p 128
2. Dark Bay horse - value 70 pounds   O.B. 5, p 129
3. Service of waggon, team and driver for 22 days,
   provision found by public   O.B. 5, p 154
4. 2 Bay horses - value 60 pounds each   O.B. 5, p 129

RUFFIN, Thomas   Patriot

For Continental Use   PC May 13, 1782
1. Gun taken into service and not returned
                                           O.B. 5, p 143

RUFFIN, William   Officer Militia

Captain in second Battalion of militia 8 March 1779
Early Wills, p 75   AC 20405

RUSSELL, Jeffrey   Soldier

Recommended as an Ensign in militia 10 Dec. 1781
                                           O.B. 5, p 115

RUSSELL, Jeffrey   Patriot

For Continental Use   PC April 9, 1782
1. 275 cwt Beef   O.B. 5, p 125

RUSSELL, Jeffrey   Soldier

b. Meck. Co. d. Meck. Co. 30 Jan. 1802   Pen. W-5751
m. Sark Gill 30 Dec. 1778
Served three years in Cont. Line as private and as a
sergeant,

RUSSELL, Nathan   Soldier

Soldier in 15th Va. State Regiment. Isaac Holmes,
Ensign.   Va. Gazette, Oct. 3, 1777

RYLAND, John   Soldier

    b. 20 Oct. 1760 d. 2 Oct. 1822   Pen. W-18847
    Entered service in 1777 for duration of war. Served in
    Artillery under Capt. Drury Ragsdale, Capt. Anthony
    Singleton, Col. Charles Harrison. Rank: Corporal.
    m. 9 Jan. 1784 by Rev. James Craig to Elizabeth (   )
    who was b. 8 Oct. 1756.

RYLAND, Thomas   Patriot

    For Continental Use   PC June 10, 1782
    1. 59 days collecting beef for army   O.B. 5, p 155

RYLAND, Thomas   Soldier

    Soldier in the militia 1782   EP, 10 June 1783

SALLEY, Isaac   (Salle')   Patriot

    For Continental Use   PC April 9, 1782
    1. 375 cwt Beef   O.B. 5, p 125

SALLEY, Isaac (Jr.) (Salle')   Soldier

    Soldier in first Battalion of militia
                                        EP, 10 June 1783

SAMSON, Benjamin (Sampson)   Patriot

    Public Service - Served as a Juror 13 Nov. 1775
                                           O.B. 4, p 326

SANDIFER, Henry   Patriot

    Public Service - Served as a Juror 12 Aug. 1783
    Moved to Mercer Co., Ky. 1796   O.B. 5, p 415

SANDIFER, James (Senr.)   Patriot

    Public Service - Served as a Juror 15 Sept. 1778 and
    10 Nov. 1783   O.B. 4, p 439 - 5, p 442

SANDIFER, James (Junr.)   Soldier

    b. 1750 - d. 1824   Pen. W-8698
    Entered service in 1776 under Capt. Samuel Hopkins.
    Served two years in 6th Va. Reg. Discharged at
    Williamsburg 1778.
    m. Martha Coleman in Meck. Co. 6 Jan. 1781. Martha
    Coleman b. 1758. Moved to Mercer Co., Ky. in 1796.

SANDERLAIN, James   Patriot

    For Continental Use   PC April 9, 1782
    1. 275 cwt Beef   O.B. 5, p 126
    Early Wills, pp. 76-77

SAUNDERS, James   Patriot

    Public Service - Served as a Juror 12 May 1781
                                              O.B. 5, p. 95

SAUNDERS, Jesse   Officer Militia

    Recommended as a Captain in room of Howell Taylor,
    resigned 8 March 1779   O.B. 4, p 457
    Took oath as militia officer 12 April 1779
                                              O.B. 4, p 459

SAUNDERS, Jesse   Patriot

    For Continental Use   PC May 14, 1782
    1. Smooth gun taken into service and not returned
                                              O.B. 5, p 148
    2. 275 cwt Beef   O.B. 5, p 151

SAUNDERS, Jesse   Patriot

    Gentleman Justice 12 Nov. 1781
    Appointed to take a list of tithables, slaves and cer-
    tain taxable commodities 14 March 1782   O.B. 5, p 121
    (Personal property tax list)
    Appointed to take annual list of tithables in Upper
    District 13 May 1782 (Tithe list)   O.B. 5, p 144
    Appointed to take a list of the number of people, both
    white and black, in 1st Precinct 9 Sept. 1782
    (Meck. Co. Census 1782)   O.B. 5, p 209

SAWYER, Lewis   Soldier

    Muster Roll, Captain Reuben Vaughan's Company 1779 -
    Hubard Papers.

SCOTT, Francis   Soldier

    Soldier in militia from 17 June 1780 until 14 Nov.1780
                        Court 9 April 1784 - O.B. 5, p 530

SEARS, Joseph   Soldier

    Private in 1st Reg. of Light Dragoons disabled in ser-
    vice by wounds in knee and shoulder
                              Meck. Deed Book 7, p. 307

SHIPP, McTyre   Patriot

    For Continental Use
    1. Smooth gun taken into service and not returned -
       value 2 pounds specie   O.B. 6, p.48

SHIPP, Thomas   Patriot

    For Continental Use   PC April 10, 1782
    1. Smooth gun taken into service and not returned
                                             O.B. 5, p 136

SHIPP, Thomas   Officer Militia

    Recommended as a second Lieutanant in second Battalion
    of militia, under Capt. William Leigh, 13 Oct. 1777
                                             O.B. 4, p 374
    Took oath of militia officer 9 March 1778
                                             O.B. 4, p 394
    Recommended as first Lieutenant 8 March 1779
                                             O.B. 4, p 457

SHORT, Jacob   Patriot

    For Continental Use   PC April 9, 1782
    1. 250 cwt Beef   O.B. 5, p 124

SHOTWELL, John   Patriot

    For Continental Use   PC May 14, 1782
    1. 350 cwt Beef   O.B. 5, p,146
    Early Wills, p 78

SHOTWELL, John (Junr)   Soldier

    Soldier in first Battalion of militia 1782
                                             EP, 10 June 1783

SIMMONS, John   Patriot

    For Continental Use   PC April 10, 1782
    1. Saddle for army   O.B. 5, p 136

SIMMONS, Samuel   Patriot

    For Continental Use   PC April 9, 1782
    1. 825 cwt Beef, 213 cwt Bacon   O.B. 5, p 128

SINGLETON, Christopher   Soldier

    Soldier who died in service - 12 Jan. 1778
                                             O.B. 4, p 389

SIZEMORE, Ephraim   Soldier

    b. 1748 in S. C. Res. Meck. Co.   Pen. R-9625
    Entered service in Meck. Co. under Capt. James Ander-
    son, served six months. Drafted in 1780, served three
    months. Moved to Spartanburg Dist, S. C. 1790.

SIZEMORE, John   Patriot

    For Continental Use
    1. Rifle furnished Capt. James Anderson for Minutemen
       Company.   VMH, Vol. 13, p. 19

SKELTON, Mark   (Shelton)   Patriot

    Public Service - Served as Constable   O.B. 4, p 395

SKIPWITH, Sir Peyton   Patriot

    Member of the Committee of Safety 8 May 1775
    Gentleman Justice 13 Nov. 1775
    Appointed to take the annual list of tithables in
    Upper District 8 April 1776   O.B. 4, p 334
    Appointed Sheriff 10 March 1777   O.B. 4, p 346

SKIPWITH, Sir Peyton   Patriot

    For Continental Use   PC April 9, 1782
    1. 2575 cwt Beef, 61 cwt Bacon   O.B. 5, p 125
    2. Service of waggon 20 days, provision found by the
       Public   O.B. 5, p 155

SMALL, James   Patriot

    For Continental Use   PC April 9, 1782
    1. 225 cwt Beef   O.B. 5, p 125

SMITH, Anderson   Patriot

    For Continental Use   PC April 10, 1782
    1. Waggon and team - value 104 pounds O.B. 5, p 135
    2. 70 days service as an artificer   O.B. 5, p 138

SMITH, Benjamin   Patriot

    Public Service - Served as a Juror 10 Sept. 1782
                          O.B. 5, p 221

SMITH, Drury   Officer Militia

    Recommended as first Lieutenant in militia 13 Oct.
    1777   O.B. 4, p 374
    Took oath as militia officer 9 Mar. 1778 O.B. 4, p 394

SMITH, Drury   Patriot

        For Continental Use   PC April 9, 1782
        1. 1200 cwt Beef   O.B. 5, p 128

SMITH, Jeremiah   Soldier

        Muster Roll, Captain Reuben Vaughan's Company 1779 -
        Hubard Papers.

SMITH, Jeremiah   Soldier

        Received pay as soldier in militia - Aud. Acct Book 22
        page 20.
        Soldier in militia 1782   EP, 10 June 1783

SMITH, John   Patriot

        For Continental Use   PC April 10, 1782
        1. 680 cwt Beef   O.B. 5, p 134
        2. 200 cwt Beef   O.B. 5, p 151
        3. 1 Flat (boat) destroyed by General's orders
                                           O.B. 5, p 152
        4. Smooth gun taken into service and not returned
                                           O.B. 5, p 216
        5. Storage 35 bbls Shad 10 April to 29 Sept.
                                           O.B. 5, p 216

SMITH, John   Soldier

        Received pay for militia service - Aud. Acct Book 22,
        page 18.

SMITH, Robert   Officer Militia

        Recommended as first Lieutanant in first Battalion of
        militia, under Capt. Asa Oliver, 13 Otc. 1777
                                           O.B. 4, p 374
        Took oath as militia officer 12 Jan. 1778
                                           O.B. 4, p 388

SMITH, Robert   Officer Militia

        Recommended as first Lieutenant in first Battalion of
        militia, under Capt. John Murray, 13 Oct. 1777
                                           O.B. 4, p 374
        Recommended as Captain in room of John Murray, pro-
        moted 8. March 1779   O.B. 4, p 457
        Took oath as Captain in militia 13 Sept. 1779
                                           O.B. 4, p 517

SMITH, Robert   Soldier

    Private in 6th Va. State Regiment under Capt. James
    Anderson - died before 3-10-1777
    Early Wills, p 81   Meck. Will Book 1, p. 219

SMITH, Sherwood   Soldier

    b. in Brunswick Co. 1761   Pen. S-1591
    Res. Meck. Co. 1786. Enlisted in Brunswick Co.
    Placed on Pension Roll in 1831
    M.R. 1765-1810, p 114

SMITH, Thomas   Soldier

    Soldier in Continental service 1778-1780
                         O.B. 5, p. 79

SMITH, Timothy   Patriot

    For Continental Use   PC May 14, 1782
    1. 325 cwt Beef   O.B. 5, p 146

SMITH, William   Soldier

    Soldier in the militia 1782   EP, 10 June 1783

SMITHSON, Micajah   Patriot

    For Continental Use   PC May 14, 1782
    1. 3 3/4 bu. Corn   O.B. 5, p 150

SPARROW, Henry   Soldier

    b. 9 Oct. 1765 Meck. Co.   Pen. S-31384
    Drafted in spring 1781 under Capt. Thomas Shipp and
    Col. Robert Munford. Later stationed at Taylor's Ferry
    as a guard for the ferry and nearby magazine. Stated
    that James Clark served with him. Moved to Mercer Co.
    Ky. about 1790.

SPARROW, James B.   Patriot

    For Continental Use   PC May 14, 1782
    1. 30 cwt Fresh pork   O.B. 5, p 149

SPARROW, James R.   Patriot

    For Continental Use
    1. 250 cwt Beef   Meck. Book Lists, p. 15

SPEED, Henry   Patriot

    Member of the Committee of Safety 8 May 1775
    Appointed with Lewis Parham to carry into execution an
    Act of Assembly laying a tax payable in certain enum-
    erated commodities   O.B. 4, p 526

SPEED, Henry   Patriot

    For Continental Use   PC April 9, 1782
    1. 325 cwt Beef   O.B. 5, p 124
    2. 30 cwt Beef, 30 cwt Flour, 6 bu. Corn O.B. 5, p 126
    3. 118 days of pasturage for stock   O.B. 5, p 132

SPEED, Henry   (Junr ?)   Soldier

    Soldier in first Battalion of militia.
                                         EP, 10 June 1783

SPEED, James   Patriot

    For Continental Use   PC May 14, 1782
    1. 350 cwt Beef   O.B. 5, p 146

SPEED, John   Patriot

    Chairman of the Committee of Safety 8 May 1775
    Gentleman Justice 8 May 1775
    Appointed to take the annual list of tithables in the
    Lower District 12 May 1777   O.B. 4, p 356

SPEED, John   Patriot

    For Continental Use   PC April 9, 1782
    1. 655 cwt Beef, 25 bu. Wheat, 7 bu. Corn, 150 cwt
       Fodder, Breakfast for 8 men and pasturage for 28
       horses   O.B. 5, p 130

SPEED, Joseph   Patriot

    Member of the Committee of Safety 8 May 1775

SPEED, Mathias   Patriot

    Public Service - Took oath of fidelity as required for
    office of under sheriff 12 Aug. 1776   O.B. 4, p 338

SPEED, Sarah   Patriot

    For Continental Use   PC May 14, 1782
    1. 200 cwt Beef   O.B. 5, p 151

SPURLOCK, Agnes   Patriot

    For Continental Use   PC April 9, 1782
    1 225 cwt Beef   O.B. 5, p 129

STANBACK, George   Patriot

    Public Service - Served as a Juror 10 Sept. 1782
                                           O.B. 5, p 227

STANDIFER, Benjamin (Sandifer ?)   Soldier

    Soldier as shown by pension of James Aiken who served
    with him.   Pen. W-26780

STANDLEY, James   (Stanley)   Patriot

    For Continental Use   PC April 9, 1782
    1. 250 cwt Beef   O.B. 5, p 127
    2. Smooth gun taken into service and not returned
                                           O.B. 5, p 234

STARLING, William, Gent.   Officer Militia

    Recommended as a Major in militia 12 Aug. 1782
                                           O.B. 5, p 181
    Took oath as a Major 9 Dec. 1782   O.B. 5, p 249

STARLING, William   Patriot

    Member of the Committee of Safety
    Gentleman Justice 11 Oct. 1779   O.B. 4, p 524
    Appointed to take the annual list of tithables in
    Lower District 12 May 1781   O.B. 5, p. 91
    Appointed as a commissioner for carrying into effect
    the Act of Assembly laying a tax payable in certain
    commodities 10 Sept. 1781   O.B. 5, p 100
    Appointed to rake a list of tithables, slaves and cer-
    tain taxable commotities 14 March 1782   O.B. 5, p 121
    (Personal property tax list)

STARLING, William   Patriot

    For Continental Use   PC April 9, 1782
    1. 300 cwt Beef   O.B. 5, p 129
    2. Waggonage Suffolk to South Quay -   O.B. 5, p 381
    3. Service of waggon and team, provision found by the
       public   O.B. 6, p 482

STARLING, William   (Junr. ?)   Officer Militia

    Recommended as first Lieutenant in militia 10 Dec.
    1781   O.B. 5, p 115

STEVENS, John   (Stephens)   Soldier

    Muster Roll, Captain Reuben Vaughan's Company 1779 -
    Hubard Papers.

STEVENS, John   Patriot

    For Continental Use   PC May 14, 1782
    1. 250 cwt Beef   O.B. 5, p 146
    Early Wills, p 83

STEVENS, Thomas   Patriot

    For Continental Use   PC April 9, 1782
    1. 250 cwt Beef   O.B. 5, p 125
    Early Wills, p 83

STOKES, David   Patriot

    Took oath as Deputy Attorney for Meck. Co. 12 July,
    1779   O.B. 4, p 479

STONE, Benjamin   Patriot

    Appointed surveyor of road in room of William Hunt.
                                         O.B. 4, p 441

STONE, Eusebius   Patriot

    For Continental Use   PC April 15, 1783
    1. 19½ cwt Bacon   O.B. 5, p 289
    Early Wills, p 83

STONE, Hezekiah   Officer Militia

    Recommended as an Ensign in militia 12 Dec. 1780
                                         O.B. 5, p. 90
    Took oath as a militia officer 12 May 1781
    Early Wills, p 83   O.B. 5, p. 96

STONE, John   Patriot

    For Continental Use   PC May 12, 1782
    1. 260 cwt Beef, 32 cwt Bacon   O.B. 5, p 146
    Early Wills, p 83

STONE, Thomas   Patriot

    For Continental Use   PC April 9, 1782
    1. 375 cwt Beef   O.B. 5, p 126
    Early Wills, p 84

STOVALL, George   Patriot

    For Continental Use   PC May 14, 1782
    1. 13 cwt Bacon   O.B. 5, p 147

STOVALL, John   Patriot

    For Continental Use   PC May 14, 1782
    1. 20 bu. Corn, 9 diets, 100 bundles fodder, 1½ bbl.
       Corn   O.B. 5, p 147

STRANGE, Stephen   Soldier

    Soldier in militia stationed at Cabin Point.
               Ex. Comm⸗, 23 Feb. 1781

STREET, Richard   Patriot

- For Continental Use   PC April 9, 1782
    1. 980 cwt Beef, 24 bu. Wheat, 6½ bu. Corn, 9 bu. Oats
      13 diets, Service of horse, provision found by the
      public, Blacksmith's and Carpenter's work on wagons
                    O.B. 5, p 148

STROUD, William   Patriot

    For Continental Use   PC April 9, 1782
    1. 475 cwt Beef, 65 cwt Bacon   O.B. 5, p 125

STUART, James   Patriot

    For Continental Use   PC April 9, 1782
    1. Black stallion - value 150 pounds   O.B. 5, p 131

SUGGETT, Edgecomb   Patriot

    For Continental Use   PC April 9, 1782
    1. 650 cwt Beef, 44 cwt Bacon   O.B. 5, p 127

SUGGETT, Edgecomb   (Junr ?)   Soldier

    Soldier in first Battalion of militia 1782
                  EP, 10 April 1783

SWEPSON, John   Patriot

    Clerk of the Committee of Safety   CJV. Vol. 2, p. 210
    For Continental Use   PC June 10, 1782
    1. Service of a waggon, team and driver for 23 days,
      provision found by the public   O.B. 5, p 154

    Early Wills, p 84

SWEPSON, Richard, Senr.   Patriot

    For Continenta Use   PC April 9, 1782
    1. 800 cwt Beef, 18 bbls Corn, 14 diets O.B. 5, p 148
       Swepson, Richard for his rations and waggon hire to
       Capt. Lucas's militia 26 Dec. 1776.
    Early Wills, p 84   VMH, Vol. 13, p. 19

SWEPSON, Richard, Junr.   Officer Militia

    Recommended as a Captain in the second Battalion of
    militia 13 Oct. 1777   O.B. 4, p 374
    Took oath as a militia officer 11 May 1778
                           O.B. 4, p 403

SWEPSON, Richard, Jr.   Patriot

    For Continental Use   PC April 9, 1782
    1. 350 cwt Beef   O.B. 5, p 124
    Early Wills, p 84

SUTTON, Thomas   Soldier

    Soldier in 15th Va. State Regiment. Isaac Holmes,
    Ensign.   Va. Gazette, Oct. 3, 1777

TABB, John   Patriot

    Member of the Committee of Safety 8 May 1775
    Note: Died June 1775 - Early Wills, p 121

TABOR, Hezekiah   Patriot

    For Continental Use   PC April 9, 1782
    1. 350 cwt Beef   O.B. 5, p 125

TANNER, Josiah   Soldier

    Res. Meck. Co. d. 1807 Jefferson Co., Ky. Pen. W-9503
    Entered service in May 1780 and served until fall 1781
    Wounded in arm at Kings Mt.

TANNER, Thomas   Officer Militia

    Recommended as an Ensign in second Battalion of Meck.
    Co. militia 13 Oct. 1777   O.B. 4, p 374
    Took oath as a militia officer 8 Dec. 1777
                           O.B. 4, p 382

TANNER, Thomas   Patriot

```
        For Continental Use                  PC April 9, 1782
        1. 300 cwt Beef                        O.B. 5, p 124
```

TANNER, Thomas (Junr)   Soldier

```
        b. 9 May 1763 in Meck. Co.              Pen. R-10391
        d. 29 Oct. 1839 in Meck. Co.  m. 5 Feb. 1795 Elizabeth
        Murphy, dau. of William and Elizabeth I. Murphy, of
        Dinwiddie Co.  Enlisted in May 1779, served three mon-
        ths under Capt. Stephen Mabry. Enlisted in Feb. 1781
        under Capt. William Lucas and served three months.
```

TARRY, George   Officer Militia

```
        Recommended as a Captain in first Battalion of Meck.
        Co. militia 13 Oct. 1777               O.B. 4, p 374
        Took oath as a militia officer 8 Dec. 1777
                                               O.B. 4, p 382
```

TARRY, George   Patriot

```
        For Continental Use                    PC May 14, 1782
        1. 1350 cwt Beef                        O.B. 5, p 146
        2. 91 bu. Corn, 300 bundles fodder      O.B. 5, p 150
        Early Wills, p 85
```

TAYLOR, Clark   Soldier

```
        b. Meck. Co. 1759  d. Oglethorpe Co. Georgia 1846
        Served as a Revolutionary War soldier. Received bounty
        land in Georgia for his service.
        M.R. 1765-1810, p 119                   Ga. DAR Roster
```

TAYLOR, David   Patriot

```
        For Continental Use                    PC May 14, 1782
        1. Three empty casks                    O.B. 5, p 152
        M.R. 1765-1810, p 119 - Early Wills, p 86
```

TAYLOR, Edmund   Patriot

```
        Member of the Committee of Safety 8 May 1775
        Gentleman Justice 8 May 1775
        Appointed to take the annual list of tithables on the
        south side of Roanoke River 8 April 1776 O.B. 4, p 334
        Appointed to take the annual list of tithables in the
        Middle District 12 May 1777             O.B. 4, p 356
        Removed to Granville Co., N. C.  d. 1808
```

TAYLOR, Goodwyn   Patriot

```
        For Continental Use                    PC May 14, 1782
        1. 300 cwt Beef                         O.B. 5, p 152
        Early Wills, pp. 85-86
```

TAYLOR, Goodwyn   (Junr)   Officer Militia

   Recommended as first Lieutenant in second Battalion of
   Meck. Co. militia 13 Oc. 1777   O.B. 4, p 374
   Took oath as a Lieutenant in the militia 13 April 1778
   Early Wills, p 85   O.B. 4, p 398

TAYLOR, Howell   Officer Militia

   Recommended as a Captain in second Battalion of Meck.
   Co. militia 13 Oct. 1777   O.B. 4, p 374
   Took oath as a militia officer 8 Dec. 1777
                                        O.B. 4, p 382

TAYLOR, Howell   Patriot

   For Continental Use   PC April 10, 1782
   1. 725 cwt Beef, 7 bbls. Corn, 6 bu. Oats
                                        O.B. 5, p 135
   2. 300 bundles of fodder, pasturage for 547 beeves and
      12 head of horses   O.B. 5, p 136

TAYLOR, Howell   (Junr ?)   Officer Militia

   Recommended as an Ensign in militia 10 March 1783
                                        O.B. 5, p 276

TAYLOR, James   Patriot

   For Continental Use   PC April 10, 1782
   1. 525 cwt Beef   O.B. 5, p 134
   2. 325 cwt Beef   O.B. 5, p 151
   3. Rifled gun taken into service and not returned
                                        O.B. 5, p 154

TAYLOR, Jesse   Officer Militia

   Recommended as first Lieutenant in second Battalion of
   militia 13 Oct. 1777   O.B. 4, p 374
   Took oath as militia officer 12 Jan. 1778
                                        O.B. 4, p 388
   Recommended as a Captain in room of John Brown, resi-
   gned, 8 March 1779   O.B. 4, p 457
   Took oath as a Captain in militia 9 Aug. 1779
                                        O.B. 4, p 493

TAYLOR, Jesse   Patriot

   For Continental Use   PC June 10, 1782
   1. Gun taken into service and not returned
                                        O.B. 5, p 154

138

TAYLOR, Jesse   Soldier

    b. Meck. Co. 1758 d. 24 Feb. 1832   Pen. W-11598
Enlisted in Meck. Co. for 12 months. Served to close
of war. In 3rd Va. Regiment in Capt. Ballard's Com-
pany under Col. Samuel Meredith. m. 31 Aug. 1792 Mary
Brandon who was b. 1776. Moved to Rutherford Co. Tenn.
Mary Taylor, widow, living in 1855 in Hamilton County,
Illinois.

TAYLOR, John   Patriot

    For Continental Use   PC May 14, 1782
    1. 325 cwt Beef   O.B. 5, p 151

TAYLOR, Jones   Patriot

    For Continental Use   Meck. Book Lists, p. 25
    1. 325 cwt Beef
    Early Wills, p 86

TAYLOR, Joshua   Patriot

    Public Service - Served as a Juror 13 Aug. 1783
                       O.B. 5, p 417

TAYLOR, Richard   Patriot

    For Continental Use   PC April 10, 1782
    1. 575 cwt Beef, 14 bbls Corn, 30 bu. Oats
                       O.B. 5, p 135

TAYLOR, Richard   (Junr)   Soldier

    Soldier in the milita 1782   EP, 10 June 1783

TAYLOR, Robert   Soldier

    Soldier in the militia 1782   EP, 10 June 1783

TAYLOR, Samuel   Patriot

    For Continental Use   PC Oct. 14, 1782
    1. Rifled gun taken into service and not returned
                       O.B. 5, p 234

TAYLOR, William   (Flatt Creek)   Patriot

    For Continental Use   PC May 14, 1782
    1. 20 bu. Wheat   O.B. 5, p 151
    Early Wills, p 86

TAYLOR, William, Gent.   Patriot

    For Continental Use   PC May 14, 1782
    1. One bbl Corn meal, 700 cwt Beef   O.B. 5, p 149
    2. Ferriage of 15 2-wheeled carriages over Roanoke
       River, 966 waggons and team, 860 men, 2061 horses
                                               O.B. 5, p 151
    3. Ferriage of 167 men, 105 horses, 41 waggons and
       team over Roanoke River   O.B. 5, p 152

TAYLOR, William   Soldier

    Received pay for service in militia - Aud. Acct Book
    22, page 19.

TAYLOR, William   Soldier

    b. Meck. Co. 1762   Pen. S-31407
    Entered service in Meck. Co. in 1779 under Capt.
    Thomas Shipp, served three months, after discharge en-
    listed in 1779 in 1st Va. Regiment and served fifteen
    months. Entered service again in Aug. 1781 under Capt.
    Elijah Graves and Col. Lewis Burwell. At Yorktown at
    the surrender of Lord Cornwallis.

TENCH, John R.   Soldier

    b. 9 March 1758 near Annapolis, Maryland, later moved
    to Virginia. Entered service from Meck. Co. under Capt
    James Anderson in 1776 in 3rd Va. Regiment. Moved
    from Meck. Co. to Brunswick Co. and then to Lunenburg
    Co. Served two more tours of duty in war. Moved
    after war to Oglethorpe Co. Ga., where he lived four
    years, and then moved to Rutherford Co. Tenn.

THOMAS, Daniel   Patriot

    Public Claim - Gun furnished Capt. J. Ballard in Dec.
    1776.   VMH, Vol. 15, p. 88

THOMAS, John   Soldier

    John Thomas a Continental soldier who died in service.
    Left widow Hannah Thomas.   O.B. 5, p 239

THOMAS, Peter   Patriot

    For Continental Use   PC April 9, 1782
    1. Dark bay horse - value 90 pounds
    2. 350 cwt Beef   O.B. 5, p 127

THOMAS, Peter   Officer Militia

    Recommended as a second Lieutenant in second Battalion
    of Meck. Co. militia 13 Oct. 1777   O.B. 4, p 374
    Took oath as a militia officer 12 Jan. 1778
                                          O.B. 4, p 389

THOMPSON, Amey   Patriot

    For Continental Use   PC April 9, 1782
    1. 325 cwt Beef   O.B. 5, p 125
    Early Wills, p 87

THOMPSON, Harmon   Patriot

    For Continental Use   PC April 10, 1782
    1. 375 cwt Beef   O.B. 5, p 134
    2. 83 bu. Corn, 42 bu. Oats   O.B. 5, p 137

THOMPSON, Harmon   Officer Militia

    Recommended as an Ensign, in first Battalion of Meck.
    Co. militia, under Capt. Charles Clay, 13 Oct. 1777
                                          O.B. 4, p 374
    Took oath as a militia officer 8 Dec. 1777
                                          O.B. 5, p 382

THOMPSON, James   Patriot

    For Continental Use   PC April 9, 1782
    1. 125 cwt Beef   O.B. 5, p 125

THOMPSON, John   Patriot

    Public Service - Appointed surveyor of road from
    Buckhorn Creek to Benjamin Whitehead's, 9 March 1778
                                          O.B. 4, p 394

THOMPSON, John   Soldier

    Mentioned in pension application of James Pool.
                                          Pen. W-9233

THOMPSON, Peter   Patriot

    For Continental Use   PC April 9, 1782
    1. 125 cwt Beef   O.B. 5, p 125

THOMPSON, Richard   Patriot

    For Continental use   PC April 9, 1782
    1. 300 cwt Beef   O.B. 5, p 129

THOMPSON, Stith   Officer Militia

    Recommended as an Ensign to fill vacancy in the militia
    14 June 1779   O.B. 4, p 476
    Took oath as a Lieutenant in the militia 10 July 1780
                                          O.B. 5, p. 81

THOMPSON, Stith   Patriot

    For Continental Use   PC May 14, 1782
    1. 350 cwt Beef   O.B. 5, p 145

TILLOTSON, Thomas   Patriot

    For Continental Use   PC April 9, 1782
    1. 225 cwt Beef   O.B. 5, p 128

TOONE, Argelon   Soldier

    b. 1754 - Res. Meck. Co.   Pen. S-41263
    Private for 5 years. Served in 6th Va. Regiment under
    Capt. Samuel Hopkins - Enlisted in March 1776. In bat-
    tles at Princeton, Trenton, Germantown and Brandywine.

TOONE, Argelon   Officer Militia

    Recommeded as an Ensign 12 Feb. 1781   EP (G) p. 778

TOONE, James   Patriot

    Public Service - Served as a Juror 15 Sept. 1778
                                          O.B. 4, p 439

TOONE, James   (Junr)   Officer Militia

    Recommended as an Ensign in second Battalion of militia
    under Capt. Richard Swepson, 13 Oct. 1777 O.B. 4, p 374
    Recommended as a second Lieutenant in militia 10 July
    1780   O.B. 5, p. 60

TOONE, Lewis   Patriot

    Public Service - Served as a Juror 12 Oct. 1779
                                          O.B. 4, p 537

TOONE, William   Soldier

    Mentioned in pension application of Clement Blackbourn
                                          Pen. S-10388

TOWNES, Joseph   Officer

Revolutionary Soldier. Died 11 June 1824 in Meck. Co.,
age 65, Captain Joseph Townes.
Richmond Enquirer, 25 June 1824.   VHM, Vol.36, p. 269

TRAYLOR, Cary   Soldier

    b. 1752 Res. Meck. Co.   Pen. R-10670
Entered the army in Meck. Co. under Captain Reuben
Vaughan. Moved to South Carolina where married. Moved
to Clarke Co. Kentucky. Living in Bath Co. Kentucky
in Oct. 1850 - age 98 years.

TUCKER, George   Soldier

    b. Amelia Co. 1758   Res. Meck. Co.
Enlisted 4 Sept. 1780 in 2nd Va. Regiment. Blacksmith:
fair hair, grey eyes, fair complexion, 5ft 11in.
                                  CS(E), p. 18

TUCKER, Hudson   Patriot

    For Continental Use   PC May 14, 1782
1. Bay horse - value 55 pounds   O.B. 5, p 150

TUCKER, James   Patriot

    Public Service - Served as a Juror 11 May 1778
                              O.B. 4, p 402

TUREMAN, Martin   Patriot

    For Continental Use   PC May 14, 1782
1. 300 cwt Beef   O.B. 5, p 146

TUREMAN, Thomas   Patriot

    For Continental Use   PC May 14, 1782
1. 250 cwt Beef   O.B. 5, p 146

TURNER, James   Patriot

    For Continental Use   PC April 10, 1782
1. Smooth gun taken into service and not returned
                             O.B. 5, p 133

TURNER, Matthew   Patriot

    For Continental Use   PC April 9, 1782
1. 250 cwt Beef   O.B. 5, p 129
Public Service - Served as a Grand Juror 12 May 1783
                             O.B. 5, p 294

TURNER, William   Patriot

    For Continental Use   PC April 9, 1782
    1. 300 cwt Beef   O.B. 5, p 125

VANDYKE, John   (Van Dyke)   Patriot

    For Continental Use   PC April 10, 1782
    1. 44 diets   O.B. 5, p 135
    2. Rent of three houses at the Magazine near Taylor's
       Ferry for one year   O.B. 5, p 150
    3. Four empty casks   O.B. 5, p 151

VANDYKE, Mary   Patriot

    For Continental Use   PC May 14, 1782
    1. Making 2 pr. overalls and 2 shirts   O.B. 5, p 149

VAUGHAN, Ingram   Officer

    Recommended as a first Lieutenant in militia 12 Aug.
    1782   O.B. 5, p 181
    Took oath as a militia officer 9 June 1783
                                      O.B. 5, p 370
    b. 1757 in Meck. Co. d. 1836 in Alabama.
    Served in Continental Line as a private and sergeant,
    and as officer in militia.

VAUGHAN, James   Soldier

    Soldier in service in Georgia 1779   O.B. 4, p 474

VAUGHAN, James   Patriot

    Appointed under (deputy) sheriff 9 Sept. 1782.
                                      O.B. 5, p 215

VAUGHAN, John   Patriot

    For Continental Use   PC June 10, 1782
    1. Use of horse and wagon at the Magazine near
       Taylor's Ferry.   O.B. 5, p 155

VAUGHAN, Joshua   Patriot

    For Continental Use   PC May 14, 1782
    1. 98 cwt Bacon   O.B. 5, p 147

VAUGHAN, Peter   Patriot

    For Continental Use   PC May 14, 1782
    1. 225 cwt Beef   O.B. 5, p 146

VAUGHAN, Reuben   Officer Militia

    Recommended as a Captain in second Battalion of Meck.
    Co. militia 13 Oct. 1777   O.B. 4, p 374
    Took oath as a militia officer 8 Dec. 1777
                                            O.B. 4, p 382

VAUGHAN, Reuben   Patriot

    Member of the Committee of Safety 8 May 1775
    Gentleman Justice 8 May 1775
    Appointed to take the annual list of tithables in the
    Lower District 8 April 1776   O.B. 4, p 334
    Appointed to take the list of tithables, slaves and
    certain taxable commodities 14 March 1782
                                            O.B. 5, p 121
    Appointed and took oath as sheriff 12 Aug. 1782
                                            O.B. 5, p 177

VAUGHAN, Reuben   Patriot

    For Continental Use   PC April 9, 1782
    1. 300 cwt Beef   O.B. 5, p 125
    2. 1400 cwt Beef, 1400 cwt Flour   O.B. 5, p 126
    3. Sorrel horse - Value 50 pounds   O.B. 5, p 129

VAUGHAN, Samuel   Patriot

    For Continental Use   PC April 9, 1782
    1. 300 cwt Beef   O.B. 5, p 129

VAUGHAN, Thomas   Patriot

    For Continental Use   PC April 10, 1782
    1. Services of two horses, provision found by the
       public   O.B. 5, p 134
    2. Service of a waggon, team and driver for 16 days,
       provision found by the public.   O.B. 5, p 138

VAUGHAN, William   Patriot

    For Continental Use   PC May 14, 1782
    1. 700 cwt Beef   O.B. 5, p 146
    Early Wills, p 89

VOWELL, William   Patriot

    For Continental Use   PC April 9, 1782
    1. 200 cwt Beef   O.B. 5, p 128
    2. Gun impressed by Samuel Lark, Quartermaster of the
       militia, ordered to be paid 10 March 1783
                                            O.B. 5, p 278

WADE, Elizabeth   Patriot

    For Continental Use   PC May 14, 1782
    1. 600 cwt Beef   O.B. 5, p 146

WADE, George   Patriot

    For Continental Use   PC April 10, 1782
    1. Bay stallion - value 175 pounds   O.B. 5, p 134

WADE, Martha   Patriot

    For Continental Use   PC April 9, 1782
    1. 300 cwt Beef   O.B. 5, p 127

WAGSTAFF, Basil   Patriot

    For Continental Use   PC April 9, 1782
    1. 200 cwt Beef   O.B. 5, p 127

WAGSTAFF, John   Patriot

    For Continental Use   PC April 9, 1782
    1. 225 cwt Beef   O.B. 5, p 127

WALKER, David   Patriot

    Public Service - Appointed surveyor of road 9 Nov.
    1779.   O.B. 5, p 8

WALKER, Daniel   Soldier

    Mecklenburg Pensioner   - Roll 1831   (G) p. 799

WALKER, Henry   Officer Militia

    Recommended as a Captain in first Battalion of militia
    13 Oct. 1777.   O.B. 4, p 374
    Took oath as a militia officer 8 Dec. 1777
                                           O.B. 4, p 382
    Recommended as a Colonel 10 Dec. 1781 O.B. 5, p 115
    Took oath as a Colonel in militia 8 July 1782
                                           O.B. 5, p 159
    "Henry Walker, Gent., made oath that he served in the
    militia at the siege of Yorktown 41 days as a Major".
                                           O.B. 5, p 530

WALKER, Henry   Patriot

    Gentleman Justice - 11 Aug. 1777   O.B. 5, p 365
    Appointed to take the annual list of tithables on the

south side of the Roanoke River 11 May 1778

O.B. 5, p 400

Took oath required by law as a Vestryman of St. James
Parish 9 Nov. 1778   O.B. 4, p 445
Appointed to take a list of the number of people, both
white and black, in the 4th Precinct 9 Sept. 1782
(Meck. Co. Census 1782)   O.B. 5, p 209

WALKER, Henry   Patriot

    For Continental Use   PC April 10, 1782
    1. 675 cwt Beef   O.B. 5, p 138

    Col. Henry Walker (1740-1792) m. Martha Bolling Eppes
                                   Va. Gazette, April 18, 1952

WALKER, Richard   Soldier

   - b. Amelia Co. 1745 - d. Meck. Co. 1801
    Private in Company of Capt. Joseph Spencer, 7th. Va.
    Regiment, commanded by Col. Alexander McClendian.
    On list of soldiers of the Va. Line on Continental
    Establishment who received certificate for the balance
    of their pay. Received April 20, 1785 pay for services
                                                   War Dept.

WALKER, Sylvanus   Patriot

    For Continental Use   PC May 14, 1782
    1. 275 cwt Beef   O.B. 5, p 148

WALKER, Tandy   Patriot

    Public Service - Served as a Juror 12 May 1783
                                                   O.B. 5, p 294

WALL, Henry   Soldier
    Received pay for service in militia - Aud. Acct Book
    22, page 18.

WALL, Mial   (Michael)   Patriot

    Public Service - Served as a Juror 12 Aug. 1783
                                                   O.B. 5, p 415

WALLACE, William   Soldier

    Ordered that Robert Munford, Gent., supply Elizabeth
    Wallace, wife of William Wallace, a poor soldier in
    the service of this state with such necessaries as she
    may want for herself and children.   O.B. 4, p 370

WALLER, Daniel   Soldier

    Meck. Co. Pens.   Pen. S-41303
    Enlisted in Meck. Co. in 1777 under Col. Lewis Burwell
    for 3 years. Served under Capt. Henry Dudley, Col.
    William Brent. In battles at Stony Point and Monmouth.

WALLER, Edward   Patriot

    For Continental Use   PC April 9, 1782
    1. 1850 cwt Beef   O.B. 5, p 127
    (Moved to Tennessee)

WALTON, Edward   Patriot

    For Continental Use   PC April 10, 1782
    1. One horse - value 50 pounds   O.B. 5, p 133

WARD, Henry   Patriot

    For Continental Use   PC April 9, 1782
    1. 600 cwt Beef   O.B. 5, p 126

WATKINS, Charles   Patriot

    For Continental Use   PC May 14, 1782
    1. Smooth gun taken into service and not returned
                                           O.B. 5, p 147

WATKINS, George   Patriot

    For Continental Use   PC May 14, 1782
    1. Smooth gun taken into service and not returned
                                           O.B. 5, p 147

WATKINS, James   Patriot

    PC Jan. 1776 - Plank for Meck. Co. Battalion of mili-
    tia.   Acct Book 1775-76, p. 16

WATKINS, Thomas   Patriot

    For Continental Use   PC May 14, 1782
    1. 225 cwt Beef   O.B. 5, p 146

WATSON, Burwell   Patriot

    For Continental Use   PC May 14, 1782
    1. 200 cwt Beef   O.B. 5, p 147

WATSON, Elizabeth   Patriot

```
     For Continental Use              PC April 9, 1782
1. 400 cwt Beef                     O.B. 5, p 128

WATSON, Isaac  (Senr)                          Patriot

     For Continental Use              PC April 9, 1782
1. 300 cwt Beef                     O.B. 5, p 129

WATSON, Isaac                          Private Militia

     Muster Roll, Captain Reuben Vaughan's Company 1779 -
     Hubard Papers.

WATSON, Jacob                                   Patriot

     For Continental Use              PC May 14, 1782
1. 275 cwt Beef                     O.B. 5, p 147

WATTS, Richard                                  Patriot

     For Continental Use              PC May 14, 1782
1. 425 cwt Beef                     O.B. 5, p 151

WEATHERFORD, Benjamin                          Soldier

     d. in Meck. Co. 18 April 1832           Pen. W-1520
     Served as a private in North and South Carolina and in
     Georgia.  Taken prisoner at Charleston.
     Nancy Weatherford, his widow, moved to Rutherford Co.
     Tenn. after death of her husband.

WEATHERFORD, William                           Patriot

     For Continental Use              PC April 10, 1782
1. Gun taken into service and not returned
                                     O.B. 5, p 136

WESTBROOK, James                               Patriot

     For Continental Use              PC Aug. 12, 1782
1. Smooth gun taken into service and not returned
                                     O.B. 5, p 182

WESTMORELAND, Jesse                            Soldier

     Res. Meck. Co. 1782                     Pen. S-3526
     Private in Va. Line.  Moved to Fentress Co. Tenn.

WESTMORELAND, Joseph                           Soldier

     b. Dinwiddie Co.  Res. Meck. Co.     Ga. DAR Roster
     Enlisted in Meck. Co. and served as a private in the
     Continental Line.  Received bounty land in Kentucky.
```

WHITE, George   Patriot

    For Continental Use   PC May 14, 1782
    1. 375 cwt Beef   O.B. 5, p 146
    2. 29 diets, 8 bbl Corn, 12 bu Oats, 400 bundles of
       fodder   O.B. 5, p 149

WHITE, John   Soldier

    b. 1761 Derry, Ireland. Res. Meck. Co. Trade: Tailor
    Enlisted 22 Oct. 1780 for 18 months. 5ft 8 in, hair
    dark brown, eyes gray, fair complexion. CS(E), p. 46

WHITE, William   Patriot

    For Continental Use   PC April 9, 1782
    1. 250 cwt Beef   O.B. 5, p 127

WHITEHEAD, Benjamin   Patriot

    For Continental Use   PC April 9, 1782
    1. 375 cwt Beef   O.B. 5, p 129
    2. Pasturage for 21 horses   O.B. 5, p 182

WHITEHEAD, Benjamin   Patriot

    Member of the Committee of Safety 8 May 1775
    Recommended as Coroner for Meck. Co. 12 April 1779
                         O.B. 5, p 460
    Took oath of office as Coroner 14 June 1779
                         O.B. 5, p 475
    Appointed with Edward Finch and John Brown to examine
    and deface all counterfeit money produced to them und-
    er Act of Assembly against counterfeiting.
    Recommended as a Justice - Died 1781 - Early Wills, p.
    92

WHITEHEAD, Richard   Patriot

    For Continental Use
    1. 300 cwt Beef   Meck. Book Lists, p. 13

WILBOURN, Thomas   Patriot

    For Continental Use   PC April 9, 1782
    1. 325 cwt Beef   O.B. 5, p 125

WILES, Luke   Soldier

    Soldier in Revolutionary War   Meck. Pet. (G), p. 827

WILKERSON, Elisha   Private Militia

b. in Sussex Co. 1763. Res. Meck. Co. d. Franklin Co.
Ga. 1837.
Entered service in Sussex Co. militia. Moved to Meck.
Co. Listed in Meck. Co. Personal Property Tax list in
1800. m. Lucy Abernathy, dau. of Signal Abernathy of
Meck. Co. Moved to Franklin Co., Ga., in 1807.

WILKERSON, William   (Wilkinson)   Patriot

    For Continental Use   PC April 9, 1782
    1. 275 cwt Beef   O.B. 5, p 128

WILKINS, Arabella   Patriot

    For Continental Use   PC April 9, 1782
    1. 225 cwt Beef   O.B. 5, p 128
    Early Wills, p 94

WILKINS, Charles   Patriot

    For Continental Use
    1. Gun furnished for service   Comm. Book IV, p. 350
    Early Wills, p 94

WILKINS, Clement   Patriot

    For Continental Use   PC May 14, 1782
    1. Repairing public arms   O.B. 5, p 150

WILKINS, James   Patriot

    Public Service - Surveyor of road 10 Nov. 1777
                                     O.B. 4, p 381

WILKINS, William   Patriot

    For Continental Use   PC April 9, 1782
    1. 200 cwt Beef   O.B. 5, p 146

WILLIAMS, Henry   Patriot

    For Continental Use   PC April 9, 1782
    1. Horse for army - value 100 pounds   O.B. 5, p 132

WILLIAMS, James   Patriot

    For Continental Use   PC April 9, 1782
    1. 400 cwt Beef   O.B. 5, p 128
    2. 295 cwt Beef   O.B. 5, p 136

WILLIAMSON, John   Patriot

For Continental Use   PC April 9, 1782
1. 350 cwt Beef   O.B. 5, p 128

WILLIS, William   Patriot

For Continental Use   PC April 9, 1782
1. One horse, 2 bu Corn, 300 bundles Fodder
                                           O.B. 5, p 131

WILLS, Isham   Patriot

Gun furnished Meck. Battalion Acct Book 1775-76, p. 9
Dec. 1775

WILMORE, Robert   Private Militia

Muster Roll, Captain Reuben Vaughan's Company 1779 -
Hubard Papers .

WILSON, Archibald   Soldier

Res. Meck. Co. 1820   Pen. W-4863
b. 1756. Moved to Guilford Co. N. C. d. 21 Dec. 1828
M.R. 1765-1810, p 133

WILSON, Edward   Soldier

b. 1759 Res. Meck. Co.   Pen. S-41362
Enlisted in March 1776. Served two years in Va. Line
under Capt. Ralph Faulkner and Col. Richard Parker.

WILSON, Elimeleck   Officer Militia

Recommended as an Ensign in militia 12 Dec. 1780
                                           O.B. 5, p. 90
Recommended as a first Lieutenant in militia 12 May
1781   O.B. 5, p. 95
Took oath of militia officer 12 May 1781 O.B. 5, p. 96

WILSON, John   Patriot

Public Service - Served as a Juror at various dates
from 11 May 1778 until 11 Nov. 1782   O.B. entries
Appointed surveyor of road from Thomas Berry's line to
Sir Peyton Skipwith's ferry road 14 April 1783
                                           O.B. 5, p 283

WILSON, John   Private Militia

Muster Roll, Captain Reuben Vaughan's Company 1779 -
Hubard Papers.

WILSON, James   Patriot

    For Continental Use   PC April 9, 1782
    1. 275 cwt Beef   O.B. 5, p 127

WILSON, James   Ensign Militia

    Muster Roll, Captain Reuben Vaughan's Company 1779 -
    serving as an Ensign - Hubard Papers.

WILSON, James   Officer Militia

    Recommended as an Ensign in second Battalion of Meck.
    Co. militia, under Capt. William Leigh, 13 Oct. 1777
                                         O.B. 4, p 374
    Took oath as a militia officer 9 March 1778
                                         O.B. 4, p 394
    Recommended as Lieutenant in militia 8 March 1779
                                         O.B. 4, p 457

WILSON, Lemuel   Patriot

    Public Service - Appointed surveyor of road in room of
    David Royster 9 Nov. 1778   O.B. 4, p 449

WILSON, Lemuel   Soldier

    Soldier in first Battalion of militia 1782
                                EP, 10 June 1783

WILSON, Wallis   Pen. S-64181

    b. 1755. Res. Meck. Co. Soldier in Virginia militia.
    On pension roll 1835. In service at Yorktown at the
    surrender of Lord Cornwallis. Mentioned in Pen. R-4307

WINFIELD, Peter   Officer Militia

    Recommended as second Lieutenant in second Battalion
    of militia, under Capt. Samuel Marshall, 13 Oct. 1777
                                       O.B. 4, p 374
    Took oath as a militia officer 9 Feb. 1778
                                       O.B. 4, p 391
    Recommended as a first Lieutenant 14 June 1779
                                       O.B. 4, p 476

WINKFIELD, Peter   Patriot

    For Continental Use   PC April 9, 1782
    1. 275 cwt Beef   O.B. 5, p 124

WINKLER, John   Patriot

    For Continental Use   PC April 10, 1782
    1. Pasturage for 534 beeves
    2. Services of a cart with three horses O.B. 5, p 136
    3. Allowed 5 pounds damage done orchard by the beeves
       with the troops under command of Major Gen. St.
       Clair (sic) (Sinclair)   O.B. 5, p 137

WINN, John   Patriot

    For Continantal Use   PC May 14, 1782
    1. 250 cwt Beef   O.B. 5, p 146

WINN, John   Officer Militia

    Recommended as an Ensign in first Battalion of militia
    under Capt. Henry Walker, 13 Oct. 1777   O.B. 4, p 374
    Took oath as a militia officer 11 May 1778
                                             O.B. 4, p 403
    Recommended as a second Lieutenant 14 June 1779
                                             O.B. 4, p 476
    Took oath as a lieutenant in militia 10 July 1780
                                             O.B. 5, p. 81

WINN, Richard   Officer Militia

    Recommended as an Ensign in first Battalion of militia
    under Capt. James Hall 13 Oct. 1777   O.B. 4, p 374
    Took oath as a militia officer 8 Dec. 1777
                                             O.B. 4, p 382

WITTON, Richard   Patriot

    For Continental Use   PC April 9, 1782
    1. 300 cwt Beef   O.B. 5, p 127
    Early Wills, p 96

WITTON, Richard, Junr.   Officer Militia

    Recommended as first Lieutenant in first Battalion of
    militia, under Capt. William Green, 13 Oct. 1777
                                             O.B. 4, p 374
    Took oath as a militia officer 11, May 1778
                                             O.B. 4, p 403
    Recommended as a Captain in militia 11 Dec. 1780
                                             O.B. 5, p. 90
    Took oath as a militia officer 12 May 1781
                                             O.B. 5, p. 96

WOOD, Archibald   Soldier

    Declaration made for a pension as a Revolutionary sol-
    dier.   Meck. Co. Court Nov. 1832, C.B. 29, p. 347

154

WOODY, John   Patriot

    For Continental Use   PC April 10, 1782
    1. Horse for army - value 40 pounds   O.B. 5, p 133

WOOTEN, Samuel   Patriot

    Public Service - Appointed assistant surveyor under
    Edward Lewis   O.B. 5, p 302

WORSHAM, Ludwell   Patriot

    For Continental Use   PC May 14, 1782
    1. 335 cwt Beef   O.B. 5, p 151

WORSHAM, Ludwell (Junr ?)   Soldier

    Soldier in militia 1782   EP, 10 June 1783

WRIGHT, Austin   Patriot

    For Continental Use   PC April 10, 1782
    1. 900 cwt Beef   O.B. 5, p 135

WRIGHT, George   Patriot

    For Continental Use
    1. 375 cwt Beef   Meck. Book Lists, p. 15

WRIGHT, Laban   Patriot

    For Continental Use   PC April 9, 1782
    1. 275 cwt Beef   O.B. 5, p 125

WRIGHT, Nathan   Soldier

    b. Lunenburg Co. 7 Nov. 1760   Pen. S-32083
    Volunteered in Meck. Co. 4 April 1779 for 18 months.
    Served two years under Col. Richard Parker in Georgia
    and South Carolina. In battles at Savannah, Siege of
    96 and Charleston. Res. Meck. Co. Moved to Wilkes Co.
    and then to Lincoln Co., Ga. Died 17 Feb. 1836.

WRIGHT, Thomas   Soldier

    Muster Roll, Captain Reuben Vaughan's Company 1779 -
    Hubard Papers. Enlisted in regular service.

WRIGHT, William   Patriot
    For Continental Use   PC April 9, 1782
    1. 325 cwt Beef   O.B. 5, p 129

YANCEY, Absolam   Soldier

    Cornet in (10 VR) WD 286,1; (14 VR) WD 259, 10; (10 &
    14 VR) WD 213, 1 Rev. Soldiers, Eckenrode Supp., 1912
    Early Wills, p. 97

YANCEY, Mary   Patriot

    For Continental Use   PC May 14, 1782
    1. 650 cwt Beef   O.B. 5, p 146
    Early Wills, p. 97

YANCEY, Zachariah   Patriot

    Appointed surveyor of road in room of William Culbre-
    ath, Jr. 10 July 1780   O.B. 5, p. 80

YOUNG, Allen   Patriot

    Public Service - Served as a Juror 13 Aug. 1782, 10
    Sept. 1782, 13 May 1783 and 12 Aug. 1783
                  O.B. 5, pp. 193, 227, 348, 419

YOUNG, Samuel   Patriot

    For Continental Use   PC April 9, 1782
    1. 100 cwt Bacon   O.B. 5, p 123
    2. 36 bu. Wheat   O.B. 5, p 125
    3. 2150 cwt Beef   O.B. 5, p 131
    4. 2 horses for army   O.B. 5, p 135
    5. 2 empty hogsheads   O.B. 5, p 136

YATES, Edward Randolph *   Soldier

    Enlisted 5 June 1777 for duration of war. Served as a
    private in Captain Robert Gamble's Company in 8th Va.
    Regiment commanded by Colonel James Wood. Served in
    the 4th, 8th and 12th Va. Regiments.
    Resided in Meck. Co. m. Elizabeth Murray of Meck.
    Co. in 1783. d. 1792 in Meck. Co.
    M.R. 1765-1810, p. 136 - Early Wills, p. 98

    * Muster Rolls of Colonel James Wood's Regiment from
      Virginia. Included in this volume through the cour-
      tesy of Mrs. S. Wirt Yates, Mechanicsville, Va.

MECKLENBURG COUNTY COMMITTEE OF SAFETY
8 May 1775

John Speed, Chairman

William Lucas	Bennett Goode
Francis Ruffin	Henry Speed
Robert Burton	Lewis Burwell
Cluverius Coleman	Edmund Taylor
Sir Peyton Skipwith	Thacker Burwell
George Baskervill	Benjamin Whitehead
Joseph Speed	Reuben Vaughan
John Jones	John Tabb
Robert Ballard	William Leigh
John Ballard, Junr.	Samuel Hopkins, Junr.

Isaac Holmes, Clerk

John Tabb, one of the original members of the Committee of Safety, died in June soon after appointment to the committee

George Baskervill, a member of the committee, died in 1777, and William Lucas, another member, died in 1778. John Jones, Joseph and Henry Speed resigned. Robert Ballard, Samuel Hopkins, Junr., John Ballard, Junr. and Isaac Holmes entered service. Robert Burton, Sir Peyton Skipwith, Edmund Taylor and William Leigh removed from the county.

While there is no record found in the Order Books of the appointment of a new clerk to succeed Isaac Holmes, the Journals of the Council of State show that Daniel Hutt and John Swepson served subsequently as clerks of the committee. The Committee of Safety was reorganized and new members were appointed.

NEW MEMBERS OF THE COMMITTEE OF SAFETY

Robert Munford	James Anderson
Henry Delony	Henry Walker
John Camp	Lewis Parham
William Davis	Samuel Goode
John Murray	William Starling
William Green	John Burton
Samuel Dedman	William Taylor

Thompson Fowlkes

Daniel Hutt, Clerk	John Swepson, Clerk

Isaac Holmes, first clerk of the committee, was commissioned as an Ensign in the 15th Virginia Regiment. Robert Ballard was an officer in the Continental Line. John Ballard, Junr. commanded one of the first companies of Minutemen called out from Mecklenburg County. Samuel Hopkins, Junr. commanded a company of regulars with Obia Clay and Hutchins Burton serving as Lieutenants and William Dawson serving as an Ensign.

ALEXANDER
  Robert
ANDERSON
  James
BUGG
  Samuel
BURTON
  John
BURWELL
  Lewis
  Thacker
CAMP
  John
CHRISTOPHER
  David
COLEMAN
  Cluverius
COX
  John
CLAUSEL
  Clausel
DAVIS
  William
DEDMAN
  Samuel
DELONY
  Henry
ERSKINE
  Thomas
FINCH
  Edward
FOWLKES
  Thompson
GOODE
  Bennett
  Samuel

GREGORY
  Roger
JOHNSON
  William
LUCAS
  William
MUNFORD
  Robert
MURRAY
  John
PARHAM
  Lewis
POTTER
  John
RANDOLPH
  William
ROYSTER
  Jacob
RUFFIN
  Francis
SAUNDERS
  Jesse
SKIPWITH
  Sir Peyton
SPEED
  John
STARLING
  William
TAYLOR
  Edmund
VAUGHAN
  Reuben
WALKER
  Henry

NOTES: Thacker Burwell died in 1780. William Lucas died
in 1778. John Murray died in 1782. John Camp died
in 1782. Samuel Bugg died in 1777.

Edmund Taylor removed to Granville County during
this period.

Sir Peyton Skipwith moved from Mecklenburg County
to Surry County in 1779.

After the Revolutionary War, James Anderson and
John Potter moved to North Carolina. Jesse Saunders
moved to Georgia in 1785. William Starling removed
to Henry County, Virginia.

GENTLEMEN JUSTICES - 1775-1783

Date on which they were sworn in as Justices, or date on which they first appeared in court.

ORDER BOOK 4

8 May 1775
    John Speed
    Edmund Taylor
    Samuel Bugg
    Reuben Vaughan
    Robert Munford
12 June
    Lewis Burwell
19 June
    John Cox
    John Potter
10 July
    William Davis
    Henry Delony
11 Sept.
    Robert Alexander
13 Nov.
    Sir Peyton Skipwith
11 Dec.
    John Camp
11 March 1776
    David Christopher

11 Aug. 1776
    Cluverius Coleman
12 Aug.
    Jacob Royster
12 May 1777
    Thomas Erskine
11 Aug.
    Bennett Goode
    Francis Ruffin
    James Anderson
    Henry Walker
    Thacker Burwell
8 Sept.
    John Murray
    Lewis Parham
13 Oct.
    William Lucas
    Samuel Goode
11 Oct. 1779
    Samuel Dedman
    William Starling

ORDER BOOK 5

8 Nov. 1781
    John Burton
12 Nov.
    William Randolph
    William Johnson
    Jesse Saunders

10 Feb. 1783
    Roger Gregory
10 April
    Edward Finch
    Thompson Fowlkes
29 April
    Clausel Clausel

In addition to their service as Justices, the following served as militia officers:

Reuben Vaughan, Robert Munford, Lewis Burwell, William Davis

Bennett Goode, James Anderson, Henry Walker, Thacker Burwell

John Murray, Lewis Parham, William Lucas, William Starling

Samuel Dedman, John Burton, Jesse Saunders, Thompson Fowlkes

SELECTED LIST OF PENSION APPLICATIONS

It was not possible for the compilers to consult every pension application made by soldiers who served in the Revolutionary War from Mecklenburg County. A list considered representative, however, was made, and these applications now filed in the National Archives were searched for information to augment the scanty records now preserved. These applications reveal that soldiers from Mecklenburg County took part in battles from Georgia to New York.

ALPHABETICAL LIST OF ENGAGEMENTS

Augusta, Ga.

Brandywine, Pa.

Brier Creek, Ga.

Broad River, S. C.

Camden, S. C.

Charleston, S. C.

Charlotte, N. C.

Eutaw Springs, S. C.

Guilford Courthouse, N. C.

Hillsborough, N. C.

Jamestown Ford, Va.

Monmouth Courthouse, N. J.

Ninety-Six, S. C.

Paulus Hook, N. J.

Princeton, N. J.

Rugley's Mills, S. C.

Savannah, Ga.

Stono Ferry, S. C.

Stony Point, N. Y.

Trenton, N. J.

White Plains, N. Y.

Yorktown, Va.

In addition to the engagements listed above, these applications reveal that many spent the hard winter at Valley Forge. It has been questioned, because of the loss of the records, whether any of the companies of Mecklenburg County Militia served at Yorktown.

The limited number of applications searched reveal that eight companies of Mecklenburg County Militia were called out in August 1781, and marched to Yorktown. Not all of the companies took part in the seige of Yorktown. Some of the companies were stationed across the York River in Gloucestor County as a precautionary measure to prevent any attempt of the British to escape by that route.

Some of the pensions reveal that the applicant was detached from his company and placed in the detail to guard the prisoners taken to Winchester after the surrender of Cornwallis.

From these applications, it appears that the Mecklenburg County Militia, which marched to Yorktown, was commanded by Colonel Lewis Burwell and Major Henry Walker.

Company Commander	Pension Applicant
Captain William Drumright	Abel Dortch
Captain Thompson Fowlkes	Joseph Butler
	Peter Crawford
Captain Elijah Graves	Thomas Brandon
	Francis Farrar
	William Taylor
Captain Achilles Jeffries	James Barnes
Captain Stephen Mabry	Joseph Bennett
	Robert Brooks
	Stephen Ellis
Captain Samuel Marshall	John Bowen
Captain William Roffe	John Adams
Captain Richard Witton	Jordan Bennett
	Ansel Cunningham

The pension application of Thomas Brandon refers to Colonel Samuel Dedman at Yorktown. This indicates that a part, at least, of both battalions of Mecklenburg County Militia were ordered to Yorktown.

The pension application of Robert W. Fitz of Mecklenburg County states that he substituted for William Watkins of Halifax County in a company of Halifax County Militia, and that the company under the command of Captain Fleming Bates marched by the most direct route to Yorktown. The company was there at the surrender of Lord Cornwallis.

The pension applications searched are particularly revealing in another way for they show subsequent migration of many Mecklenburg County people to other states.

The application of Abel Dortch was made from Illinois; that of Peter Crawford from Rockingham County, N. C. Robert Brooks made application from Marion County, Georgia, which was later transferred to Pike County, Alabama.

John Adams moved to Montgomery County, Tennessee; James Barnes moved first to Burke County, N. C., then to Blunt County, Tennessee and finally to Vigo County, Indiana; Joseph Bennett went to Rutherford County, Tennessee.

MUSTER ROLL OF CAPTAIN REUBEN VAUGHAN

A list of Men Marched Out Under the Command of Captain Vaughan from Mecklingburg (sic) on a detachment to the Southard Under the Immediate Command of David Mason, Col. Command. A. D. 1779

Rubin (sic) Vaughan		Capt.
Jno. Holmes		Lieut.
James Wilson		Ensign
Samuel Lark		Serg. Maj.
Wm. Holloway		Serg.
James Ladd		do

Thos. Adams		
Wm. Mason		
Wm. Cradle		
Robt. Crowder		
Sterling Dixon		
James Arnold	Capt. Vaughan List Returned	
Wm. Brandum		
Wm. Cunningham		
Francis Hinton		
Wm. Archer		
Howell Hargrove		
Wm. Hudson		
John Hall		(Sick Abstant)
Mark Evans		
John Holloway		
John Parks		
James Hy. Kidd		(On furlough sick)
Wm. Conell		do
Thos. Crage		do
Richard Lewis	Sustituted by Wm.	Adkins (Deserted)
Jeremiah Lucas	do	Jno. Adams
Jeremiah Smith	do	Barnet Burnit (Deserted)
Ezekiah Crowder	do	Epheram Andrews
John Steevens	do	Ansel Cunningham
Josiah Cunningham	do	Jno. Cunningham
John Guy	do	Christopher Guy
Jesse Bowin	do	Bracey Bowin
James Bowin	do	David Bowin
Hicks Bowin	do	Alexander Bowin
Wm. Roberts	do	Abel Dortch
Isaac Watson	do	Joseph Cradle
John Cook Taylor *	do	David Dortch
Ray Moss	do	Robt. Wilmore
Wm. Hatchell	do	Willis Hatchell
Jesse Bugg	do	Jno. Mallit
John Goode	do	Wm. Guy
James Hicks	do	Wm. S. Roberts
James Ramey	do	(Wm.) Delafield

Charles Kelley	Substituted by John Farrar
Dick Evans	do Godfrey Evans
Thos. Meares	Discharged at Saulsbery May 10th 1779
Thos. Wright	Inlisted in the Reagulars Servis
Wm. Epps	do
Edwd Giles	do
John Mize	do
John Burnit	Deserted
John Wilson	do
Benj. Burnit	do
Lewis Sawyer	do
John Decker	do
Wm. Mealer	do

/s/ Reuben Vaughan Capt

Note: The foregoing Muster Roll of Captain Reuben Vaughan is with the Hubard Papers, Southern Historical Collection, University of North Carolina Library, Chapel Hill, N. C.

Note: How this muster roll came into the possession of Edmund W. Hubard of Buckingham County is not known to the compilers.

The list has been preserved in the Edmund W. Hubard Papers and is now, with that collection, some 31,000 items in all, in the Southern Historical Collection of the University of North Carolina Library, Chapel Hill.

History of Prince Edward County,
Herbert Clarence Bradshaw.

* John Cook Taylor. It is uncertain whether this was John Cook a tailor, or John Cook Taylor. Other Mecklenburg County records have John Cook (Taylor).

C O M M I S S I O N

THE COMMONWEALTH OF VIRGINIA

REUBEN VAUGHAN, Gent.   Greeting,

"Know you, that from the special Trust and Confidence which is reposed in your Patriotism, fidelity, courage and good conduct, you are by these presents, constituted and appointed Captain of Militia in the County of Mecklenburg.

You are therefore carefully and diligently to discharge the Duty of Captain of Militia, by doing and performing all Manner of Things thereunto belonging; and you are to pay a ready Obedience to all Orders and Instructions which from Time to Time you may receive from the Governour, or Executive Power of this State for the time being, or any of your Superior Officers, agreeable to the Rules and Regulations of the Convention or General Assembly.

All Officers and Soldiers under your Command are hereby Strictly charged and required to be obedient to your Orders, and to aid you in the Execution of this Commission, According to the Intent and Purport thereof".

WITNESS Patrick Henry, Esquire, Governour or Chief Magistrate of the Commonwealth, at Williamsburg, this 29 day of October in the second year of the Commonwealth Anno Domini 1777.

                                                /s/ P. Henry

List of Officers found in the order books of Mecklenburg County or in other records pertaining to the county.

It should be <u>noted</u>, however, that some of those whose
names appear in the <u>following</u> list <u>cannot be documented</u> as
having served in the Revolutionary War. Some of the ranks
given do not appear to have been attained during the Revolutionary War, but in the militia after the war.

Capt. James Anderson
Ensign Knacy H. Andrews
Capt. Henry Ashton

Capt. James Ballard
Capt. John Ballard
Capt. Robert Ballard
Lieut. John Baskervill
Capt. William Baskervill
Capt. Fleming Bates *
Ensign John Bevill
Lieut. James Bilbo
Col. Thomas Bland *
Col. William Blunt *
Lieut. Thomas Booth
Ensign Thomas Browder
Lieut. James Brown
Capt. John Brown
Ensign Mordecai Brown
Ensign Jacob Bugg
Lieut. Hutchins Burton
Col. John Burton
Lieut. Peter Burton
Col. Robert Burton *
Col. Lewis Burwell
Lt. Col. Thacker Burwell
Capt. Turner Bynam *

Lieut. Thomas Carleton
Lieut. Thomas Carleton, Jr.
Ensign Carter Clarke
Lieut. Clausel Clausel
Col. Charles Clay
Lieut. John Clay
Lieut. Obia Clay
Ensign John Cox
Ensign Samuel Cox
Lieut. Henry Cunningham

Capt. Josiah Dailey
Lieut. David Darden

* Col. William Davies
Lieut. Baxter Davis
Capt. Charles Davis
Lieut. Hardaway Davis
Capt. William Davis
Ensign William Dawson
Col. Samuel Dedman
** Col. Henry Delony
Capt. Henry Delony, Jr.
Lieut. William Delony
Lieut. Edward Dodson
Lieut. Noah Dortch
Capt. William Drumright
* Capt. Henry Dudley
Lieut. William Eastland
* Col. John Eaton
Capt. Richard Epperson
* Col. Richard Elliott
Lieut. Stephen Evans, Jr.

Lieut. Laughlin Fanning
Capt. John Farrar
* Capt. John Faulkner
* Capt. Ralph Faulkner
Capt. Benjamin Ferrell
Lieut. James Ferrell
* Capt. Charles Fleming
* Col. James Fleming
Lieut. Thompson Fowlkes
Ensign Arthur Fox
Ensign George Freeman

* Capt. Peter Garland
* Lieut. William Gill, Jr.
* Capt. George Glenn
Col. Bennett Goode
Lieut. Edward Goode
Lieut. Edward Goode, Jr.
Capt. Elijah Graves
Capt. William Green
Col. William Wills Green

Capt. Thomas Greenwood
Capt. James Gunn *

Capt. James Hall
Lieut. Miles Hall
Col. Charles Harrison *
Capt. Wyatt Hawkins *
Capt. Francis Hester (a)
Capt. James Hester
Capt. Isaac Hix
Lieut. Nicholas Hobson *
Ensign William Holloway
Lieut. Isaac Holmes
Lieut. John Holmes
Lieut. Samuel Holmes, Jr.
Col. Samuel Hopkins, Jr.
Lieut. Samuel Hopson, Jr. *
Lieut. James Hudson
Lieut. John Hudson
Lieut. William Hundley
Capt. James Hunt
Ensign William Hunt, Jr.
Lieut. John Hutcheson
Lieut. Peter Hutcheson
Capt. Richard Hutcheson

Capt. Achilles Jeffries
Capt. Andrew Jeter *
Lieut. Caleb Johnson
Lieut. Isaac Johnson
Capt. James Johnson *
Lieut. William Johnson
Capt. Benjamin Jones
Major Binns Jones *
Ensign James Jones
Major Peter Jones *
Capt. Richard Jones
Lieut. Robert Jones
Capt. Thomas Jones, Jr.
Lieut. Tignal Jones, Jr.
Ensign William Jones

Capt. John Kendrick
Capt. Abraham Keen (a)

Capt. William Leigh
Capt. James Lewis
Capt. Abner Lockett
Lt. Col. William Lucas
Capt. William Lucas, Jr.

Capt. Joshua Mabry (a)

Capt. Stephen Mabry
* Col. Frederick Maclin
Lieut. Benjamin Malone
Lieut. Nathaniel Malone
Lieut. Daniel Marrow
* Capt. Benjamin Marshall
Capt. Francis Marshall
(a) Capt. James Marshall
Capt. Robert Marshall
Capt. Samuel Marshall
Major William Marshall
* Col. David Mason
* Capt. James Mason
* Col. Samuel Meredith
* Lieut. William Moseley
Col. Robert Munford
Col. John Murray

Ensign Thomas Nash
Ensign Thomas Neal
Lieut. Thomas Neal
Lieut. William Neal

Capt. Asa Oliver
* Capt. John Overton

Capt. Lewis Parham
* Capt. Joseph Peebles
Ensign Edward Pennington
Ensign Henry Pennington
Lieut. Samuel O. Pettus
Lieut. Thomas Pettus, Jr.
Ensign Walter Pool

* Capt. Drury Ragsdale
Col. William Randolph
Lieut. Philip Rix (Reekes)
Lieut. William Robinson
Capt. William Roffe
* Capt. Howell Rose
* Capt. Thomas Rowlett
Capt. Charles Royster
Lieut. David Royster
Lieut. Joseph Royster
* Col. John Ruffin
Capt. William Ruffin
Ensign Jeffrey Russell

Ensign James Sandifer, Jr.
Capt. Jesse Saunders
Lieut. Thomas Shipp
* Lieut. Anthony Singleton

Lieut. Drury Smith
Lieut. Robert Smith
Capt. Robert Smith
Capt. Joseph Spencer *
Major William Starling
Capt. John Stokes *
Col. David Stokes *
Ensign Hezekiah Stone
Capt. Richard Swepson, Jr.

Lieut. Josiah Tanner
Ensign Thomas Tanner
Capt. Anderson Taylor
Lieut. Goodwyn Taylor
Capt. Howell Taylor
Ensign Howell Taylor, Jr.
Capt. Jesse Taylor
Col. Joseph Taylor *
Capt. William Taylor
Col. George Tarry
Lieut. Peter Thomas
Lieut. Harman Thompson
Lieut. Stith Thompson

Ensign Argelon Toone, Jr.
Lieut. James Toone
* Capt. Joseph Townes

Lieut. Ingram Vaughan
Capt. Reuben Vaughan

Lt. Col. Henry Walker
Lieut. Edward Walton
* Lieut. Richard Walton
** Capt. James Wilkins
* Major John Willis
Lieut. Elimileck Wilson
Ensign James Wilson
Lieut. Peter Wingfield
Lieut. John Winn
Lieut. Richard Winn
(a) Lieut. John Wise
Capt. Richard Witton, Jr.
(a) Capt. Bennett Wood
* Col. James Wood

*** Col. Thornton Yancey

* Not residents of Mecklenburg County, but mentioned in records pertaining to the county.

** Rank in militia at beginning of Revolutionary War, but
did not served as active officers in war.

*** Col. Yancey, a native of Granville County, N. C., served in North Carolina forces, but moved to Mecklenburg
County in 1794.

(a) Rank in militia after the war, but no record found to
document Revolutionary War service though they undoubt-
edly served in some capacity.

BRUNSWICK COUNTY: Capt. Turner Bynam, Col. Richard Elliott
                     Major Binns Jones, Col. Frederick Maclin
                     Capt. Joseph Peebles, Major John Willis
CUMBERLAND COUNTY: Capt. Charles Fleming, Lt. William Mose-
                     ley
HALIFAX COUNTY: Capt. Fleming Bates, Capt. John Faulkner
                     Capt. Ralph Faulkner, Lt. Samuel Hopson,
                     Jr., Capt. Joseph Townes
LUNENBURG COUNTY: Capt. Peter Garland, Capt. James Gunn,
                     Capt. James Johnson, Capt. Drury Rags-
                     dale, Capt. John Stokes, Col. David
                     Stokes
SUSSEX COUNTY: Capt. James Mason, Col. David Mason

AUDITORS' ACCOUNT BOOK - 27 May 1784 - Richmond, Virginia.

Pay for Militia Service in this State - Mecklenburg County

Page 18

ARNOLD
    William
BALLARD
    William
BENNETT
    Jordan

BENNETT
    Joseph
BOWEN
    Bracey
CLEATON
    John

KELLY
    James
LADD
    William
NANNEY
    William

Page 19

ANDREWS
    Ephraim
BILBO
    Nathan
BOWEN
    Isham
BOWEN
    James
BOWEN
    John
BOWEN
    Starling
BROOKS
    Robert
BROWN
    Aries
BROWN
    Thomas
BURNETT
    Nathan
COLLIER
    William
CRADLE
    Joseph
EDMUNDSON
    Benjamin
EDWARDS
    Isaac
EPPES
    Peter

EZELL
    Lewis
FERRELL
    William
GREEN
    Thomas
HATCHELL
    Edward
HOLLOWAY
    William
HOLMES
    John
JOHNSON
    James
JOHNSON
    Zachariah
JOHNSTON
    Howell
JOHNSTON
    Phillip
KENDRICK
    John
KIDD
    William
KING
    William
KEETON
    Joseph
LAMBERT
    Joseph
LETT
    James

LIPFORD
    Scruggs
LUDWELL
    John
MALONE
    Benjamin
MITCHELL
    Edward
MORGAN
    John
PENNINGTON
    Henry
PENNINGTON
    Phillip
ROBERTS
    Thomas
ROFFE
    Edward
RUDDER
    Samuel
SMITH
    John
STEWART
    Robert
TAYLOR
    William
WALL
    Henry
WILLIAMS
    William

Page 20

ALLEN
    Darling

COX
    James

LOGAN
    William

BALLARD
    John
BILBO
    William
BROOKS
    Richard
BROWN
    Mordecai
BURNETT
    William
CONDRY
    John

CROWDER
    Hezekiah
DAVIS
    John
DECKER
    William
GOODE
    John
GOODE
    Thomas
HASTY
    James

INSCO
    James
MALLETT
    Stephen
McDONALD
    Crawford
ROBERTSON
    James
SMITH
    Jeremiah
WHITE
    Robert

Accounts re-audited according to law.

ACTS of the GENERAL ASSEMBLY
Regulations of the Military Forces

Excerpts:

DIVISION OF FORCES

Infantry   Artillery   Cavalry

COMPOSITION OF THE FORCES

1. Continental Line - On active duty

2. State Line - On active duty

3. Minutemen - Subject to immediate call

4. Militia - Subject to call by the General Command

5 Guards - Organized for special guard duty - Also called
      Invalid Forces

AGE LIMITS

Nearly all of those in the Continental and State Line and
Minutemen were under 35 years of age

Militia age limits - 16 to 50 years

Guards - Composed of those unfit for active duty, and inval-
      id soldiers who had previously served duty.

UNIT STRENGTH

Legion - Consisted of six companies of infantry and one
      troop of cavalry of 100 men each.
      Officers: A captain, two lieutenants and one
      ensign, except the cavalry which shall have a
      cornet in lieu of an ensign.
      Legion: A Lieut. Colonel and two Majors and
      commanded by a Brigadier General.

Artillery Company - One captain, three lieutenants, one
                  seargeant, 4 bombardiers, 8 gunners,
                  48 matrosses.

Infantry Company - Normally 50 men commanded by a captain,
                  two lieutenants and one ensign.
                  Minimum 32 men - maximum 68 men

Battalion - 500 to 1000 men commanded by a colonel, lieut.
      colonel and a major.

How Armed: Colonel, Lieutenant Colonel, Major - Sword

Captain and Lieutenants - Gun, Bayonet and
Sword   - Ensign: Sword

Non-commissioned officers and Privates -
Rifle and tomahawk, or bayonet

Each captain was required to appoint a drum-
mer and fifer for his company.

Regiment: In addition to general officers, each regiment
had a Chaplain, Paymaster, Adjutant, Quarter-
master, Surgeon, two Surgeon's Mates and a
Sergeant Major.

Other Notes from Acts of the General Assembly

State of Virginia divided into 16 Military Districts

Mecklenburg Military District: Composed of the counties of
Mecklenburg, Lunenburg,
Halifax and Charlotte

Military District: Committee of Safety composed of three
members from the Committee of Safety
for each county in the district.

Magazine: Located at Taylor's Ferry on Roanoke River.

Note: James Clark, in pension application S-30941, states
that after the battle at Guilford Courthouse he was
transferred to Taylor's Ferry, Mecklenburg County,
as a guard at the ferry and magazine which was located one-half mile from the ferry at a place called
Banks Old Store.

MECKLENBURG COUNTY MILITIA

A general return of the Militia of Mecklenburg County the
24th March 1783

      1 County Lieutenant
      2 Colonels
      2 Lieut. Colonels
      2 Majors
      19 Captains
      25 Lieutenants
      16 Ensigns
      44 Sergeants
      0 Drums & Fifers
                            Privates

      Over 18 years   Under 18 years   Fit for
      fit for duty   fit for duty   Station duty

          865   85   75

                     Total 1136

                         /s/ Lewis Burwell Co. Lieut.

Executive Papers, Mecklenburg County

        A report made by Lewis Burwell, County Lieutenant, in
reply to a request as to the status of the militia of Mecklenburg County, specifically asking that the number under
18 years old be listed separately.

        Col. Lewis Burwell was appointed County Lieutenant by
Governor Thomas Jefferson on 21 February 1781.

        As County Lieutenant, Col. Burwell was head of the
Mecklenburg County Militia and responsible for military op-
erations in the county.

        Lieut. Colonel John Burton was appointed Colonel to
succeed Col. Lewis Burwell as commander of the First Battalion of Mecklenburg County militia. The Second Battalion
was commanded by Col. Bennett Goode.

        On March 24, 1783, John Murray and William Wills
Green were Colonels, William Randolph and Samuel Dedman
were Lieut. Colonels and William Starling and William Lucas
were Majors.

At a Court for Mecklenburg County the 8th Day of Sept. 1777

Present Henry Delony Francis Ruffin) Gent. Justices
     John Camp   Henry Walker)

Ordered that the following persons be recommended to his
excellancy the Governor as proper persons for Officers to
fill up the vacancies in the two Battalions of militia in
this County, viz: In the first Battalion, Thacker Burwell,
esq. Lieutenant Colonel, James Anderson, esq. Major,
Richard Swepson, Asa Oliver, James Hall, James Wilkins, and
Howell Taylor, Captains, Tignal Jones, Junr., Robert Smith,
Richard Epperson, William Neal & Drury Smith, first Lieut-
enants, Peter Hutcheson, Stephen Evans, Junr., William
Robinson, Thomas Jones, Baxter Davis & Clausel Clausel, sec-
ond Lieutenants and James Sandifer, Junr., Thomas Carleton,
John Clay, William Gill, Junr., Elijah Graves & Caleb
Johnson, Ensigns; In the second Battalion, Henry Delony,
esq. Colonel, William Lucas, esq. Major, Lewis Parham &
Benjamin Ferrell, Captains, John Farrar, James Ferrel, David
Darden, William Roffe & Jesse Taylor, first Lieutenants;
Noah Dortch, John Baskervill, Charles Hutcheson, Thomas
Shipp, Edward Goode, Hardaway Davis, John Holmes, Peter
Thomas & Henry Pennington, second Lieutenants; & William
Lucas, Junr & Jacob Bugg, Ensigns.

Ordered that the Court be adjourned till the Court in Course
  The minutes of these proceedings were signed
            Henry Delony

At a Court for Mecklenburg County the 13th day of Oct. 1777

Present Robert Munford Thacker Burwell)
    Henry Delony   and   ) Gent. Justices
    Reuben Vaughan Cluverius Coleman)

The Order of the last Court recommending militia Officers
to his excellancy the Governor is set aside & It is Ordered
that the following persons be recommended to his excellancy
the Governor as proper for Officers to fill up the two
Battalions of militia in this County, to-wit:
     In the first Battalion

 Lewis Burwell, esq. Colonel, Thacker Burwell, esq. Lieut.
Colonel and James Anderson esq. Major

 John Murray, first Captain, Robert Smith, first Lieutenant, Thomas Carleton, second Lieutenant & Thomas Neal,
Ensign

Charles Clay, second Captain, Richard Epperson, first Lieutenant, John Clay, Junr., second Lieutenant, Harmon Thompson, Ensign

Henry Walker, third Captain, William Neal, first Lieutenant, Thomas Jones, second Lieutenant, John Winn, Ensign

George Tarry, fourth Captain, Drury Smith, first Lieutenant, Baxter Davis, second Lieutenant, Elijah Graves, Ensign

William Green, fifth Captain, Richard Witton, first Lieutenant, Edward Goode, second Lieutenant, Thomas Pettus, Junr. Ensign

James Hester, sixth Captain, Joseph Royster, first Lieutenant, Clausel Clausel, second Lieutenant, Caleb Johnson, Ensign

Asa Oliver, seventh Captain, Robert Smith, first Lieutenant, Thomas Carleton, second Lieutenant, Thomas Neal, Ensign

James Hall, eighth Captain, Charles Royster, first, Lieutenant, John Hudson, second Lieutenant, Richard Winn, Ensign

Howell Taylor, ninth Captain, Thomas Greenwood, first Lieutenant, William Hundley, second Lieutenant, Daniel Marrow, Ensign

In the second Battalion

Bennett Goode, esq. Colonel, William Lucas, esq. Lieutenant Colonel, John Burton, esq. Major

Reuben Vaughan, first Captain, Josiah Dailey, first Lieutenant, Charles Hutcheson, second Lieutenant, Richard Hutcheson, Ensign

William Leigh, second Captain, William Roffe, first Lieutenant, Thomas Shipp, second Lieutenant, James Wilson, Ensign

James Lewis, third Captain, John Kendrick, first Lieutenant, Hardaway Davis, second Lieutenant, George Freeman, Ensign

Taylor
Stephen Mabry, fourth Captain, Goodwyn,/first Lieutenant, John Holmes, second Lieutenant, Thomas Tanner, Ensign

John Brown, fifth Captain, Jesse Taylor, first Lieutenant, Peter Thomas, second Lieutenant, William Jones, Ensign

Samuel Marshall, sixth Captain, Isaac Johnson, first Lieutenant, Peter Winfield, second Lieutenant, William Drumright, Ensign

Lewis Parham, seventh Captain, Samuel Holmes, Jr.,first Lieutenant, John Farrar, second Lieutenant, William Lucas, Junr., Ensign

Benjamin Ferrell, eighth Captain, James Ferrell, first Lieutenant, John Baskervill, second Lieutenant, Jacob Bugg, Ensign

Richard Swepson, ninth Captain, Tignal Jones, Junr., first Lieutenant, William Eastland, second Lieutanant, James Toone, Ensign

Ordered that the Court be adjourned till the Court in Course

The minutes of these proceedings were signed
John Speed

Notes: The order of the court on the 8th day of September, 1777, was set aside and superseded by the order of the court of 13th day of October, 1777.

* David Darden - d. 1784; Henry Delony - d. 1785; Noah Dortch - d. 1781; James Wilkins - d. 1781.
    * Early Wills, 1765-1799, Mecklenburg County.

The names of David Darden, Henry Delony, Stephen Evans, Jr., Peter Hutcheson, William Robinson and James Wilkins do not again appear in the recommendations of militia officers. William Gill, Jr., removed to Granville County where he served as a lieutenant in the North Carolina militia.

Court 8 Dec. 1777

Bennett Goode, Lewis Burwell, Thacker Burwell, esquires, George Tarry, Henry Walker, James Anderson, John Murray, William Green, Thomas Jones, Thomas Carleton, Jr., John Burton, Charles Clay, Richard Epperson, Harman Thompson, Reuben Vaughan, Noah Dortch, William Leigh, Charles Hutcheson, Richard Hutcheson, Stephen Mabry, James Hall, Edward Goode, William Roffe, John Holmes, John Brown, Thomas Tanner, Charles Royster, Richard Winn, John Hudson & Howell Taylor, Gents., Officers in the militia of this Co.

took the oath of a militia officer as required by law.

Order Book 4, Page 382

Court 12 Jan. 1778

William Lucas, Lewis Parham, Baxter
Davis, Thomas Greenwood, Jesse Taylor & Robert Smith, Gents
Officers in the militia of this County, severally took the
oath of a militia officer as directed by law.

Order Book 4, Page 388

Samuel Marshall, Isaac Johnson, William
Drumright, Asa Oliver, Peter Thomas, William Jones, Caleb
Johnson, James Hester, Elijah Graves, officers in the mili-
tia of this County, severally took the oath of a Militia
Officer as required by law.

Order Book 4, Page 389

Court 9 Feb. 1778

Benjamin Ferrell, James Ferrell, Josiah
Dailey, William Lucas, Junr., Peter Wingfield and John
Farrar, Gents., were sworn militia officers according to
law.

Order Book 4, Page 391

Court 9 Mar. 1778

William Neal, Thomas Shipp, James Wilson
Drury Smith and John Clay were sworn militia officers according to law.

Order Book 4, Page 394

Court 13 Apr. 1778

Goodwyn Taylor, a Lieutenant in the mil-
itia of this County, took the oath of an officer according
to law.

Order Book 4, Page 398

Court 11 May 1778

John Kendrick, John Winn, Joshua Davis,
Richard Swepson, Jr., Charles Davis, Thomas Pettus, Richard
Witton, Junr. & James Bilbo, officers in the milita of this
County, took the oath of an officers according to law.

Order Book 4, Page 403

Court 8 June 1778

Baxter Davis and Thompson Fowlkes, off-
icers in the militia of this County, took the oath required
by law.

Order Book 4, Page 414

Court 13 July 1778

William Eastland and Tignal Jones, Junr.,
officers in the militia of this County, took the oath of an
officer as required by law.

Order Book 4, Page 421

Court 14 Sept. 1778

Edward Dodson and Peter Burton, officers
in the militia of this county, took the oath of an officer
required by law.

Order Book 4, Page 426

Court 12 Oct. 1778
                    Laughlin Fanning, an officer of the mil-
itia in this County, took the oath of an officer as requir-
by law
                                    Order Book 4, Page 442
Court 8 March 1779
                    The following persons are recommended by
the Court, to his excellancy the Governor, as proper officers to fill up the vacancies in the militia in this county,
to-wit:
        Jesse Saunders, a Captain, in the room of Howell
Taylor resigned, William Roffe, a Captain, in the room of
William Leigh removed, Jesse Taylor, a Captain, in the room
of John Brown resigned, Robert Smith, a Captain, in the
room of John Murray promoted, Thomas Shipp & James Wilson,
Lieutenants, Knacy Andrews, Edward Pennington & Abner
Lockett, Ensigns.
                                    Order Book 4, Page 457
Court 12 April 1779
                    Jesse Saunders, a Captain in the mili-
tia of this County, took the oath required by law.

                                    Order Book 4, Page 459
Court 14 June 1779
                    The following persons are recommended by
this Court, to his excellancy the Governor, as proper for
officers to fill up the vacancies in the militia in this
County, to-wit:
        Peter Wingfield, as first Lieutenant,
William Drumright & John Winn, as second Lieutenants and
Stith Thompson & Henry Pennington, as Ensigns.

                                    Order Book 4, Page 476
Court 12 July 1779
                    John Burton, Gent., a Lieutenant Colonel
in the militia of this County, took the oath required by
law.
                                    Order Book 4, Page 478
Court 13, July 1779
                    Jesse Taylor, a Captain, Elijah Graves,
a Lieutenant and William Hundly, an Ensign, in the militia
of this County, took the oath required by law.

                                    Order Book 4, Page 493
Court 13 Sept. 1779
                    Robert Smith, a Captain, Thomas Booth &
Benjamin Malone, Lieutenants, and William Hunt, Junr. &
Nathaniel Malone, Ensigns, in the militia of this County,
took the oath as an officer as required by law.

                                    Order Book 4, Page 517

Court 11 Oct. 1779

William Lucas (Jr), a Captain, and Thompson Fowlkes, a Lieutenant, in the militia of this County, too the oath of an officer as required by law.

Order Book 4, Page 522

Court 12 June 1780

James Jones, an Ensign, in the militia of this County, took the oath of an officer as required by law.

Order Book 5, Page 54

Court 10 July 1780

The following persons are recommended by this Court, to his excellency the Governor, as proper officers to fill up the vacancies in the militia in this County, to-wit:

James Toone, second Lieutenant, Samuel Cox & Carter Clark, Ensigns.

Order Book 5, Page 60

Court 10 July 1780

Achilles Jeffries is by the Court recommended, to his excellency the Governor, as a proper person for an Ensign in Captain Clay's Company of Militia in this County.

Order Book 5, Page 67

Court 11 Aug. 1780

The following persons are recommended by this Court, to his excellency the Governor, as proper for officers to fill up the vacancies in the militia in this County, to-wit:

Thomas Booth, first Lieutenant, Nathaniel Malone, second Lieutenant and Arthur Fox, Ensign.

Order Book 5, Page 72

Court 9 Oct. 1780

John Winn & Stith Thompson, Lieutenants, in the militia of this County, took the oath of an officer required by law.

Order Book 5, Page 81

Court 12 Dec. 1780

The following persons are recommended, to his excellency the Governor, as proper persons for officers to fill up the vacancies in the militia in this County, to-wit:

Lewis Burwell, as County Lieutenant, John Burton, as Colonel, John Murray, Charles Clay, Henry Walker, William Green, as Majors, Richard Witton, Thomas Jones, Elijah Graves, Richard Epperson, as Captains, Edward Goode, Junr., John Clay, as first Lieutenants, William Hundley, Daniel Marrow, Thomas Pettus, David Royster, Achilles Jeffries, as second Lieutenants, Hezekiah Stone, Elimileck Wilson, James Brown, John Cox, as Ensigns.

Court 12 May 1781
                    The following persons are recommended to
his excellancy, the Governor, as proper persons for officers to fill up the vacancies in the militia in this County,
to-wit:
         Charles Royster, as Captain, Robert Jones, Elimi-
leck Wilson, Samuel Holmes, Jr., John Hudson, as first
Lieutenants, Abner Lockett, as second Lieutenant and Walter
Pool & Miles Hall, as Ensigns.

Court 12 May 1781
                    Lewis Burwell, esq., Elijah Graves, James
Hunt, William Roffe, Thomas Pettus, William Hundley, Elimileck Wilson, Hezekiah Stone, Richard Witton, Officers in
the militia of this County, took the oath of an officer according to law.

Court 9 July 1781
                    Edward Goode, Junr., first Lieutenant in
the militia of this County, took the oath of office according to law.

Court 10 Dec. 1781
                    The following persons are recommended to
his excellancy, the Governor, as proper persons for officers to fill up the vacancies in the militia in this County,
to-wit:
         John Murray and Henry Walker, as Colonels, William
Green, as Lieutenant Colonel, William Randolph and Samuel
Dedman, as Majors, William Baskervill and Charles Davis, as
Captains, Achilles Jeffries and Richard Hutcheson, as Captains, Philip Rix (Reekes), Thomas Pettus and William Starling, as first Lieutenants, Jeffrey Russell and Mordecai
Brown, as Ensigns.

Court 8 July 1782
                    John Murray, Colonel, William Green, Lieu-
tenant Colonel, Henry Walker, Lieutenant Colonel, William
Randolph and Samuel Dedman, Majors, William Baskervill,
Captain, in the militia of this County, severally took the
oath required by law.

Court 12 Aug. 1782
                    The following persons are recommended to
his excellancy, the Governor, as officers to fill up the
vacancies in the militia of this County, to-wit:
       William Wills Green, as Colonel, William Randolph and
Samuel Dedman, as Lieutenant Colonels, William Lucas and
William Starling, as Majors, Thomas Greenwood, as Captain,
and Clausel Clausel, William Hundley & Ingram Vaughan, as
first Lieutenants.

Court 9 Sept. 1782

Charles Davis, a Captain in the militia of this County, took the oath required by law.

Order Book 5, Page 214

Court 9 Sept. 1782

The following persons are recommended to his excellancy, the Governor, as proper to fill up the vacancies in the militia of this County: John Farrar, as Captain, and William Delony, as first Lieutenant.

Order Book 5, Page 215

Court 11 Nov. 1782

Josiah Dailey, Richard Hutcheson, Captains, Miles Hall, Mordecai Brown, Ensigns, in the militia of this County, took the oath required by law.

Order Book 5, Page 237

Court 9 Dec. 1782

William Starling, Gent., a Major in the militia in this County, took the oath required by law.

Order Book 5, Page 249

Court 13 Jan. 1783

William Wills Green, a Colonel, and William Randolph & Samuel Dedman, Lieutenants, in the militia of this County, took the oath as required by law.

Order Book 5, Page 261

Court 10 Feb. 1783

Thomas Greenwood, a Captain in the militia of this County, took the oath required by law.

William Johnson, as a first Lieutenant, and Howell Taylor (Jr), as an Ensign, are recommended to fill vacancies in the militia.

Order Book 5, Page 276

Court 10 March 1783

William Lucas, Gent., a Major in the militia of this County, took the oath required by law

Order Book 5, Page 279

Court 12 May 1783

John Hutcheson is recommended to his excellancy, the Governor, as a proper person for an Ensign in the militia in this County.

Order Book 5, Page 209

Court 9 June 1783

Ingram Vaughan, a Lieutenant in the militia of this County, qualified according to law.

Order Book 5, Page 370

Court 9 June 1783

Abner Lockett, as a Captain, Miles Hall, as a first Lieutenant, and William Marshall, as an Ensign, are recommended to his excellancy, the Governor, as proper persons to fill up the vacancies in the militia in this County.

Order Book 5, Page 360

Court 9 June 1783

John Farrar, a Captain in the militia of this County, took the oath required by law.

Order Book 5, Page 375

SUNDRY NOTES FROM ORDER BOOKS

Court 9 March 1778

Henry Hudson, being sworn, saith that his son, Forrest Hudson, who was drafted under the late Act of Assembly, was only 16 years of age on the 19th day of January last which is ordered to be certified to the Commanding Officer of the Continental Troops in the city of Williamsburg.

Order Book 4, Page 395

Court 14 April 1783

Samuel Hopkins, Junr., came into Court and made oath that Hutchins Burton, at the time of his death, was a first Lieutenant in the Sixth Virginia Regiment on Continental establishment, which is ordered to be certified; and also that John Burton, Gent., is his legal representative. *

* Hutchins Burton, brother of Col. John Burton of Mecklenburg County, was killed in the battle at Princeton.

Order Book 5, Page 285

Court 8 Oct. 1781

Jesse Hix vs Amos Hix and Jacob Bugg - acting as executors of Samuel Bugg, deceased - on the motion of the plaintiff is awarded him to examine and take the deposition of James Hix, a witness in this cause, who is about to go into service.

Order Book 5, Page 103

Court 11 Aug. 1777

Ordered that Cluverius Coleman, Gent., furnish Susanna Smith, wife of Thomas Smith a poor soldier in the service of this state, with such necessaries as she is immediately in want of, and apply for payment of same to the Treas. of this Commonwealth.

Order Book 4, Page 367

Court 8 Sept. 1777

Ordered that Francis Ruffin, Gent., supply Judith Hamilton, wife of John Hamilton a poor soldier in the service of this state, with such necessaries as

she may want for the support of herself & children & make
return of his account to the Court.

Order Book 4, Page 370
Court 8 Sept. 1777
                    Ordered that Robert Munford, Gent.,
supply Elizabeth Wallace, wife of William Wallace a poor
soldier in the service of this state, with such necessaries as she may want for the support of herself & children
and return his account to the Court.

Order Book 4, Page 370
Court 8 March 1779
                    Ordered that John Speed, Gent., be re-
quested to furnish Mary Singleton, widow of Christopher
Singleton, a poor soldier who died in the service of this
state, with the sum of 40 pounds for her support.

Order Book 4, Page 457
Court 11 May 1779
                    Ordered that Henry Walker, Gent., Supply
the wife of James Vaughan, a poor militiaman, with such
necessaries as she may want for her support during her
husband's absence in the service in Georgia.

                    Ordered that John Puryear supply Anne
Blake, wife of Robert Blake, a poor militiaman, with such
necessaries as she may want for her support during her
husband's absence in the service in Georgia.

Order Book 4, Page 474
Court 12 June 1780
                    Ordered that John Burton, Gent., furn-
ish Sarah Booker, wife of Richard Booker a Continental
soldier, with a barrel of corn and fifty pounds of bacon
for support of herself and three children.

Order Book 5, Page 54
Court 11 Dec. 1780
                    Ordered that the treasurer pay unto
John Burton, Gent., 237 pounds, being the amount of his
account for necessaries furnished Sarah Booker, wife of
Richard Booker, a poor soldier belonging to the state's
quota of troops on Continental establishment, for support
of herself and three children.

Order Book 5, Page 86
Court 11 Nov. 1782
                    Ordered that Richard Epperson do furn-
ish Hannah Thomas, widow of John Thomas, a Continental
soldier who died in the service, with two and a half bushels of wheat and thirty pounds of bacon.

Order Book 5, Page 239

REGULATIONS UNDER THE ACT OF JUNE 7, 1832

Four general classes of cases are embraced in this law:
1. The Regular Troops
2. The State Troops, Militia, Volunteers
3. Persons employed in the Naval service
4. Indian Spies

DECLARATION,

In order to obtain the benefit of the Act of Congress of the 7th of June, 1832.

                    State of Virginia   )
                    County of Mecklenburg) ss.

On this 23rd day of October 1832 personally appear-ed before Stephen P'Pool a Justice of the Peace in the County aforesaid in the State of Virginia Robert W. Fitz a resident in the County of Mecklenburg, State of Virginia, aged 77 years, who being first duly sworn, according to law, doth on his oath make the following declaration, in order to obtain the benefit of the provision made by the Act of Congress, passed June 7th, 1832. That he entered the Service of the United States as a volunteer soldier in the year 1776 in the month of March under Capt. James Anderson, Lieut. William Baskervill and Ensign John Holmes, in the regiment commanded by Col. John Ruffin.

(The declarant was required to give the name of the general officer, the time of his discharge - and if he served more than one term of enlistment, specify the particular period, the rank and names of his officers - the town or county and State in which he resided when he entered the service; the battles, if any, in which he was engaged, and the country through which he marched.)

He hereby relinquishes every claim whatever to a pen-sion, except the present, and he declares that his name is not on the Pension Roll of any Agency in any State.
Sworn to and subscribed the day and the year aforesaid.

                              Robert W. Fitz

The acknowledgement was taken by Stephen P'Pool, Justice of the Peace for Mecklenburg County.

(The declarant was required to furnish an affidavit from a Clergyman and one other person residing in his vicinity as to his character and service. Then followed a certificate of the Clerk of the Court.)

The foregoing excerpted application for a pension was made by Robert W. Fitz in the Court of Mecklenburg County under the Act of June 7, 1832.

Under the Act, certain regulations in respect to the filing of an application were supplied the local Court of Record as a guide; and the court was required to interrogate the applicant for a pension.

THE INTERROGATORY

1. Where and in what year were you born?
2. Have you any record of your age, and if so, where is it?
3. Where were you living when called into service; where have you lived since the Revolutionary war, and where do you now live?
4. How were you called into service; were you drafted, did you volunteer, or were you a substitute? And if a substitute, for whom?
5. State the names of some of the Regular Officers, who were with the troops, where you served; such Continental and Militia Regiments as you can recollect, and the general circumstances of your services.
6. (To a soldier) Did you ever receive a discharge from the service, and if so, by whom was it given and what has become of it?
   (To an officer) Did you ever receive a commission, and if so, by whom was it signed, and what has become of it?
7. State the names of persons to whom you are known in your neighborhood, and who can testify as to your character for veracity, and their belief of your services as a soldier of the Revolution.

The applicant for a pension was required to make his declaration for such pension in Open Court unless he was incapacitated or so infirm that he could not travel to the court.

In that case, the Judge of a Court of Record, or a Justice of the Peace, could take his declaration for a pension at the home of the applicant, or at a place convenient to the applicant. The Judge, or Justice of the Peace, was required to certify that the applicant cannot, from bodily infirmity, attend the Court.

Whenever any official act is required to be done by a Judge or Justice of a Court of Record, or by a Justice of the Peace, in connection with an application for a pension, the certificate of the proper Clerk of the Court or County, under his seal of office, was required to be annexed, stating that such person is a Judge or Justice of a Court of Record, or a Justice of the Peace, and that the signature annexed was his genuine signature.

WAR DEPARTMENT

Revolutionary Claim

I certify that in conformity with the Law of the United
States, of the 7th June 1832, Robert W. Fitz of the State
of Virginia, who was a private in the Army of the Revolution, is entitled to receive,-- - - Eighty - - - - dollars
and - - - - - - cents per annum, during his natural life,
commencing on the 4th of March, 1831, and payable semi-an-
nually, on the 4th of March, and 4th of September, in each
year.

Given at the War Office of the United States,
this --- 3rd. ------ day of   December,
one thousand eight hundred and thirty two.

Lew Cass
Examined and)
Countersigned)   Secretary of War.

J. L. Edwards

The foregoing certificate was issued to Robert W.
Fitz on his application for a pension under the
Act of June 7, 1832 through the Virginia Agency.

VIRGINIA 2578

Robert W. Fitz, Mecklenburg County, State of Virginia, who
was a Private in the Company commanded by Captain Anderson
of the Regiment commanded by Col. Ruffin in the Virginia
Line for 18 months.

Inscribed on the Roll of Virginia at the rate of 80
Dollars ------ Cents per annum, to commence on the 4th day
of March 1831.

Whenever a declaration submitted for a pension was incomplete, incorrect, did not meet all requirements of the regulations or required additional proof of service, it was returned to the Court of Record to be delivered to the applicant for correction and resubmission.

WAR DEPARTMENT

Pension Office

(Date)

Sir:

The evidence in support of your claim, under the Act of (June 7, 1832), has been examined, and the papers are herewith returned. The following is a statement of your case in a tabular form. On comparing these papers with the following rules, and the subjoined notes, you will readily perceive that objections exist, which must be removed, before a pension can be allowed. The notes and the regulations will shew what is necessary to be done. Those points to which your attention is more particularly directed, you will find marked in the margin with a brace (Vius:). You will, when you return your papers to this Department, send this printed letter with them; and you will, by complying with this request, greatly facilitate the investigation of your claim.

I am respectfully,

Your obedient servant,

J. L. Edwards,

Commissioner of Pensions

BOUNTY LAND

Act enacted 3 October 1779:

    Colonel, 5000 acres; Lieut. Colonel, 4500 acres; Major 4000 acres; Captain, 3000 acres; Subaltern, 2000 acres; Non Com. Officers, who enlisted in the war and served to the end thereof, 400 acres.   like
    Every soldier and sailor under/conditions 200 acres.
    Every officer of the Navy, the same quantity of land as an officer in the army, of equal rank.
    Where any officer, soldier or sailor has died in the service, his heirs or legal representatives, shall be entitled to the same quantity of land as would have been due to such officer, soldier or sailor, had he been living.

TROOPS AT VALEY FORGE

Brig. Genl. Peter Muhlenburg's Brigade:

1st Va. Reg. Col. James Hendricks, <u>Lieut. Col. Robert Ballard</u>, Major Edmund B. Dickinson.

6th Va. Reg. Col. George Gibson, Lieut. Col. Charles Simms, <u>Major Samuel Hopkins.</u>

Note: Lieut. Col. Robert Ballard and Major Samuel Hopkins
      were from Mecklenburg County.

CLAIM FOR BOUNTY LAND

William Gordon, Mecklenburg County, Sergeant in the First Virginia Regiment commanded by Colonel Richard Parker.

    William Pully, personally appeared before me, and made oath that William Gordon and himself were both soldiers in Capt. Samuel Hopkins' Company, and that William Gordon served as a Sergeant in said Company until he was taken prisoner at the surrender of Charleston, South Carolina.
    Sworn to before me this 1st November 1811.
                      M. Alexander, Justice
                      Meck. Co. Court

    I do hereby certify that William Gordon served as a Sergeant in the Continental Virginia Line in the Revolutionary War; that he marched with a detachment of 400 men commanded by Col. Richard Parker to the State of Georgia in 1779, that he belonged to the platoon commanded by me in the attack on Savannah, that he was taken prisoner at Charleston when it surrendered to the British under command of Sir Henry Clinton. Given under my hand 3rd September 1811
              Sam'l Hogg, (then) 1st. Lt., 1st. Va. Reg.

James McCarter, a Revolutionary soldier, appeared in Court and presented his declaration to enable him to obtain a pension under the Act of Congress passed 7 day of June, 1832. Ordered to be certified.
August Court 1832   O.B. 29, p. 281

James McCarter, pensioned under the Act of 7 June 1832 died 18 April 1841, and left widow Nancy who is still alive and a resident of this County. Ordered that the same be certified to the War Department.
Sept. Court 1841.   Minute Book 3, p. 153

Ordered that it be certified that Daniel F. Thomas and Maria, wife of Henry Pettus, are the only heirs at Law of Daniel Thomas, a private soldier in the Revolutionary War, who died intestate.
Sept. Court 1834   Minute Book 1, p. 168

Ordered that record be certified (on evidence of John Waller, administrator of Daniel Waller, deceased) that John Waller, Isaac Waller, William Waller, Frances Wilson, and the children of Rebecca Toone, deceased, are the only heirs at Law of Daniel Waller.
Jan. Court 1835   Minute Book 1, p. 204

It appears to the Court that satisfactory evidence was produced that Daniel Waller, a Revolutionary pensioner late of this County, departed this life 7 May 1834, leaving no widow at time of his death; and that Isaac Waller, John Waller, Fanny Wilson widow of James Wilson and William Waller, all of lawful age, are his only living children and heirs of Daniel Waller, deceased. Ordered that same be certified.
July Court 1837   Minute Book 2, p. 92

Susanna Arrington, widow of John Arrington, appeared to the satisfaction of the Court to be the widow of John Arrington, a Revolutionary soldier who died 6 November 1837 Ordered same to be certified.
March Court 1838   Minute Book 2, p. 186

Royall Lockett, Senr., a Revolutionary soldier, died July 1, 1842, leaving no widow. Ordered to be certified that Royall Lockett, Junr. and Sarah B. Puryear, the wife of Achilles Puryear, were his only children living at the time of his death; and that Mary Malven, wife of William Malven, Susan Malven, wife of John Malven, Elvira Cardwell and Elizabeth Cardwell were his only grandchildren, and the children of his deceased daughter Patience Cardwell.
June Court 1843   Minute Book 3, p. 366

DECLARATIONS FOR PENSIONS

Declaration of Varney Andrews
William Baber
Joseph Bennett
Thomas Brandon
Hutchins Burton
Joseph Butler
William Coleman
Isham Coley
William Collier
Bartlett Cox
James Cunningham
Stephen Ellis
Abel Farrar
Robert W. Fitz
Elijah Griffin
Michael Gwaltney
Daniel Hicks

Charles Hudson
William Insco
James Johnson
John Jones
Royall Lockett
James McCarter
Moses Parrish
William Pully
Williamson Rainey
John Ryland
Sherwood Smith
Thomas Tanner
Argelon Toone
John Wagstaff
Daniel Waller
Edward Wilson
Archibald Wood

The foregoing filed declarations for pensions in the Mecklenburg County Court.

Margaret Brandon presented her declaration for pension as the widow of Thomas Brandon, who died on or about the 17th day of December, 1834, in this county. He was the same Thomas Brandon who was a pensioner under the Act of 7th June 1832. Margaret, his widow, has not since intermarried. Ordered to be certified.
October Court 1840   Minute Book 3, p. 37

John Ryland, a pensioner and resident of this county, died 2 October 1822 leaving widow Elizabeth Ryland, still living and a resident of this county. She is the only person entitled to the arrears of said John Ryland's pension. Ordered to be certified.
Court August 17, 1840   Minute Book 3, p. 14

Jane J. Whittemore, resident of this county and of lawful age, is a daughter and sole surving heir at Law of John Ryland, deceased, late a corporal of artillery on Va. Continental Line in the War of Revolution. Elizabeth Ryland, widow of John Ryland, deceased, died on August 29, 1840, leaving only one surviving child by her late husband, John Ryland, to-wit: Jane J. Whittemore. Ordered to be certified.
Court Sept. 1840   Minute Book 3, p. 26

Rebecca Rowlett, widow of William Rowlett a pensioner who died June 2, 1839, a resident of this county has not since intermarried, applies for rest of pension of her late husband formerly of Chesterfield County.
Court Sept. 1840   Minute Book 3, p. 30

189

MECKLENBURG COUNTY, 15 Feb. 1781

The enemy Cornwallis is at Boyd's Ferry on the Dan River. The Militia has been called out and the people will fight, but there is only a little ammunition and few guns.

Excerpt from a letter from Col. Lewis Burwell to Governor Jefferson. Note: Boyd's Ferry at present South Boston, Halifax County.

The enemy being in the neighborhood of this County, and the Court thinking the records of this County within the reach of the excursions, it is ordered that the Clerk hire a Cart or Wagon to convey them to some place of security. The payment of which hire the Court will provide at the laying of the next County levy.
Court 12 May 1781   O.B. 5, p. 96

The enemy being removed from the neighborhood of this County - It is ordered that the records which were removed to New London, as a place of secutity, be brought back again; and that the Clerk employ a Wagon for that purpose for defraying the expense of which the Court will provide at the laying of the next County levy.
Court 9 July 1781   O.B. 5, p. 98

Ordered that the Sheriff pay out of the depositum in his hands to Philip Mealer eight pounds five shillings being the amount for carrying the records of this County to Bedford Court House as a place of security during the invasion last year.
Court 11 May 1782   O.B. 5, p. 144

George M. Norvell presented his declaration as one of the children of Margaret Norvell. Margaret Norvell became a widow on 26 Jan. 1824 when her husband, a Revolutionary soldier, died. She died on 28 Aug. 1840, before her pension papers could be arranged. George M. Norvell, James Norvell, Thomas A. Norvell, William H. Norvell, Margaret B. Whobry and Mary B. Meacham, all of whom are of legal age, are her children. Ordered to be certified.
Court Oct. 1840   Minute Book 3, p. 37

BRITISH DESERTERS

Ordered that claim of John Speed be certified for 24 pounds paid .. to Benjamin Arnold and John McDole, deserters from the British Legion, on an order for that sum payable to them and drawn on the Quarter Master of the Southern Army by Benjamin Brooke, Brigade Major, for two horses delivered by them for the use of Gen. Morgan's detachment.
Court 9 April 1782   O.B. 5, p. 130

CERTIFICATE AS A PENSIONER

William Baber, late private in the Militia of Mecklenburg County, Virginia, and whose pay was at rate of 24 pou▀
nds per annum, was disabled in the service of the United
States by illness which wholly deprived him of his sight.
He is allowed the sum of 12 pounds annually from the 1st of
January 1786.
    Given under my hand as Gov. of the Commonwealth of Va.
at Richmond 20 August 1788.

                        Edmund Randolph

Teste: T. Meriwether

    At Court for Meck. Co., 8 Sept. 1788, was ordered re-
corded.   John Brown, Clk.
Deed Book 7, Page 307

    Joseph Sears, age 26 years, private in First Regiment
of Light Dragoons, whose pay was at rate of 30 pounds per
annum, was disabled in the service of the United States, by
a wound in knee and one in shoulder. He is allowed the sum
of 10 pounds yearly to commence from 1st day of January,
1786.
    Given under my hand as Gov. of the Commonwealth of Va.
at Richmond 9 January 1788.

                        Edmund Randolph

1788 April 15. Joseph Sears made oath that he is the person
certified.
    Given under my hand at Court 12 day of May 1788, and
ordered recorded.   John Brown, Clk.
Deed Book 7, Page 307

Richard Booker - Pensioner No. 39

    Richard Booker enlisted as a private in the 3rd Va.
Regiment in the Continental Line. He died in said Regiment
while quartered in Petersburg leaving Sarah Booker, his
widow and three small children in distressed circumstances
living in this County.
Meck. Co. Court Sept. 1788

    Sarah Booker, widow of Richard Booker a private in the
Va. Line who died while in service, was placed on the pen-
sion roll at 8 pounds per annum from 1 January 1789.
Executive Order 28 July 1789

Bartlett Cox - Pensioner No. 98

    Bartlett Cox, a private in the Militia, received a
wound from which he lost a leg. Placed on pension roll.
Meck. Co. Court December 1787

BRANDON, Thomas   Pen. W-4643

Nancy Brandon daughter of Thomas & Margaret
                              was born Sept. 2, 1771
Agnes Brandon daughter of Thomas & Margaret
                              was born June 2, 1773
Walden Brandon son of Thomas & Margaret
                              was born July 5, 1775
Suckey Brandon daughter of Thomas & Margaret
                              was born Sept. 12, 1777
Edward Brandon son of Thomas & Margaret
                              was born Nov. 10, 1779
Elizabeth Brandon daughter of Thomas & Margaret
                              was born Feb. 3, 1782
Peter Brandon son of Thomas & Margaret
                              was born June 30, 1784
Thomas Brandon son of Thomas & Margaret
                              was born Aug. 30, 1786
Margaret Walden Brandon daughter of Thomas & Margaret
                              was born Jan. 22, 1790
John Brandon som of Thomas & Margaret
                              was born Sept. 30, 1792
Jesse Brandon son of Thomas & Margaret
                              was born May 7, 1796
Note: No record found, but Thomas Brandon is believed to
      have married Margaret Walden.

ELLIS, Stephen

Pen. R-3322: Sally Ellis, widow of Stephen Ellis applied
for a pension and submitted what was purported to be a family record as follows: *

Stephen Ellis was born Oct. 19, 1760 in Prince George Co.,
and was married Dec. 13, 1790
Sally Ellis, his wife, was born July 9, 1770
Polly Ellis their daughter was born Oct. 19, 1791
John Ellis   born Feb. 18, 1793
Cynthia S. Ellis and Patsy B. Ellis born Dec. 20, 1795
Green B. Ellis   born April 3, 1798
Byron Ellis   born Jan. 12, 1800
Wyatt Ellis   born Jan. 8, 1802
Lucy S. Ellis   born Dec. 20, 1803
Ira Ellis   born Feb. 3, 1806
Tatnai Ellis   born April 8, 1808
William I. Ellis   born Dec. 17, 1811

* Her claims for a pension were never allowed because she
  never proved definitely her age or date of marriage.
  Sally Ellis died January 23, 1853.

HAMNER, John

Pen. W-10081: Mary Hamner, widow

John Hamner was born Jan. 2, 1761 in Mecklenburg County and died Oct. 28, 1836. Married about 1790. *
Mary Hamner was born Aug. 4, 1770 and died Nov. 14, 1842

James Hamner born Jan. 25, 1793
Ann Hamner born Nov. 28, 1795 - wife of Liberty Noel
Rebecca Hamner born July 28, 1797 - wife of James Coffelt
Sarah Hamner born Feb. 14, 1799 - widow of William Doone
Polly Hamner   wife of John A. Rogers
John Hamner
George Hamner

* Marriage Records - 1765-1810, page 57. M.B. Dec. 22,
  1790 - John Hamner and Molly Whobery
Note: Name Whobery is spelled Whobry and Hoobry in Meck.
      Co. Records also. See: Early Wills, page 41.

NELSON, Major John

Pen. W-5414: Nancy Nelson, widow   -   Family records.

Thomas Manduit Nelson born 27 Sept. 1782
John Nelson born 31 March 1784
Lucy Nelson born 11 Sept. 1785
Robert Nelson born 30 Jan. 1787
Hugh Nelson born 22 Nov. 1788 - died 25 Feb. 1830
Nancy Carter Nelson born 27 Sept. 1790
William Nelson born 31 July 1792 - and his daughter Anna
                         Matilda Nelson was born 15 Nov. 1817
Mary Nelson born 16 March 1794 - died 20 April 1795
Nathaniel Nelson born 9 April 1796 at Oak Hill
Caroline Matilda Nelson born 27 Dec. 1798 -
                                    died 5 April 1802
Sarah Nelson born 14 Aug. 1802 - died 25 Nov. 1802

John Nelson died 18 Feb. 1827

Nancy C. Kennon, wife of E. Kennon, died 24 May 1831

See: Marriage Records - 1765-1810, page 174.

See also: Marriage Records - 1811-1853, page 123.

William Nelson married on December 23, 1816 Martha L. Walker.

See: Marriage Records - 1765-1810, page 77.

POOL, James

Pen. W-9233: Ursula Pool, widow   -   Family record.

Ursula Pool born 1 Jan. 1762, married James Pool in Mecklenburg County 11 July 1782
James Pool died 29 July 1839

Rebekah Pool was born April 22, 1783
C (illegible) Pool was born Jan. 18, 1785
William Pool was born Feb. 21, 1787
Sally Pool was born March 9, 1789
Gabriel Pool was born Nov. 9, 1793
Betsy Pool was born Nov. 6, 1796
John Pool was born July 16, 1799
James Pool was born March 15, 1804

RYLAND,.John

Pen. W-18847: Elizabeth Ryland, widow

Elizabeth Russell was born October 8th 1756
John Ryland was born Octr. 20th 1760
Departed this life Octr. the 2nd 1822

John Ryland was married to Elizabeth Russell Jany 9th 1784

Jincy Ivason Ryland Daughter of the above two was born Nov.
the 5th 1786

William H. Ryland Son of the above two was born May the
16th 1788

Harrison M. Ryland Son of the above two was born Feby the
27th 1790

Nancy Hundly Ryland Daughter of the above two was born Dec.
the 4th 1794

RUSSELL, Jeffrey

Pen. W-5751: Sarah Russell, widow

Family Register

Jeffrey Russell & Sarah his wife was married by Parson
Craig the 30th day of December 1778

Children Ages

Richard Russell son of Jeffrey & Sarah Russell was born 20th March 1780

Elizabeth B. Russell daughter of same was born 12th of April 1782

Martha Russell daughter of the same was born 18th March 1784

Mary Russell daughter of the same was born 17th May 1787

Tabby Russell daughter of the same was born 2nd of February 1792

Rebecca Russell daughter of the same was born April 14th 1794

Note: Attached was a part of the title page from a Bible headed "New Testament", Third Philadelphia Edition, Philadelphia. The date and publisher not included on the partial page.

SANDIFER, James

Pen. W-8698: Martha Sandifer, widow

James Sandifer married Martha Coleman Jan. 6, 1781

Martha Sandifer was born Nov. 13, 1786 - daughter of James and Martha

Martha Ann Sandifer was born Sept. 25, 1787

Robert Sandifer was born May 10, 1790

Note: The record states that 10 children were born to James and Martha Sandifer, but only these three were living in 1836. The names of the other children were not given.

TANNER, Josiah

Pen. W-9503: Martha Tanner, widow

Josiah married Martha 1 Dec. 1771 in Mecklenburg County, Virginia. Died in Oct. or Nov. 1807 in Jefferson County Kentucky.

Children:

Sally Tanner born 30 October 1773
Lucy Tanner born 25 April 1775

Martha Tanner born 7 August 1777
Matthew Tanner born 11 January 1779
Samuel Tanner born 15 August 1780
Ann Tanner born 11 October 1783
Elizabeth Tanner born February 18, 1786
Creed Tanner born 24 February 1788
Mary Tanner born 16 December 1789
Kezia Tanner born 29 April 1792
John Tanner
Eleanor Tanner born in March 1797
Thomas Tanner born 3 December 1803

TAYLOR, Jesse

Pen. W-11598: Mary Taylor, widow

Record from annexed book *

"Jesse Taylor his book June 26, 177_ (torn)"

Charles Taylor his hand and pen he was born July 19, 1796
this is Sept. 1812

Henry Taylor was born 1798 December 4

Lewis Taylor was born Friday October 4 (paper faded)

Mourning Taylor was born January 10, 1801

William Taylor born February 25 1803

James Taylor born April 21 1805

John Taylor born April   1807

Elizabeth Taylor born 1810

One name born 1812 - other names illiegible

Signed "Charles Taylor"

* Charles Taylor, son of Jesse and Mary Taylor, appears to
  have copied in 1812 the above records from an old Bible
  belonging to his father.

Lt. Isaac Holmes

Ensign 2nd Va. State Reg. Sept. 2, 1777; 1st Lieut. 15th Sept. 1778; served to Jan. 1781.

Probably same as Isaac Holmes, Cadet, in Capt. John Ballard's Minute Men in Aug. 1776.

Ordered to Richmond to take command as Lieut. March 3rd, 1781; shown as supernumerary at half pay April 1, 1782; awarded 2,666 acres as Lieut.

Gwathmey

Captured by English forces in spring of 1781 - Prisoner of war until the end of Revolutionary War.

Bounty Land Application

Qualified as Clerk of the Court of Nottoway County May 7 1789, with William Yates and Vivion Brooking as his securities.

Nottoway County Records

Married Elizabeth Brooking, daughter of Vivion Brooking. Children: Vivion B. Holmes, John B. Holmes, Frances T. Holmes, Margaret B. Holmes, Lucy Holmes.

Col. Samuel Hopkins (Jr)

Captain 6 CL Feb. 26, 1776; Major Nov. 29, 1777; wounded at Germantown Oct. 4, 1777; Lieut. Col. 14 CL June 19, 1778; regiment designated as 10 CL Sept. 14, 1778; taken prisoner at Charleston May 12, 1780; exchanged and transferred to 1 CL Feb. 12, 1781; served to close of war. Awarded 7,833 acres.

Gwathmey

Col. Samuel Hopkins died 9 Nov. 1819 at Henderson, Ky.

Burgess Vol. 1, page 336

HOPKINS, Samuel (Jr)   Betty Bugg
   M.B. Jan. 18, 1783   Surety: George Nicholas
   Note: Betty, daughter of Jacob Bugg, Sr.

Marriage Records 1765-1810, page 66

Col. Samuel Hopkins moved to Christian County, Kentucky. The city of Hopkinsville, and county seat of Christian Co., was named for him.

ACTS of the GENERAL ASSEMBLY
Chapter XVIII - - - May 1779

An Act for laying a tax payable in certain enumerated Commodities -

Be it enacted by the General Assembly, That for every man above 16 years old, and every woman slave of like age ..
......

SPECIFIC TAX

there shall be delivered by him or her .... one bushel of wheat, or 2 bushels of good Indian Corn, Rye or Barley, or 10 pecks of Oats, or 15 pounds of Hemp, or 28 pounds of inspected Tobacco ... to the commissary to be appointed for that purpose at the place or places hereafter by this Act directed to be accounted in the county in the month of March in the year 1780, and in each of the four succeeding years.
Be it enacted, That the court in each county, on some of their several court days in the months of August, September or October ... appoint two commissioners, who shall have power to fix on some one certain place .... for the receipt and delivery of such commodities ... as to the purpose of safekeeping & storing, manufacturing and removal to the public magazines... and the sheriffs shall have power to collect in the same manner as other taxes.

Chapter XXXII - November 1781

Be it enacted, That there shall be delivered to the Commissioners ... 2 pounds of good sound bacon for each free person above the age of 21, and for each slave above the age 16 years ... (the act provides for those responsible to the Commissioners for delivery).... and further provides, That in lieu of 2 pounds of bacon they may pay in money at the rate of 6 pence per pound in gold or silver coin for each pound. *

* Paper currency was, apparently, not accepted in payment.-
  This was probably due to the inflation in the currency,
  or current money of Virginia, as at that time the paper
  money was exchanged at the rate of 600 pounds of currency
  for 1 pound specie - gold or silver.

Court 10 Sept. 1781
William Starling and Richard Epperson, Gentlemen, are appointed Commissioners for carrying into execution the Act of Assembly laying a tax payable in certain enumerated commodities for the ensuing year.

Order Book 5, Page 100

SPECIFIC TAX MECKLENBURG COUNTY

A return of grain issued by Henry Delony, Dep. Comm. Law
for Mecklenburg County from 30 March to 8 September 1781

To Whom Delivered	By Whose Order	Use (Corn and Oats)
Anthony Hilton	Wm. Brown	Artillery going to South
Captain Patrick	Capt. Patrick	Light Infantry
Edward Smith	James Anderson	3 teams in public service
Wm. Watlington	James Anderson	A Continental Team
Thomas Goode	Wm. Starling	Corn exchange
Lewis Ballard	Br. General Allen Jones	For N. C. Troops
Howell Edmonds	do	do
John Prochit	do	do
Nicolas Parham	Capt. Jones	Post at Taylor's Ferry
James Anderson	do	do
Abraham Mitchell	James Anderson	For post riders
Charles Hood	do	do
Maj. Richard Call	Major Call	For his horse
Pascal Grindale		The horses impressed for service
Ebenezer Vaughan	Express Rider	For his horse
Thomas Matthews and		For horses going
Jouman Wagner		to Paytonsburg
Thomas Matthews		For 2 Pub. Wagons
Wm. Watlington		do
G. W. Carlile		Express
Wm. Watlington		For Public Service
Wm. Boswell		For Public use
Benj. Ferrell Q.M.		For horses impressed for service
Capt. James Gunn	Capt. Gunn	For part of his Company
Lt. James Cannady	Lt. Cannady	For the South Troops
James Anderson D.Q.M.	Capt. Anderson	Post at Taylor's Ferry

Receipts for the delivery of grain was included with this
report filed by Henry Delony, Deputy Commissioner. Capt.
James Anderson acted as Deputy Quarter Master at the Post
at Taylor's Ferry where military travel through Mecklenburg
County crossed the Roanoke River.

Captain Benjamin Ferrell acted as Quarter Master for Meck.
lenburg County.

ACTS of the GENERAL ASSEMBLY
Chapter IV - October 1780

An Act for supplying the Army with Clothes, provisions
& Waggons:

Excerpts: And, Be it enacted by the authority aforesaid ..

Note: Under this act, the county courts were authorized to
      appoint commissioners for the purpose of collecting
      specified articles of clothing and beef to clothe and
      provision the army in the field; and each county was
      required to furnish a waggon (sic), team and driver
      for public use at the expense of the county.

Court 6 Feb. 1781
                     At a Court held at the Courthouse of Meck-
lenburg County, the 6th day of February 1781, pursuant to
an Act of Assembly entitled An Act for supplying the Army
with Clothes, provisions & Waggons:
Present
          John Speed   Cluverius Coleman)
          Reuben Vaughan   John Burton   ) Gentlemen
          James Anderson   &   ) Justices
          Lewis Parham   William Starling   )

        Ordered that the sum of 30432 pounds 8 shillings be
levied on the tithable persons of this County, being 3169 in
number, for the purpose of paying for a Waggon, team, Driver
& all necessary Charges attending the same; that the Sherif
collect by the first day of March next the sum of 9 pounds
12 shillings for each of the said tithables and out of the
money arising thereby pay to the person that shall be appointed to purchase the said Articles such a sum as will enable
him to make payment for the same and that he retain in his
hands a commission as in case of collecting taxes and account
for the balance to the Court.

                                        Order Book 5, Page 88

Ordered that John Burton, Gent., be appointed to purchase
for the publick Service by the first day of March next a good
and serviceable Waggon with a good cover and a team of four
good horses complete harness and to employ a driver to serve
for one month from the time he takes charge of said Waggon &
team & on the said first day of March the said John Burton is
directed to apply to the Sherif of this County for such sum
of money as will enable him to pay for the said Articles, the
wages of the Driver and expenses attending the purchase.

                                        Order Book 5, Page 88

Court 11 June 1781

Ordered that Henry Delony, Gent., take in to the publick Service one good and serviceable Waggon with a good cover and Team of four horses and complete harness with a Driver who is to serve as a Driver for one month at the expence of this County, being the Wagon etc purchased on behalf of this county by John Burton, Gent., for the use of the publick.

Ordered that the expences and expenditure of the said Wagon & Team be furnished to Henry Delony, Gent., that he may settle with the commissioners.

Order Book 5, Page 97

SPECIFIC TAX

Commissioners appointed in Mecklenburg County under the act Henry Delony, James Hughes and Caleb Johnson

Specific Tax Return to Governor & Council

An account of the grain received in Mecklenburg County in the year 1781 agreeable to an Act of Assembly entitled -

An Act for laying a tax in certain enumerated commodities:

Total received by 3 Commissioners

Tobacco	1176 cwt
Corn	1352 bu.
Wheat	260 bu.
Oats	2806 bu.
Rye	8 bu.

Copy grain rec'd

15 May 1781   /s/ Richard Epperson) CST
                     William Starling)

201

Pursuant to the Act of the Gen. Assembly for adjusting
claims for property impressed or taken for public service,
the Court doth ascertain the value of the several srticles
taken or impressed as follows, to-wit:

To breakfast or dinner	2 shillings
pasturage 24 hours for a horse	6 pence
a waggon, team and driver, if	
found provision by the Public	15 shillings per day
ditto if found	
provision by the owner	20 ditto
waggon and gear	3 ditto
waggon and team, if found	
provision by the Public	12 ditto
fresh pork	25 shillings per 100 cwt
salt pork	40 ditto
a cart	2 shillings 6 pence per day
a driver for the samw	2 do 6 do
the hire of a horse, if	
found provision by owner	2 do 6 do
bacon	1 shilling per pound
grass beef	3 ditto
vinegar	3 shillings a gallon
fodder	5 shillings 100 cwt or 100 bundles
corn	2 shillings 6 pence per bushel
wheat	5 shillings do
oats	2 do do
bolted flour	25 shillings per cwt
a pole axe	12 shillings
a mutton	20 do
lodging 1 night	$7\frac{1}{2}$ do
tar	$7\frac{1}{2}$ shillings per gallon
meal	2 shillings 6 pence per bu.

9 April 1782   O.B. 5, p. 123

    At a Court held for Mecklenburg County, 9 April 1782,
the foregoing prices were set as a basis for settling public claims arising from articles impressed or taken for
public service during the Revolutionary War.

    In the case of horses, guns and other articles impress-
ed or taken for public service, the owner was permitted to
set a value. The Court, if it considered the claim, or
value set, reasonable, ordered the claim to be certified as
just.

    If the Court considered the value set as unreasonable,
it set a price from which it appears there was no appeal.
The judgement of the Court was final. The claims were paid
by the Sheriff out of tax funds in his hands. The claims
were subsequently sent to the Commonwealth where they were
audited by the Public Auditor.

LEGISLATIVE PETITION No. 392
Mecklenburg County, Virginia
May 14, 1777

To the Honorable the Speaker, and Gentlemen of the House of
Delegates of Virginia:

The petition of the Inhabitants of the County of Mecklenburg humbly beseech, That your petitionare highly approve
of the several Acts and Resolutions of Conventions, and Assembly, but conceive that some amendment might be made to
those, relating to the natives of Great Britain, and to the
establishment of the paper currency of this Commonwealth.
   We conceive that it would tend to unite more firmly, the
natives of this State, were the resolution respecting the
Factors of British merchants extended to the married as
well as the single natives of Great Britain, who were factors for, or partners with, merchants residing in Great
Britain, and have not uniformly manifested a friendly disposition to the American cause; and who notwithstanding
their connexions in this County by marriage, declare that
the paper currency of this State, now in circulation, is of
very little, or no value, and absolutely refuse to receive
same in discharge of the debts due to the British merchants
with whom they are concerned as factors or partners.
   Your petitioners do not mean to be exculpate, many of
their own Countrymen who esteem Gold or Silver so much more
than paper, as to demand a very considerable advance in ex-
changing one for the other, notwithstanding the penalty inflicted to prevent the depreciating of the paper currency
of these states.
   Wherefore your Petitioners pray that all the natives of
Great Britain, who have not uniformly shown their friendly
disposition to the American cause, may be compelled to
leave this State, and that some more severe punishment may
be inflicted upon those who depreciate the paper currency
of the United States, and this Commonwealth, upon the credit
of which depends the support of the American War.
   And your Petitioners as in duty bound shall ever pray

Bennett Goode	Isaac Gordin	Buckner Rainey
Thos. Mitchell	Buckner Whittemore	Wm. Taylor
John Farrar	Wm. Lucas, Jr.	Jordan Bennett
James Bilbo	Adam Overbee	Benj. Malone
Wm. Lawrence	Henry Delony, Jr.	Robt. Allen
Frank Lightfoot	Richard Hanserd	Wm. Epps
Sam'l Holmes	Thomas Gregory	Isham Nance
Rich'd Crowder	Edgcomb Suggitt	Jones Taylor
William Cook	Jeremiah Crowder	Edward McDonald
Anthony Evans	Isaac Watson	Thomas Crowder
William Ballard	Peyton Skipwith	James Insco
Frank Collins	John Daly	William Mason

John Hubbard	Jas. Holmes	John Russell
Thomas Craig	Stephen Mabry	Charles Pistole
Joshua Gordin	David Taylor	Wm. Crutchfield
Ephraim Gordin	Joseph Bennett	Joel Johnson
Benj. Fargeson	Nathaniel Malone	David Tucker
James B. Davis	James Standley	Leonard Cardin
John Waller	Isham Eppes	James Cardin
William Moore	James Adams	Phil Poindexter, Jr.
William Insco	Peter Ragsdale	Will F. Bassy
John Cardin	Newman Bragg	John Lipford
Jeremiah Lucas	John Thompson	Abram Forrest
Joel Traler	Edward Bevill	Gideon Freeman
Nath. Burnett	Wm. Weatherford	Thomas Burton
James Johnson	James Westbrooke	John Wilson
William Hightower	Charles Clay	Joseph Goode
James Cash	Richard Epperson	Edw. Colley
Zachariah Johnson	Thomas Pettus, Jr.	Thos. Greenwood
John Calthorpe	James Brown	Joshua Edwards
John Mackcasie	Charles Royster	Thomson Fowlkes
Reuben Vaughan	Samuel Cox	James Tucker
Rich'd Edmondson	Asa Oliver	Edw. Goode, Junr.
James Willson	Thos. Berry	Cuthbert Russell
Samuel Johnson	Abram Crowder	David Smith
David Darden	James Wilkins	Thomas Vaughan
Joseph Powers	Baxter Davis	John Hayes, Junr.
Ellis Carroll	William Oliver	Jerry Smith
John Willis	Samuel Marshall	Edward Walton
James Hargrove	Wm. Drumright	Matthew Tanner, Jr,
James Gordin	Wm. Leigh	Thos. Haile
Wm. Hudson	John Bugg	Jno. Avory
Robert Hicks	Wm. Hunt, Jr.	Hugh Lambert
Peter Thomas	Benjamin Doggett	Cluverius Coleman
Ephraim Hutson	James Hester	William Mason
Jno. Webb	Wingfield Hayes	John Brame
Abraham Burton	Joseph Royster	Peter Hutcheson
Charles Burton	Moses Overton	James Brame
Edward Tisdale	Phil Poindexter, Sr.	Elijah Graves
Caleb Johnson	William Hunt	Frank Moore Neal
Charles Wells	John Bottom	Zachariah Yancey
Isaiah Turner	Joel Chandler	Joel Elam
John Baskervill	Leonard Murray	John Walden
John Evans	Thos. Howell	Alex'r Elam
George Minor	Jesse Taylor	Harman Thompson
Thos. Matthews	Benj. Burton	David Adams
Hudson Tucker	Thomas Westbrook	Jno. Burton
Edward Roffe	John Kitchen	John Goode
Peter Burton	Feilds Read	John Bradley
Clem Whittemore	Wm. Bottom	Will Baskervill
David Royster	William Hatsel	Robert Brooks
Peter F. Jefferson	John Puryear, Jr.	Roger Gregory, Junr.
Peter Farrar	Edward Pennington	Sam'l Brame

Mecklenburg Pet'n 1777
May 14. Ref'd to Prop'r
Chairman to move that this
Comm. be discharged from
proceed'g on this Petition, &c.
May 16th.
Ref'd to Com. of the whole on
State of Commonwealth

Note: The original petition bearing the signatures of the
foregoing citizens of Mecklenburg County is in the
Archives, Virginia State Library.

Abercromby,
  Robert   11
Abernathy,
  Lucy   151
  Signal   151
Adams,
  Calarine   11
  David   11,204
  James   204
  John   11,161,162
  Lucy   11
  Thomas   11,162
Adkins,
  Thomas Durham   11
  William   11,162
Aiken,
  James   133
Akin,
  Thomas   11
Alexander,
  M. (Mark)   187
  Col. Robert   12
  Robert   158,159
Allen,
  Darling   12,168
  David   12,61
  James   117
  Robert   12,203
  Thomas   12
  William   12
Allgood,
  John, Sr.   13
  John   13,(2)
  Moses   13
  Spencer   13
  William   13,35
Allin,
  Philip   12
Anderson,
  Capt. James   12
  James   14,22,24,35,(2),
            53,63,101,121,
            125,129,131,140,
            157,158,159,165,
            173,175,183,199,
            (4),200
  Sarah   14
  Thomas, Sr.   14
  Thomas, Jr.   14
Andrews,
  Ephraim, Sr.   14
  Ephraim,   15,162,168
  Ephraim, Jr.   14
  George   15
  Knacy H.   15,165
  Knacy   177
  Nancy   64
  Rowland   15
  Varney   15,(2),189
  William   15,(2)
Archer,
  William   15,162
Armistead,
  John   15
Armstrong,
  James   15
Arnold,
  Benjamin   190
  Elisha   16,(2)
  James   16,162
  James, Jr.   16
  John   16,(2)
  Mary   16
  William   168
Arrington,
  John   16,188
  Susanna   16,188
Ashby,
  Stephen   100

Ashton,
  Henry   167
Avery,
  Henry   17
  John   17
Avory,
  John   204

Baber,
  William   17,189,191
Bagley,
  William   17
Bagwell,
  Lunsford   17
Bailey,
  George   17
  Howard   17
  Peter   17
  William   18
  William, Jr.   18
Bails,
  David   18
Baker,
  Jane   18
  William   63
Ballad,
  Dudley   18
Ballard,
  J.   140
  James   165
  John, Sr.   18
  Captain   18,89,110
  John   21,165,169,197
  John, Jr.   18,157
  Lewis   199
  Robert   15,19,(2),116,
             157,165,187
  William   19,168,203
  William, Jr.   19
Baptist,
  William Glanvil   19
Barbee,
  William   19
  Captain   20
Barnes,
  James   19,161
Baskervill,
  George   19,157
  John   20,165,173,175,
            204
  William   20,63,165,179,
            183,204
Bassy,
  Will F.   204
Bates,
  Fleming   63,161,165,167
Baugh,
  Daniel   20
  James   20
Baxter,
  Peter   20
Beavers,
  John   20
Bennett,
  Anthony   21
  Jordan   21,161,168,203
  Joseph, Sr.   21
  Joseph   21,31,90,161,
             168,189,204
Bentley,
  Samuel   21
Berry,
  Andrew   21
  Hugh   21
  John   22
  Thomas   22,152,204
Bevill,
  Edward   22,(2),56,204
  John   13,23,165

Bilbo,
  James, Sr.   23
  James   165,176,203
  James, Jr.   23
  John   23
  Joseph   23
  Nathan   23,168
  William, Sr.   23
  William   23,169
Blackbourn,
  Clement   24,97
  Thomas   24
Blake,
  Anne   182
  Robert   24,182
Bland,
  Colonel   110
  Thomas   43
Blanton,
  James   24
  John   24
Blunt,
  William   101
Booker,
  Richard   24,182,191
  Sarah   182,191
Booth,
  Thomas, Sr.   24
  Thomas   24,165,177,178
Boswell,
  David   25,105
  John   25
  Joseph   25
  Robert   25,(2)
  William   199
Bottom,
  James   25
  John   25,204
  William   25,204
Bowen,
  Alexander   25,162
  Bracey   26,162,168
  Charles   26
  David   26,162
  Hicks   25,26,162
  Isham   26,168
  James   26,(2),162,168
  Jesse   26,162
  John   26,161,168
  Starling   168
  Sterling   26
  William   27
Boyd,
  Alexander   - 27
Bradley,
  John   204
Bragg,
  John   27
  Newman   27,204
Brame,
  James   27,204
  John   27,204
  Richins, Sr.   27
  Samuel   27,204
Brandon,
  Agnes   192
  Edward   192
  Elizabeth   192
  Jesse   192
  John   192
  Margaret   189,192
  Margaret Walden   192
  Mary   139
  Peter   192
  Suckey (Susanna)   192
  Thomas   27,161,189,(2),
            192,(2)
  Walden   192
  William   28,162

Brasfield,
  Elizabeth   22
Brent,
  Colonel   59
  William   148
Bridgewater,
  William   28
Brodie,
  John   28
Brooke,
  Benjamin   190
Brooking,
  Elizabeth   197
  Vivion   197
Brooks,
  David   28
  Richard   169
  Robert 28,(2),161,168,
      204
Brough,
  Robert   28
Browder,
  Thomas   165
Brown,
  Aries   168
  Aris   29
  Henry   29
  James 19,29,165,178,204
  John   20,29,(2),35,37,
      63,92,93,138,150,
      165,175,(2),177,
      191
  Mordecai 29,165,169,
      179,180
  Thomas   29,30,168
  William   199
Bruce,
  John   30
Buchanan,
  William Willis   30
Bugg,
  Betty   197
  Jacob, Sr.   197
  Jacob 30,(2),165,173,
      175,181
  Jesse   30,(2),162
  John   21,30,31,204
  Samuel 31,(2),158,159,
      181
  William   31
Bullington,
  William   31
Burnett,
  Barnett   31,162
  Benjamin   31,162
  John   31,162
  Nathan   31,168
  Nathaniel   204
  William   31,169
Burrus,
  William Jennings   32
Burt,
  Matthew   32
  William   32
Burte,
  Moody   32
Burton,
  Abraham   32,204
  Benjamin   32,204
  Charles   32,204
  Horace A.   34
  Hutchins 32,33,(2),34,
      157,165,181,
      (2),189
  John   19,33,(3),35,86,
      121,157,158,159,
      165,172,174,175,
      177,178,181,182,
      (2),200,(3),201,
      204
  Noel Hunt   34
  Peter 33,(2),165,176,
      204

Burton, cont'd.
  Col. Robert   34
  Robert 34,157,165,167
  Thomas   34,204
Burwell,
  Col. Lewis   12,13,17
  Lewis 19,21,22,24,26,28,
      34,(2),35,58,63,
      65,73,74,101,120,
      140,148,157,158,
      159,161,165,172,
      173,175,178,179,
      190
  Mary   34
  Thacker 34,35,157,158,
      159,165,173,(3),
      175
Butler,
  James   35
  John   35
  Joseph   35,65,161,189
  Patrick   35
  Zachariah   35
Bynum,
  Turner   72,165,167

Call,
  Richard   199
  William   36
Calthorpe,
  John   204
Camp,
  John 36,157,158,159,173
Cannady,
  James   199,(2)
Gardin,
  James   204
  John   36,204
  Leonard   204
Cardwell,
  Elizabeth   188
  Elvira   188
  Patience   188
Carleton,
  Gabriel   36
  Henry   36
  Thomas 36,165,173,(2),
      174
  Thomas, Jr. 36,165,175
Carlile,
  G.W.   199
Carroll,
  Ellis   204
Carter,
  Alexander   36
  James   37
  John   37
  Matthew   37
  Thomas   37
Cash,
  James   204
Cass,
  Lew   185
Cavaniss,
  Henry   37
Chamberlain,
  Thomas   37
Chandler,
  Joel   37,(2),204
  John   38
Chavers,
  Anthony   38
Chavis,
  John   38
Cheatham,
  Daniel   38
  Elizabeth   38
  James   38
  Leonard   38
Christopher,
  David 38,39,158,159
  Robert   39
  William   39

Christy,
  Hannah   46
Clark,
  Alexander   39
  Archibald   39
  Bolling   39
  Carter   39,165,178
  Edward   39
  James 39,40,90,131,171
  John   40
Clausel,
  Clausel 40,158,159,165,
      173,174,179
  Richard   40
Clay,
  Charles 22,(2),24,40,
      58,87,97,165,
      174,175,178,(2),
      204
  John 28,33,35,(2),41,
      165,173,174,176,
      178
  John, Jr.   41
  Obia   157,165
  Samuel   41
Cleaton,
  John   41,(2)
  Poythress   41
  Thomas   41
  William   41
Clemonds,
  William   42
Clemons,
  Edmund   41
Clibourn,
  William   42
Clinton,
  Sir Henry   69,187
Cocke,
  Nathaniel   113
Cockerham,
  Benjamin   42
Coffelt,
  James   193
Coleman,
  Cluverius 42,157,158,
      159,173,181,
      200,204
  James   42
  Martha   126,195
  Obadiah   42
  Richard   42
  William   21,42,121,189
Coley,
  Isham   43,189
Colley,
  Daniel   43
  Edward   43,204
Collier,
  Frederick   43
  Howell   43
  William   43,168,189
Collins,
  Frank   203
Condry,
  John   169
Conell,
  William   162
Conery,
  John   43
Connel,
  Avery   44
  James   44
  William   44
Connell,
  Morris   44
Cook,
  John   44
  Nathaniel   44
  William   44,203
Copeland,
  John   44

Coppage,
  Charles   44
Cornwallis,
  Lord 16,21,28,35,46,54,
    58,61,63,72,(2),
    73,140
Cox,
  Bartlett 21,44,45,189,
    191
  Francinia   45
  James   45,168
  John, Sr.   45
  John 45,158,159,165,178
  John, Jr.   45
  Lucretia   45
  Samuel 46,165,178,204
  Thomas   46
Craddock,
  Edmund   46
Cradle,
  Joseph   162,168
  William   162
Crage,
  Thomas   46,162
Craig,
  James   126,194
  Thomas   204
Crawford,
  Peter   46,161,(2)
Crawley,
  Robert   46
Credle,
  Joseph   46
  William   46
Crocksin,
  Joanna   29
Crook,
  James   47
  William   47
Crowder,
  Abraham   47
  Abram   204
  Bartholomew   47
  Bartholomew, Jr.   47
  Batt   47
  Dorcas   47
  George   47
  Godfrey   47
  Hezekiah   48,162,169
  Jeremiah   48,203
  John   48
  Richard   48,203
  Robert   48,162
  Thomas   203
  William   48
Culbreath,
  Thomas   48,103
  William   48,49
  William, Jr.   48,49,73
Crutchfield,
  William   204
Cunningham,
  Ansel   49,161,162
  Henry   167
  James   49,189
  John   162
  Josiah   49,162
  William   49,162

Dailey,
  John   49,50,203
  Josiah, Sr.   49
  Josiah 49,165,174,176,
    180
Daniel,
  William, Sr.   50
  William   14
  William, Jr.   50
  William Powell   50
Darden,
  David 50,165,173,175,
    204
  David, Jr.   50

Davies,
  William   64,165
Davis,
  Baxter 50,165,173,174,
    176,(2),204
  Baxter, Jr.   50
  Charles 50,51,165,176,
    179,180
  Edward   51
  Ensign   21
  Hardaway 51,165,173,174
  James   51
  James B.   204
  John   51,169
  Joshua   51,176
  Lieut.   115
  Randolph   51
  William, Gent.   52
  William 52,(2),101,157,
    158,159,165
Dawson,
  William   157,165
Davis,
  William, Jr.   52
Daws,
  John   52
Day,
  James   52
Decker,
  Fanny   52
  John   52,162
  William   53,169
Dedman,
  Samuel 28,53,157,158,
    159,161,165,172,
    179,(3),180
Delafield,
  William   53,162
Delony,
  Henry 53,(2),157,158,
    159,165,167,173,
    (3),175,(2),199,
    (2),201,(3)
  Henry, Jr.   53,165,203
  William   53,165,180
Dick,
  William   63
Dickinson,
  Edmund B.   187
Dixon,
  Sterling   53,162
Dodson,
  Edward   54,(2),165,176
  William   54
Doggett,
  Benjamin   54,204
  John   54
Doone,
  William   193
Dortch,
  Abel   54,161,162
  Anne   54
  David, Sr.   54
  David   162
  David, Jr.   54
  Noah 54,55,165,173,175,
    (2)
Douglas,
  John   55
Draper,
  Joshua   55
  Solomon   55
  Sol   55
  William   55
Drumright,
  William 54,55,161,165,
    175,176,177,204
Dudley,
  Henry   59,148
Duncan,
  George   56
Dunston,
  Charles   56

Durham,
  John   56
  Samuel   56
  Thomas   56

Easter,
  Enos   56
  John   22,56
  Richard   56
Eastland,
  Sarah   57
  William 57,(2),165,175,
    176
Eaton,
  John   165,167
Edmonds,
  Howell   199
Edmondson,
  Richard   204
  Samuel   57
Edmundson,
  Benjamin   57,168
Edwards,
  Isaac   57,168
  J.L.   185,186
  John   57
  Joshua   204
Elam,
  Alexander   57,204
  Joel   58,204
Elliott,
  Richard   72,165,167
Ellis,
  Byron   192
  Cynthia S.   192
  Green B.   192
  Ira   192
  John   192
  Lucy S.   192
  Polly   192
  Sally   192
  Stephen 58,161,189,192
  Tatnai   192
  William I.   192
  Wyatt   192
Epperson,
  Richard 58,75,165,173,
    174,175,178,182,
    198,201,204
Eppes,
  Isham   204
  Martha Bolling   147
  Peter   168
Epps,
  John   - 58
  William   58,162,203
Erskine,
  Thomas   58,158,159
Evans,
  Anthony   58,203
  Charles   58,59
  Dick   59,162
  Godfrey   59,162
  John   59,204
  Ludwell   59
  Major   59
  Mark   59,162
  Richard   59
  Stephen, Jr. 59,165,173,
    175
  Thomas   59,60
  William   60,(2)
Ezell,
  Balaam   60
  John   60
  Lewis   168
  Michael   60

Fann,
  Willebee 60
  Willoughby 60
Fanning,
  Laughlin 28,33,35,60,
       165,177
Fargeson,
  Benjamin 204
Farrar,
  Abel 60,189
  Francis 12,61,161
  John 61,74,162,165,173,
       175,176,180,181,203
  Peter 204
  Thomas 61
  William 61
Faulkner,
  John 16,61,120,165,167
  Ralph 72,152,165,167
Fegins,
  Henry 61
Feild,
  Thomas 62
Ferguson,
  Benjamin 62
Ferrell,
  Benjamin 20,26,30,62,93,
       165,173,175,
       176,199
  James 62,165,173,175,176
  William 168
Finch,
  Adam 62
  Edward, Gent. 63
  Edward 62,150,158,159
  John 63
  William 63
Fitz,
  Robert W. 63,161,183,
       (2),184,185,
       (2), 189
Fitzhugh,
  Beverly 64
Fleming,
  Charles 98,165,167
  James 13,28,165,167
  John 19
Flinn,
  James 64
Flood,
  Burwell 64
Floyd,
  Charles 64
  John 64
  Richard 64
Ford,
  Calvin 64
Forrest,
  Abram 204
Fowler,
  Alexander 64
  Thomas 65
Fowlkes,
  Thompson 28,35,46,65,
       157,158,159,
       161,165,176,
       178,204
Fox,
  Arthur 65,165,178
  Ensign 21
  Jacob 65
  Richard 65
  William 65
  William, Jr. 65
Franklin,
  Hugh 66
  Owen 66
Freeman,
  George, Sr. 66
  George 165,174
  George, Jr. 66
  Gideon 204
  Holman 66

Garland,
  Peter 81
Garner,
  James 66
  James, Jr. 66
Gibson,
  George 187
Giles,
  Edward 66,162
Gill,
  Sarah 125
  William, Jr. 17,66,165,
       167,173,175
Glaspy,
  Martin 67
Glass,
  Josiah 67
Glasscock,
  Robert 67
  Zachariah 67
Glenn,
  George 165
Gobor,
  John 67
Goddin,
  William 67
Gold,
  Daniel 67
Goode,
  Bennett 50,67,(2),68,
       157,158,159,165,
       172,174,175,203
  Edward 13,68,165,173,
       174,175
  Edward, Jr. 68,165,178,
       179,204
  Jack 68
  John 68,162,169,204
  Joseph 204
  Richard 68
  Samuel, Gent. 68
  Samuel 68,69,157,158,159
  Thomas 69,169,199
  Thomas, Jr. 69
Gomer,
  John, Sr. 67
Goodwin,
  Peter 69
Gordon,
  Ephraim 204
  Isaac 203
  James 204
  Joshua 204
  Thomas 69,81
  William 69,187
Grant,
  Daniel 69
  Edward, Jr. 69
Graves,
  Elijah 17,19,28,61,69,
       70,(2),140,161,
       165,173,174,176,
       177,178,179,204
Green,
  Garner 70
  Matthew 70,(2)
  Thomas 70,(2),168
  William 43,70,(2),116,
       154,157,165,174,
       175,178,179,(2)
  William Wills 71,165,172,
       179,180
Greenwood,
  James 71
  Thomas 71,72,165,174,
       176,179,180,204
Gregory,
  Joseph 72
  Richard 72
  Roger, Sr. 72
  Roger 158,159
  Roger, Jr. 204
  Thomas 203

Griffin,
  Elijah 16,72,189
  James 72
Grinage,
  James 71
  Joshua 71,(2)
Grindale,
  Pascal 199
Gunn,
  James 50,165,167,199,
Guy,
  Christopher 72,162
  John 73,162
  William 73,120,162
Gwaltney,
  Michael 72,189

Haile,
  John 73
  Thomas 73,204
Hailey,
  Thomas 73
  William 73
Hall,
  James 73,74,82,124,154,
       165,173,174,175
  John 73,162
  Miles 74,165,179,180,
       181
Hamblin,
  Thomas 74
Hamilton,
  John 74,181
  Judith 74,181
Hamner,
  Ann 193
  George 193
  James 74,193
  John 74,193,(2)
  John, Jr. 193
  Mary 193,(2)
  Polly 193
  Rebecca 193
  Sarah 193
Handserd,
  Richard 74
Hanserd,
  Richard 203
Hardy,
  John 74
Hargrove,
  Howell 75,162
  James 204
Harper,
  John 75
Harris,
  Benjamin 75
  Judith 75
  Philip 75
  Sarah 22
Harrison,
  Charles 126
  James 75
  William 75
Hasty,
  Henry 75
  James 76,169
  Thomas 76
Hatchell,
  Edward 168
  William 76,162
  Willis 76,162
Hatcher,
  Phebe 103
Hatsell,
  John 76
  William 76,204
Hawkins,
  Matthew 76
  Wyatt 165,167

Hayes,
 John   76
 John, Jr.   204
 Winkfield   76
 Wingfield   204
Hazelwood,
 Daniel   77
Hendricks,
 James   187
Henry,
 Patrick   164
Hepburn,
 Dr. William   77
Hester,
 Abram   77
 Ann   77,106
 Barbara   77
 Francis   77,165
 Henry   77
 James 24,77,78,87,165,
      174,176,204
Hicks,
 Amos   78
 Daniel, Sr.   78
 Daniel   189
 Isaac   78
 James, Sr.   78
 James   78,162
 Robert   204
Hightower,
 William   204
Hill,
 Matthew   78
 William   78
Hilton,
 Anthony   199
Hinton,
 Francis   78,162
Hix,
 Amos   181
 Isaac   165
 James   181
 Jesse   181
Hobson,
 Nicholas   81
Hogan,
 Edward   79
Hogg,
 Major   24
 Samuel   69,187
Holloway,
 Bennett   79
 Edward   79
 John   19,162
 William, Sr.   79
 William   162,165,168
 William, Jr.   79
Holmes,
 Frances T.   197
 Isaac 79,82,88,101,104,
      105,157,165,197,
      204
 James   204
 John 11,63,79,162,165,
      168,173,174,175,
      183
 John B.   197
 Lucy   80,197
 Margaret B.   197
 Pennington   80
 Samuel, Sr.   80
 Samuel   80,203
 Samuel, Jr. 80,165,175,
      179
 Vivion B.   197
 William   80
 William, Jr.   80
Homes,
 John   80
Hoobry,
 Jacob   80
Hood,
 Charles   199

Hopkins,
 John   81
 Samuel, Sr.   81
 Samuel 43,126,142,187,
      197,(4)
 Samuel, Jr. 81,(3),157,
            (2),165,181
Hopson,
 Samuel   167
 Samuel, Jr.   165
Howell,
 Thomas   204
Hubbard,
 John   81,204
Hudson,
 Charles   81,189
 Cuthbert   81
 Edward   81
 Forrest   82,181
 Henry   181
 James   82,165
 John, Sr.   82
 John 77,82,165,174,175,
      179
 Robert   82
 Stephen   82
 Thomas   82
 William 17,82,83,162,
      204
Hughes,
 Elizabeth   83
 James   83,201
Humphries,
 John   83
Hundley,
 William, Gent.   83
 William 165,174,178,179,
      (2)
Hundly,
 William   177
Hunley,
 William   84
Hunt,
 Berry   84
 James   84,165,179
 Presley   84
 William   84,204
 William, Jr. 84,165,177,
      204
Hurdon,
 Reuben   84
Hurt,
 Philemon   84
Hutcheson,
 Charles 84,85,173,174,
      175
 John   85,165,180
 Peter 85,166,173,175,
      204
 Richard 85,(2),166,174,
      175,179,180
Hutson,
 Ephraim   204
Hutt,
 Charles   85
 Daniel   14,85,157,(2)
Hyde,
 James   86
 John   86
 Robert   86,(2)

Insco,
 James   169,203
 James, Jr.   86
 William 86,103,121,189,
      204

Jackson,
 Jonathon   86
 Matthew   86

Jacobs,
 Sarah   --
James,
 Joshua   87
Jefferson,
 Peter Feild   204
 Gov. Thomas   190
Jeffress,
 Achilles, 13,19,28,87,
      161,166,178,
      178,179
 John, Sr.   87
 Swepson   87
Jeter,
 Andrew   166
 William   87
Johns,
 John   87
Johnson,
 Caleb 87,(2),166,173,174,
      176,201,204
 Ellis   88
 Isaac 88,167,175,176
 James 16,30,81,88,166,
      167,168,189,204
 James, Jr.   88
 Joel   204
 John, Sr.   88
 John   88,(2)
 Mary   88
 Samuel   204
 William 89,(2),158,159
 William   166,180
 William, Jr.   89
 Zachariah   89,168,204
Johnston,
 Howell   89,168
 Philip   89,168
Jones,
 Adam   89
 Allen, Brig. Gen.   199
 Balaam   89
 Benjamin   89,166
 Capt. (Binns)   199
 Binns 11,13,26,28,58,166,
      167
 Carroll   90
 Daniel   90,(2)
 Harold   40,90
 James, Sr.   90
 James   90,166,178
 John 90,(3),157,(2),189
 Peter   90,166
 Richard   91,(2),166
 Robert   91,(2),166,179
 Stephen   63,91
 Tabitha   91
 Thomas, Sr.   91
 Thomas   173,174,175,178
 Thomas, Jr.   91,166
 Tignal, Sr.   92
 Tignal, Jr. 40,91,166,
      173,175
 William 92,(2),166,175,
      176

Keen,
 Abraham   166
Keeton,
 Joseph   92,(2),168
Kelly,
 Charles   92,162
 James   92,168
Kendrick,
 James   92
 John 93,(3),166,168,174,
      176
Kennon,
 E. (Erasmus)   193
 John   93
 Nancy C.   193
 Richard   93

Kidd,
  James   93
  James H.   93,162
  William   93,168
King,
  Charles   93
  James   94
  William   94,168
Kitchen,
  John   204

Ladd,
  Garrard   94
  James   94,162
  Ursley   94
  William   168
  William, Jr.   94
Lambert,
  Hugh   94,204
  Jervis   94
  John   94
  Joseph   94,95,168
  Lewis   95
Lampkin,
  James   95
  Jeremiah   95
  Sampson   95
Langley,
  Thomas   95
Lankford,
  Seleta   13
Lark,
  Robert   95
  Samuel 95,(2),145,162
Lawrence,
  William   203
Leigh,
  Walter   96
  William 96,123,(2),128,
       153,157,(2),166,
       174,175,177,204
Lester,
  Henry   96
Lett,
  James   168
  Joseph   96
Lewis,
  Charles   96,(2)
  Edward   96,(2)
  James 66,93,96,166,174
  John   97
  Mary   97
  Richard   11,97,162
  Thomas   97
Lightfoot,
  Francis   97
  Frank   203
Lipford,
  John   97,204
  Scruggs   97,168
Liptrot,
  John   97
  William   97
Lockett,
  Abner 97,98,166,177,
     179,181
  Royall, Sr.   188
  Royall   98,189
  Royall, Jr.   188
Logan,
  William   168
Lucas,
  James   98
  Jeremiah 98,162,204
  William, Gent.   98
  William, Captain 12
  William 13,21,33,35,45,
     56,98,137,157,
     (2),158,,(2),
     159,(2),166,
     172,173,174,176,
     179,180

Lucas, cont'd.
  William, Jr. 98,99,166,
       173,175,
       176,178,
       203
Ludwell,
  John   168

McCan,
  Dr. James   99
McCarter,
  James 99,187,188,189
  John   99
  Nancy   188
McClendian,
  Alexander   147
McCraw,
  Dancy   99
  Danny   99
McDaniel,
  Drury   99
  James   100
  John   100
McDole,
  John   190
McDonald,
  Crawford   169
  Edward   203
McHarg,
  Ebenezer   100
  Elizabeth   100
McKenney,
  James, Sr.   101
McKinney,
  Charles   101
McLachlin,
  Daniel   100
  John   101
McLin,
  Frances   100
  Frederick   100
  John   100
  Thomas   100
McNeil,
  John   101,(2)
McQuie,
  John   101
  William   101

Mabry,
  Joshua   166
  Stephen 21,28,58,73,74,
     90,101,102,120,
     137,161,166,174,
     175,204
Mackcasie,
  John   204
Maclin,
  Frederick 72,121,166,
     167
Mallett,
  John   102,162
  Stephen   102,169
  Stephen, Jr.   102
Malone,
  Benjamin 102,166,168,
     177,203
  Drury   102
  Isaac   102
  Lieut.   21
  Nathaniel 102,166,177,
     178,204
Malven,
  John   188
  Mary   188
  Susan   188
  William   188
Marable,
  Matthew   102
  William   103

Marrow,
  Daniel, Sr.   103
  Daniel 103,166,174,178
Marshall,
  Benjamin 86,103,121
  Francis 103,(2),166
  James   72,166
  John   103
  Robert   166
  Samuel 26,55,88,103,104,
     153,161,166,175,
     176,204
  Sarah   103
  William 104,166,181
  William, Jr.   104
Martin,
  Thomas   104
Mason,
  Captain   82
  David 162,166,167
  James   166,167
  William 104,162,203,204
Matthews,
  Nehemiah   104
  Thomas   199,204
Mayes,
  John   104
Maynard,
  Nicholas   104
  William   104
Mayo,
  Joseph   105
Meacham,
  Mary B.   190
Mealer,
  Matthew   105
  Philip 17,105,190
  William   105,162
Meanley,
  Richard   105
Meares,
  Thomas   105,162
Melton,
  Richard   105
Meredith,
  Samuel   139
Meriwether,
  T.   191
Millender,
  William   105
Miller,
  Hugh   105
Minor,
  George   204
  Hannah   116
  William   25,105
Mitchell,
  Abram   106
  Abraham   199
  Edward 106,(3),168
  Elijah   106
  Thomas   203
  William   106
Mize,
  John   106,162
Moody,
  Francis   106
Moon,
  Gideon   107
Moore,
  Feild   107
  Mark   107
  Thomas   107
  William   204
Morgan,
  General   190
  John   107,168
  Reuben 100,107,(2)
Morrison,
  Alexander   107
Morton,
  James   107

Moseley,
  William   98,166,167
Moss,
  Joshua   107
  Nathaniel   108
  Ray   108,162
Muhlenburg,
  General   59
  Peter   187
Munford,
  Col. Robert   108,(2)
  Robert 22,45,131,147,
      157,158,159,166,
      173,182
Murphy,
  Elizabeth   137
  Elizabeth I. 137
  William   137
Murray,
  John 36,63,108,109,130,
     157,158,(2),159,
     (2),166,172,173,
     175,177,178,179,(2)
  Leonard   204
Mustian,
  John   109

Nance,
  Daniel   109
  Isham   203
  Robert   109
  Thomas   109
Nanney,
  William   109,168
Nash,
  John   109
  Thomas   166
  William   109
Neal,
  Francis Moore 204
  John   109
  Thomas 109,110,166
  Thomas 109,166,173,174
  William, Sr.   110
  William 110,166,173,
     174,176
Nelson,
  Anna Matilda   193
  Caroline Matilda 193
  Hugh   193
  Major John   110
  John   193,(2)
  John, Jr.   193
  Lucy   193
  Mary   193
  Nancy   193
  Nancy Carter   193
  Nathaniel   193
  Robert   193
  Sarah   193
  Thomas Manduit 193
  William   193
Newport,
  Jane   61,110
  Peter   110
Newton,
  Robert B.   110
  Thomas, Jr.   110
Nicholas,
  George   111,197
Noblin,
  Thomas   111
Noel,
  Liberty   193
Norment,
  William   111
Northington,
  Chavis   111
  Jabez   111
Norvell,
  George M.   190
  James   190

Norvell, cont'd.
  Margaret   190
  Thomas A.   190
  William H.   190
Nowell,
  Thomas   111

Ogburn,
  John   111
Oliver,
  Asa 11,13,21,22,28,36,
    58,90,101,109,111,
    130,166,173,174,176,
    204
  John, Sr.   111
  John, Jr.   112
  William   204
Oslin,
  Jesse   112
Overby,
  Adam   203
  Drury   112
  Jeremiah   112
  Peter   112
Overton,
  John   13,166
  Moses   112,204
Owen,
  John   112
  John, Jr.   112
  Thomas   112

Parham,
  Lewis 61,80,112,113,132,
    157,158,159,166,
    173,175,176,200
  Nicolas   199
Parker,
  Richard 69,152,155,187
Parks,
  James   113
  John   113,162
Parrish,
  John   113
  Moses   113,189
Parson,
  Sarah   116
Patillo,
  Austin   67,113,114
Patrick,
  Captain   199
  John   114
Peebles,
  Joseph   72,166,167
Pegram,
  Alice   114
  William   114
Pennington,
  Benjamin   114
  Edward, Sr.   114
  Edward 73,114,116,177,
    204
  Henry 115,(2),166,168,
    173,177
  Howell   115
  James   115
  John George   115
  Philip   115,168
Perkins,
  David   115
Perry,
  William   115
Pettus,
  Henry   188
  Maria   188
  Samuel   115
  Samuel O.   166
  Samuel Overton 115,116
  Thomas 116,174,176,178
  Thomas   179,(2)
  Thomas, Jr. 116,166,204

P'Pool,
  Stephen   183,(2)
Phillips,
  Dabney   116,(2)
  Martin   116
  Pettus   116
  Thomas   116
Pinson,
  Thomas   117
Pistole,
  Charles   117,204
Poindexter,
  Phil, Sr.   204
  Philip   117
  Phil, Jr.   202
  Philip, Jr.   117
Poarch,
  Joshua   117
Pool,
  Betsy   194
  C.   194
  Gabriel   194
  James 117,141,194,(3)
  James, Jr.   194
  John   194
  Rebekah   194
  Sally   194
  Ursula   117,194
  Walter 117,166,179
  William   117,194
Poole,
  Thomas   117
Potter,
  John 118,158,(2),159
Powell,
  Thomas   118
Powers,
  Joseph   118,204
  William   118
Price,
  Susan   25
  William   118
Prochit,
  John   199
Puckett,
  Page   118
Pulliam,
  Benjamin   118
  James   118
  John   118
Pully,
  Spettle   118
  William 119,187,189
Puryear,
  Achilles   188
  John   119,(2),182
  John, Jr.   204
  Obadiah   119
  Samuel, Sr.   119
  Samuel   119
  Sarah   119
  Sarah B.   199
  Seymour   119

Ragsdale,
  David   119
  Drury   126
  John   120
  Peter, Sr.   120
  Peter   120,204
  Richard   120
  William   120
Raiborne,
  George   120
Rainey,
  Buckner   120,203
  Francis   120
  Williamson 21,121,189
Ramey,
  James   121,162
Randolph,
  Edmund   191,(2)

Randolph, cont'd.
  Joseph   121
  William 121,(2),158,159,
    166,172,179,(2),
    180
Rawls,
  George   53
Raynor,
  John   121
Read,
  Feild   204
Reese,
  Eton   121
  John   121,(2)
Reid,
  Nathan   64
Reives,
  Thomas   121
Richardson,
  Thomas   121
Rix,
  Philip   122,166,179
Roads,
  John   122
Roberts,
  Thomas   122,168
  William   122,162
  William S.   122,162
Robertson,
  James   122,169
  John   122
  William   122
Robinson,
  Benjamin   123
  William 123,166,173,175
Roffe,
  Edward   168,204
  William 11,123,161,166,
    173,174,175,
    177,179
  William, Jr.   123
Rogers,
  Captain   --
  John A.   193
Rose,
  Howell   166
Ross,
  David   123
Rottenberry,
  Samuel   123
Rowlett,
  Rebecca   189
  Thomas   166
  William   123,189
Royster,
  Charles 123,124,166,
    174,175,179,
    204
  David 124,166,178,204
  Jacob 124,(2),158,159
  Joseph 124,166,174,204
  Joseph, Jr.   124
  William   124
Rudd,
  Feild   124
  Joseph   124
Rudder,
  Samuel   168
Ruffin,
  Francis 74,125,(2),157,
    173,181
  John   63,183,185
  Thomas   125
  William   125,166
Russell,
  Cuthbert   204
  Elizabeth   194
  Elizabeth B.   195
  Jeffrey 88,125,(3),166,
    179,194
  John   204
  Martha   195
  Mary   195

Russell, cont'd
  Nathan   125
  Rebecca   195
  Richard   195
  Sarah   194
  Tabby   195
Ryland,
  Elizabeth 126,189,194
  Harrison M.   194
  Jincy Ivason   194
  John 126,189,(4),194,(2)
  Nancy Hundly   194
  Thomas   126,(2)
  William H.   194

St. Clair,
  Major Gen.   154
Salle',
  Isaac   126
Salley,
  Isaac   126
  Isaac, Jr.   126
Samson,
  Benjamin   126
Sanderlain,
  James   127
Sandifer,
  Henry   126
  James, Sr.   126
  James   195,(2)
  James, Jr. 126,166,173
  Martha   195
  Martha, Jr.   195
  Martha Ann   195
  Robert   195
Saunders,
  James   127
  Jesse 21,63,127,(3),158,
    159,166,177,(2)
Sawyer,
  Lewis   127,162
Scott,
  Francis   127
Sears,
  Joseph   127,191
Shipp,
  McTire   128
  Thomas 128,(2),131,140,
    166,173,174,176,
    177
Short,
  Jacob   128
Shotwell,
  John   128
  John, Jr.   128
Simmons,
  John   29,128
  Samuel   128
Simms,
  Charles   187
Singleton,
  Anthony   126
  Christopher   128,182
  Mary   182
Sizemore,
  Ephraim   129
  John   129
Skelton,
  Mark   129
Skipwith,
  Sir Peyton 129,(2),152,
    157,(2),158,
    159,203
Small,
  James   129
Smith,
  Anderson   129
  Benjamin   129
  David   173
  Drury 129,130,166,173,
    174,176
  Edward   199
  Jeremiah 130,(2),162,169,
    204

Smith, cont'd
  Jerry,   204
  John   130,(2),168
  Mary   19
  Robert 22,43,61,75,130,
    131,166,173,174,
    176,177,
  Sherwood   131,189
  Susanna   181
  Thomas   131,181
  Timothy   131
  William   131
Smithson,
  Micajah   131
Sparrow,
  Henry   131
  James B.   131
  James R.   131
Speed,
  Henry 113,132,(2),157
  Henry, Jr.   132
  James   132
  John 132,(2),157,158,
    159,182,190,200,
  Joseph   132,157,(2)
  Mathias   132
  Sarah   132
Spencer,
  Joseph   147
Spurlock,
  Agnes   133
Stanback,
  George   25,133
Standifer,
  Benjamin   133
Standley,
  James   133,204
Stanfield,
  Captain   72
Starling,
  William, Gent.   133
  William 133,(2),157,158,
    (2),159,166,172,
    179,(2),180,198,
    199,200,201
  William, Jr.   133
Stevens,
  John   134,(2),162
  Thomas   134
Stewart,
  Robert   168
Stokes,
  David   134
  John   69,81
Stone,
  Benjamin   134
  Eusebius   134
  Hezekiah 134,166,178,
    179
  John   134
  Thomas   134
Stovall,
  George   135
  John   135
Strange,
  Stephen   135
Street,
  Richard   135
Stroud,
  William   135
Stuart,
  James   135
Suggett,
  Edgecomb   135,203
  Edgecomb, Jr.   135
Sutton,
  Thomas   136
Swepson,
  John   135,157,(2)
  Richard, Sr.   136
  Richard 13,28,33,35,(2)
    46,92,173,175
  Richard, Jr. 136,(2),
    166,176

Tabb,
John   136,157,(2)
Tabor,
Hezekiah   136
Tanner,
Ann   196
Creed   196
Eleanor   196
Elizabeth   196
Josiah 136,166,195,(2)
Kezia   196
John   196
Lucy   195
Martha   195
Martha, Jr.   196
Mary   196
Matthew   196
Matthew, Jr.   204
Sally   195
Samuel   196
Thomas 136,(2),166,174,
    175,189,196
Thomas, Jr.   137
Tarry,
George 69,137,(2),166,
    174,175
Taylor,
Anderson   166
Charles   196,(2)
Clark   137
David   137,204
Edmund 137,157,(2),158,
    159
Elizabeth   196
Goodwyn 137,166,174,176
Goodwyn, Jr.   138
Henry   196
Howell 71,83,127,138,
    166,173,174,175,
    177
Howell, Jr.138,166,180
James   138,196
Jesse 138,(2),139,166,
    173,175,176,177,
    196,204
Jones   139,203
John   139,196
John Cook   162
Joseph   166,167
Joshua   139
Lewis   196
Lieut.   21
Mary   139,196
Mourning   196
Richard   139
Richard, Jr.   139
Robert   139
Samuel   139
William, Gent.   140
William 139,140,(2),157,
    161,166,168,196,
    203
Tench,
John R.   140
Thomas,
Daniel   140,188
Daniel F.   188
Hannah   140,182
John   140,182
Peter 55,140,141,166,
    173,175,176,204
Thomas   60
Thompson,
Amey   141
Harman 141,(2),166,174,
    175,204
James   141
John 117,141,(2),204
Peter   141
Richard   141
Stith 142,(2),166,177,
    178
Tillotson,
Thomas   142

Tisdale,
Edward   204
Toone,
Argelon   142,(2),189
Argelon, Jr.   166
James 142,166,175,178
James, Jr.   142
Lewis   142
Rebecca   188
William   24,142
Townes,
Joseph   142,143,166
Traylor,
Cary   143
Traler,
Joel   204
Tucker,
David   204
George   143
Hudson   143,204
James   143,204
Tureman,
Ann   73
Martin   73,143
Mary   73
Thomas   143
Turner,
Isaiah   204
James   143
Matthew   143
William   144

Vandyke,
John   144
Mary   144
Vaughan,
Ebenezer   199
Ingram 144,166,179,180
James   144,(2),182
John   144
Joshua   144
Peter   144
Reuben 11,14,15,16,25,
    26,28,30,31,54,
    63,85,145,157,
    158,159,162,(2),
    164,166,173,174,
    175,200,204
Samuel   145
Susanna   16
Thomas   145,204
William   16,145
Vowell,
William   145

Wade,
Elizabeth   146
George   146
Martha   146
Wagstaff,
Basil   146
John   146,189
Walden,
John   204
Margaret   192
Walker,
David   146
Daniel   146
Henry 65,91,110,146,(2),
    147,(2),154,157,
    158,159,161,166,
    173,174,175,178,
    179,(2),182
Martha L.   193
Richard   147
Sylvanus   147
Tandy   147
Wall,
Henry   147,168
Michael   147
Wallace,
Elizabeth   147,182

Wallace, cont'd
William   147,(2),182
Waller,
Daniel 148,188,(3),189
Edward   148
Isaac   188,(2)
John   188,(2),204
William   188,(2)
Walton,
Edward   148,166,204
Richard   166
Ward,
Henry   148
Washington,
Gen. George   19
Watkins,
Charles   148
George   148
James   148
Thomas   148
William   63,161
Watlington,
William   199,(3)
Watson,
Burwell   148
Elizabeth   148
Isaac, Sr.   149
Isaac   149,162,203
Jacob   149
Watts,
Richard   149
Weatherford,
Benjamin   149
Nancy   149
William   149,204
Webb,
John   204
Wells,
Charles   204
Westbrook,
James   149
Westbrooke,
James   204
Thomas   204
Westmoreland,
Jesse   149
Joseph   149
White,
Colonel   82
George   150
John   150
Robert   169
William   150
Whitehead,
Benjamin 63,141,150,157
Richard   150
Whittemore,
Buckner   204
Clem   204
Jane J.   189,(2)
Whobry,
Margaret B.   190
Molly   193
Wilbourn,
Thomas   150
Wiles,
Luke   150
Wilkerson,
Elisha   150
William   151
Wilkins,
Arabella   151
Charles   151
Clement   151
James 151,166,167,173,
    175,(2),204
William   151
Williams,
Henry   151
James   151
William   168
Williamson,
John   151

Willis,
    John 72,167,(2),204
    William   152
Wills,
    Isham   152
Wilmore,
    Robert   152,162
Wilson,
    Archibald   152
    Edward   152,189
    Elimileck 152,167,178,
            179,(2)
    Fanny   188
    Frances   188,(2)
    James 153,(3),162,167,
        174,176,177,188,
        204
    John   152,(2),162,204
    Lemuel   153
    Wallis   153
Winfield,
    Peter   167,177,176
Winkfield,
    Peter   -   153
Winkler,
    John   154
Winn,
    John 154,(2),167,174,
       176,177,178
    Richard 154,167,174,175
Wise,
    John   167
Witton,
    Richard   11,21,22,86
          121,154,161,
          174,178,179
    Richard, Jr. 154,167,
          176
Wood,
    Archibald   154,189
    Bennett   167
    James   156
Woody,
    John   155
Wooten,
    Samuel   155
Worsham,
    Ludwell   155
    Ludwell, Jr.   155
Wright,
    Austin   155
    George   155
    Laban   155
    Nathan   155
Wright,
    Thomas   155,162
    William   155

Yancey,
    Absolam   156
    Mary   156
    Col. Thornton   17
    Thornton   167,(3)
    Zachariah   156,204
Yarbrough,
    Lieut.   77
Yates,
    Edward Randolph 156
    William   197
Young,
    Allen   156
    Samuel   156

* * *

www.ingramcontent.com/pod-product-compliance
Lightning Source LLC
Chambersburg PA
CBHW041256040426
42334CB00028BA/3039